GENERAL KNOWLEDGE
GENIUS!

DK Delhi

Senior Editor Bharti Bedi
Senior Art Editor Shreya Anand
Project Editor Neha Ruth Samuel
Art Editor Nidhi Rastogi
Assistant Editors Bipasha Roy, Manan Kapoor
Assistant Art Editors Baibhav Parida, Sanya Jain, Srishti Arora
Jacket Designer Tanya Mehrotra
Jackets Editorial Coordinator Priyanka Sharma
Senior DTP Designer Harish Aggarwal
DTP Designers Pawan Kumar, Vijay Khandwal
Picture Researcher Rituraj Singh
Managing Jackets Editor Saloni Singh
Pre-production Manager Balwant Singh
Production Manager Pankaj Sharma
Picture Research Manager Taiyaba Khatoon
Managing Editor Kingshuk Ghoshal
Managing Art Editor Govind Mittal

DK London

Editor Jessica Cawthra
Designer Gregory McCarthy
Senior Designer Rachael Grady
Editorial Team Vicky Richards, Ann Baggaley
Jacket Designers Stephanie Cheng Hue Tan, Akiko Kato
Jacket Editor Emma Dawson
Jacket Design Development Manager Sophia MTT
Producer, Pre-production Gillian Reid
Senior Producer Angela Graef
Managing Editor Francesca Baines
Managing Art Editor Philip Letsu
Publisher Andrew Macintyre
Associate Publishing Director Liz Wheeler
Art Director Karen Self
Design Director Phil Ormerod
Publishing Director Jonathan Metcalf

First published in Great Britain in 2019
by Dorling Kindersley Limited
80 Strand, London WC2R 0RL

Copyright © 2019 Dorling Kindersley Limited
A Penguin Random House Company
10 9 8 7 6 5 4 3 2 1
001–309848–April/2019

All rights reserved.
No part of this publication may be reproduced, stored in or introduced into a retrieval system, or transmitted, in any form, or by any means (electronic, mechanical, photocopying, recording, or otherwise) without the prior written permission of the copyright owner.

A CIP catalogue record for this book is available from the British Library
ISBN: 978-0-2413-3624-3

Printed and bound in China

A WORLD OF IDEAS:
SEE ALL THERE IS TO KNOW
www.dk.com

DK
GENERAL KNOWLEDGE
GENIUS!

Contributors: Peter Chrisp, Clive Gifford, Derek Harvey, Andrea Mills, and John Woodward

CONTENTS

1 SCIENCE GEEK

Space	10
Planet parade	12
Space travellers	14
The elements	16
Simply elementary	18
The human body	20
Know your bones	22
Under the microscope	24
Maths	26
Shape up!	28
Transport	30
On the road	32
All aboard!	34
Taking to the skies	36
All at sea	38

2 NATURE KNOW-IT-ALL

Dinosaurs
Clawed carnivores
Plant-eating giants
Prehistoric creatures
Mammals
Know your cats
Primate party
Aquatic mammals
Invertebrates
Insects everywhere
Under the sea
Arachnids assemble
Birds
Birds of a feather
Deadly hunters
Reptiles
Reptile room
Scaly serpents

mphibians	78
mazing amphibians	80
h	82
eshwater fishes	84
arine life	86
imal behaviour	88
cky tracks	90
t cracking	92
e spy	94
ants	96
wer power	98
it and nuts	100
nt food	102

3 GEOGRAPHY GENIUS

Earth	106
High seas	108
World waterways	110
Peak puzzle	112
Wonders of the world	114
Countries of the world	116
Cities	118
Cool constructions	120
City skylines	122
Capital cities	124
Eye in the sky	126
Flags	128
Raise the flag	130
Weather	132
Cloudspotting	134
Rocks and minerals	136
Rock stars	138
Precious gemstones	140

4 HISTORY BUFF

Ancient civilizations	144
Lost cities	146
Guess the gods	148
Mythical creatures	150
Castles	152
Hold the fort	154
Battle ready!	156
Fighting fashion	158
Leaders	160
Famous faces	162

5 CULTURE VULTURE

Art	166
Gallery of the greats	168
Playing the classics	170
Making music	172
Languages	174
Greetings!	176
Sports	178
On the ball	180
Game on!	182
Sports store	184
Your turn!	186

Index	188
Acknowledgments	192

How this book works

01. Choose your topic. There are five chapters on a wide range of subjects and lots of different quizzes. Perhaps start with one that you know all about, and then move on to something new.

Welcome to this fact-packed, quiz-filled challenge. Top up with some new knowledge and then put your brain to the test by matching the picture clues with the answers. Can you identify your insects? Do you know the names of the bones in your body? Can you work out which warrior's weapon is which? It's time to find out!

Facts first

First brush up on the basics with these pages of fun facts. Filled with both essential and curious information, these will warm up your brain for the quizzes that follow.

Next the challenge

Then it's time to test yourself. Take a look at the pictures and the list of answers in the panel down the side and try to match them up. Follow these four steps for the best way to tackle things.

02. When you've chosen a quiz, take a careful look at the pictures. Do you recognize them all? The clues will give you extra information to help you work things out.

03. Look at the "Test Yourself" panel and match the words and pictures. Don't write the answers in the book – you may want to quiz again later, to improve your score, or give it to a friend to see how they do.

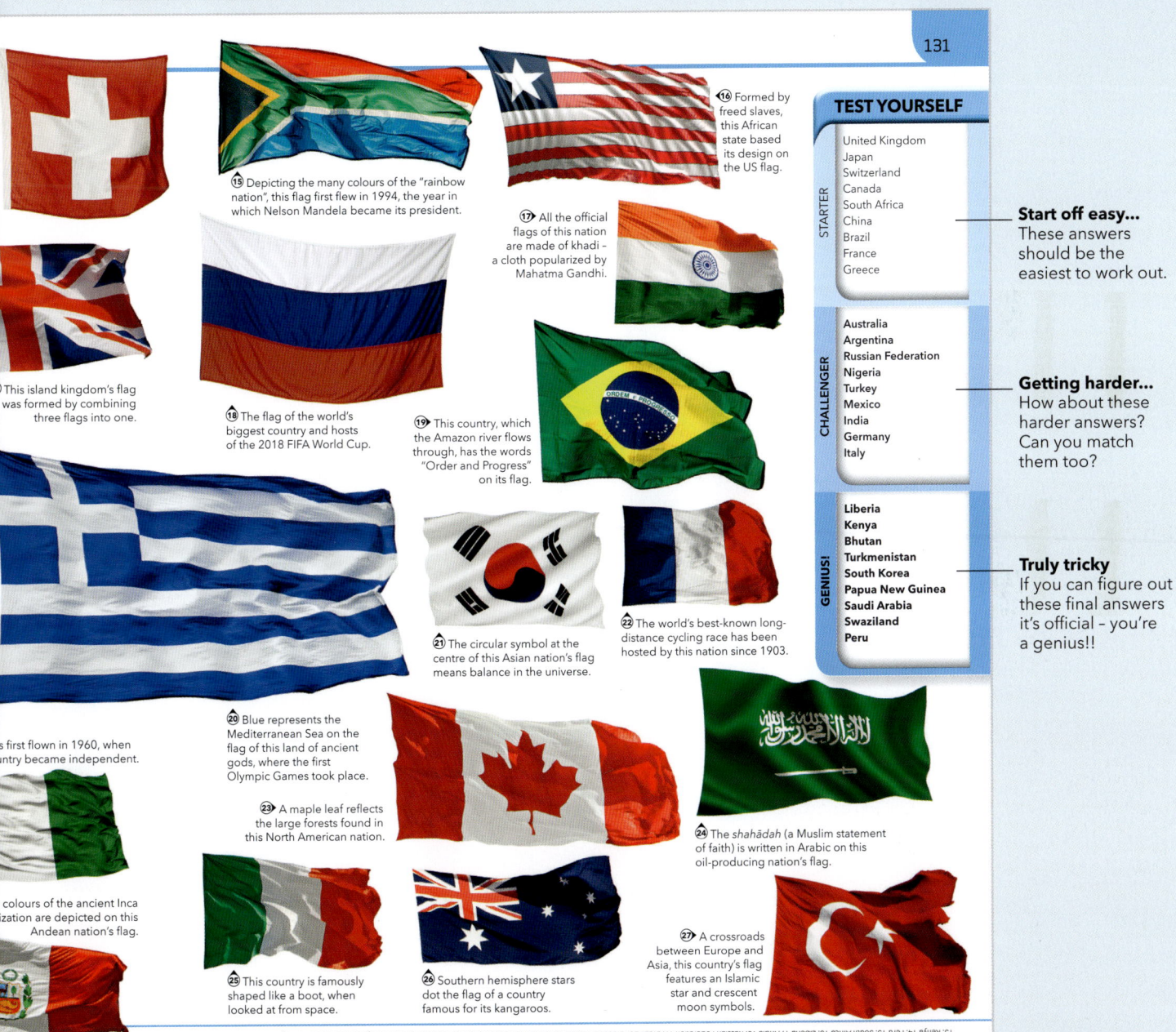

⑮ Depicting the many colours of the "rainbow nation", this flag first flew in 1994, the year in which Nelson Mandela became its president.

⑯ Formed by freed slaves, this African state based its design on the US flag.

⑰ All the official flags of this nation are made of khadi – a cloth popularized by Mahatma Gandhi.

⑱ The flag of the world's biggest country and hosts of the 2018 FIFA World Cup.

⑲ This country, which the Amazon river flows through, has the words "Order and Progress" on its flag.

This island kingdom's flag was formed by combining three flags into one.

㉑ The circular symbol at the centre of this Asian nation's flag means balance in the universe.

㉒ The world's best-known long-distance cycling race has been hosted by this nation since 1903.

as first flown in 1960, when untry became independent.

⑳ Blue represents the Mediterranean Sea on the flag of this land of ancient gods, where the first Olympic Games took place.

㉓ A maple leaf reflects the large forests found in this North American nation.

㉔ The *shahādah* (a Muslim statement of faith) is written in Arabic on this oil-producing nation's flag.

e colours of the ancient Inca ilization are depicted on this Andean nation's flag.

㉕ This country is famously shaped like a boot, when looked at from space.

㉖ Southern hemisphere stars dot the flag of a country famous for its kangaroos.

㉗ A crossroads between Europe and Asia, this country's flag features an Islamic star and crescent moon symbols.

TEST YOURSELF

STARTER
- United Kingdom
- Japan
- Switzerland
- Canada
- South Africa
- China
- Brazil
- France
- Greece

Start off easy... These answers should be the easiest to work out.

CHALLENGER
- Australia
- Argentina
- Russian Federation
- Nigeria
- Turkey
- Mexico
- India
- Germany
- Italy

Getting harder... How about these harder answers? Can you match them too?

GENIUS!
- Liberia
- Kenya
- Bhutan
- Turkmenistan
- South Korea
- Papua New Guinea
- Saudi Arabia
- Swaziland
- Peru

Truly tricky If you can figure out these final answers it's official – you're a genius!!

ANSWERS: 1. Argentina 2. Turkmenistan 3. Switzerland 4. China 5. Germany 6. Swaziland 7. United Kingdom 8. Japan 9. Papua New Guinea 10. Bhutan 11. Nigeria 12. Mexico 13. Kenya 14. Peru 15. South Africa 16. Liberia 17. India 18. Russian Federation 19. Brazil 20. Greece 21. South Korea 22. France 23. Canada 24. Saudi Arabia 25. Italy 26. Australia 27. Turkey

No peeking! You'll find the answers matched with the number of the correct picture, at the bottom of the page.

04. Work your way through the three levels of difficulty – it's not supposed to be easy! When you think you have got them all, check the answers – they're upside-down at the bottom of the page.

05. There is also a picture quiz for every chapter, from spotting an insect to finding your way through a maze. Check you've got it right in the Answers section at the back of the book.

1 SCIENCE GEEK

Star hunter
Studying the night sky has helped scientists discover many wonders in our Universe. Can you find the constellation of Orion the hunter in this starry scene? Start by looking for three bright stars in a line that make up his belt. Nearby, more stars form his body.

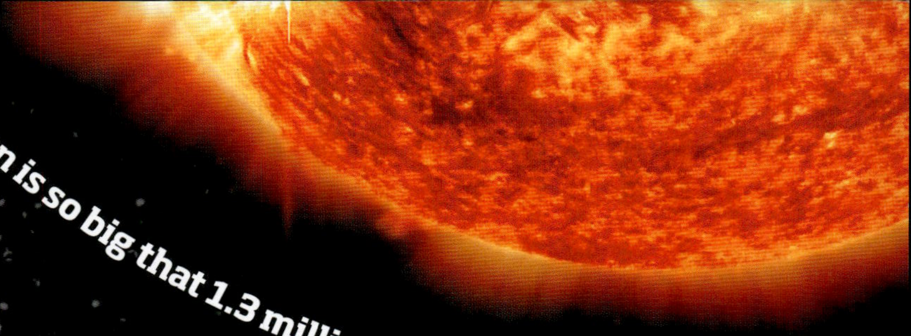

The Sun is so big that 1.3 million Earths could fit inside it.

Space

Everything in the Universe – from the tiniest specks of dust to large balls of burning gas called stars – exists in the vastness of space. Scattered throughout space are collections of millions of stars called galaxies. Within galaxies, many stars are orbited by rocky, icy, or gassy worlds called planets. Our planet, Earth, orbits a star called the Sun.

Solar System

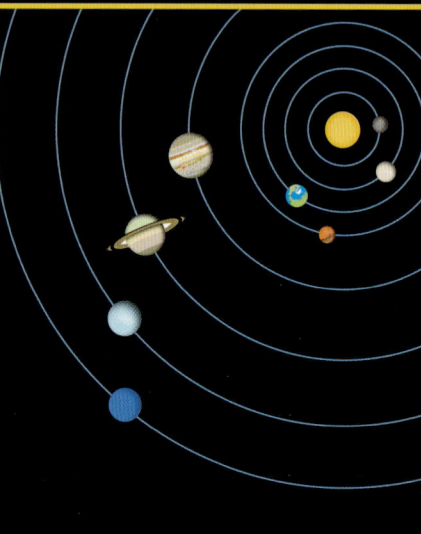

The Solar System formed around 4.6 billion years ago, from a ball of gas and dust. At its centre lies a star called the Sun. Eight planets orbit the Sun along oval-shaped paths.

What is a comet?

These dirty snowballs, made of ice and dust, travel around the Sun in oval orbits. When they pass close to the Sun, the ice heats up forming long tails of dust and gas.

Coma: A cloud of gas and dust that surrounds the nucleus, when the comet heats up.

Parker Solar Probe: This is the only part that will actually reach the Sun.

Nucleus: A solid centre made of ice, dust, and rock.

Dust tail: Dust released from the comet forms a tail, which trails behind the comet's path.

Gas tail: The gas from the comet that stretches out a long way behind the nucleus, pointing almost directly away from the Sun.

I don't believe it

A giant star, called RMC 136a1, is about 32 times larger than the Sun and shines around eight million times more brightly!

Delta IV Heavy: This powerful American launch vehicle is 72 m (236 ft) tall.

Milky Way

Our home galaxy contains between 200 and 400 billion stars!

Galaxies galore

Elliptical galaxy
Shaped like a ball or an egg, elliptical galaxies, such as Fornax, have little gas or dust.

Spiral galaxy
A galaxy shaped like a giant disc with a round centre and long, curving arms is known as a spiral galaxy. The arms of NGC 1566, for example, are full of dust and young stars.

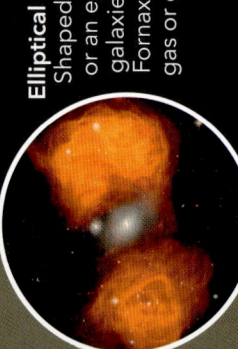

How to get to the Sun

01. Construct a suitable spacecraft, like the Parker Solar Probe that launched in 2018 and is expected to fly through the Sun's atmosphere, and make its closest approach to the Sun in 2025.

02. Make sure there are two parts to your spacecraft – a probe, to be sent to the Sun, and a giant launch vehicle, like the Delta Heavy IV shown here, to get the probe into space.

03. During the launch, the booster rockets will use their fuel and fall away, leaving the probe to travel towards the Sun.

The rocket booster contains 200,400 kg (441,806 lb) of fuel, which is all burned up in just four minutes after lift-off.

04. Once closer, the Sun's gravitational force will help the probe reach speeds of up to 690,000 km/h (428,750 mph) and pull it in – so make sure you're ready to record the data it receives and relays to Earth.

Exoplanet facts

⭐ In the 1990s, planets orbiting other stars – called exoplanets – were discovered. By 2018, around 3,791 exoplanets had been found.

⭐ The exoplanet WASP-12b takes just 26 hours to travel around its star. Earth, in contrast, takes 365¼ days to orbit the Sun.

⭐ The exoplanet HD 80606b also lies very close to its star. As a result, the temperature on its surface is almost 2,200°C (3,990°F) – enough to melt most metals.

⭐ The temperatures of Kepler-186f (right), discovered in 2014, mean liquid water could exist there – the key to supporting life. It's now hoped that another exoplanet might be found, which does host life.

In numbers

149.6 million km
(92.9 million miles) The average distance between Earth and the Sun.

800,000 km/h
(500,000 mph) The speed at which the Solar System is swirling round the core of the Milky Way galaxy.

299,792 km
(186,282 miles) The distance that light travels in a single second – a unit known as a light year.

260,000 light years
The diameter of the Andromeda galaxy – the nearest major galaxy to the Milky Way.

4.6 billion years
The average age of a comet.

4.2 light years
The distance to Proxima Centauri – the nearest star to Earth after the Sun.

Lenticular galaxy
Some galaxies, such as NGC 5010, have no curved arms, just a bulge in the middle, which makes them look like a glass lens.

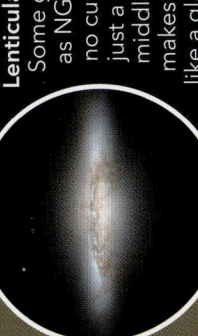

Irregular galaxy
These are galaxies with no obvious shape. They may have been pulled out of shape by a close encounter with another galaxy. Seen here is Barnard's Galaxy.

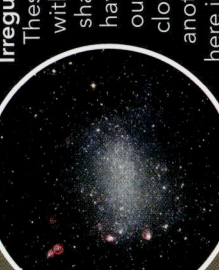

Planet parade

The Sun is a star. Around it travel eight planets, along with many asteroids, dwarf planets, and comets, all following oval paths called orbits, and known together as the Solar System. Rocky bodies called moons orbit many of the planets.

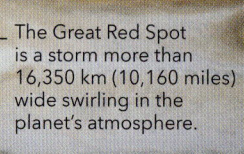

The Great Red Spot is a storm more than 16,350 km (10,160 miles) wide swirling in the planet's atmosphere.

Orbits the Sun in just 88 Earth days at 170,500 km/h (105,944 mph)

① The smallest of the planets, and the closest one to the Sun, this rocky world shares its name with a chemical element.

Surface hidden by thick clouds, some of which rain deadly sulfuric acid.

② A stormy world, the surface temperature on this planet can rocket to a blistering 464°C (867°F) which is hot enough to melt lead.

Water covers more than two-thirds of the surface of this planet.

③ The third planet from the Sun, this is the only place in the Universe where life is known to exist.

Craters scar the surface, made by impact with countless meteorites.

④ This object was visited by 12 astronauts in Apollo spacecraft between 1969 and 1972.

⑤ Also known as the Red Planet because of its rusty, iron rocks, more spacecraft have been sent to this world than any other.

⑥ The Solar System's largest planet is so big more than 1,300 Earths could fit inside. It is orbited by almost 70 moons.

The surface temperature of the Sun is 5,500°C (9,930°F).

This gas giant is the least dense planet in the Solar System – it is lighter than water.

The band of main rings extends for 280,000 km (174,000 miles), but for the most part is just 10 m (33 ft) thick.

Most planets rotate upright, like a top, but this one spins on its side.

TEST YOURSELF

STARTER
- Earth
- Mars
- Moon
- Jupiter

CHALLENGER
- Saturn
- Venus
- Mercury
- Neptune

GENIUS!
- Titan
- Uranus
- Io
- Ganymede

⑦ The largest moon in the Solar System, it is 5,262 km (3,270 miles) across.

⑧ Discovered by the Italian astronomer Galileo in 1610, this yellow moon is home to more than 400 active volcanoes.

⑨ Spectacular rings of dust, rock, and ice encircle this gas giant.

⑩ Second largest in the Solar System, this moon is bigger than the planet Mercury.

⑪ This giant ball of gas with an icy core takes 84 Earth years to orbit the Sun.

⑫ The farthest planet from the Sun, it was named after a god of the sea for its deep-blue colour.

ANSWERS: 1. Mercury 2. Venus 3. Earth 4. Moon 5. Mars 6. Jupiter 7. Ganymede 8. Io 9. Saturn 10. Titan 11. Uranus 12. Neptune

Space travellers

The development of powerful rocket engines in the 1950s enabled spacecraft and, later, people to explore space. The voyages made by these remarkable spacecraft – both manned and unmanned – have taught us much about the Universe.

1 Launched in 1973, this was the first probe to fly close to the planet Mercury. It also travelled to Venus!

2 This 1972 American space probe was the first to travel past Mars and through the Asteroid Belt to take photos of Jupiter.

3 Launched in 1957, the first human-made object to travel into space made 1,400 orbits around Earth. It gets its name from the Russian word for "fellow traveller".

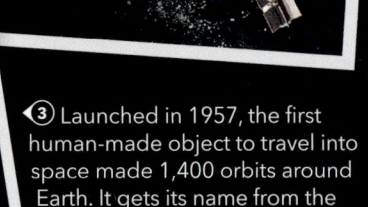

4 The size of a motor car, this rover has been exploring the surface of Mars since 2012. It carries 17 cameras and a host of scientific instruments.

A laser in the head turns rocks into dust and gas, to reveal the rocks' composition.

Cone-shaped Command Module held three astronauts

Antenna dish sent signals from the Moon to Earth

Solar panels generate electricity

The spacecraft was almost 111 m (364 ft) tall – as high as some 36-floor buildings.

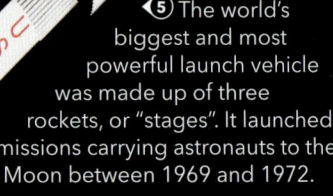

5 The world's biggest and most powerful launch vehicle was made up of three rockets, or "stages". It launched missions carrying astronauts to the Moon between 1969 and 1972.

6 This small Chinese rover landed on the surface of the Moon in 2013 and explored it for 31 months. Its name comes from the Chinese for "jade rabbit".

ANSWERS: 1. Mariner 10 2. Pioneer 10 3. Sputnik 1 4. Curiosity 5. Saturn V 6. Yutu 7. Cassini-Huygens 8. Space Shuttle 9. Apollo 11 Lunar Module 10. Voyager 1 11. International Space Station 12. Long March 3A

15

TEST YOURSELF

STARTER
International Space Station
Space Shuttle
Sputnik 1
Saturn V

CHALLENGER
Pioneer 10
Voyager 1
Apollo 11 Lunar Module
Curiosity

GENIUS!
Yutu
Cassini-Huygens
Long March 3A
Mariner 10

⑧ Five of these reusable spacecraft flew more than 130 NASA space missions between them. They launched like rockets but glided back to Earth to land on runways like planes. The last of these spacecraft retired in 2011.

⑦ The largest spacecraft to visit another planet, this probe had two parts – one that orbited Saturn for 13 years and another that was parachuted down onto Saturn's largest moon Titan.

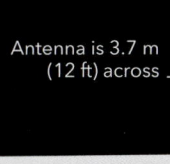

Antenna is 3.7 m (12 ft) across

⑩ Now more than 21.7 billion km (13½ billion miles) away, this probe is the farthest spacecraft from Earth. It was launched in 1977 to explore the giant planets Jupiter and Saturn.

⑨ Nicknamed "Eagle", this spacecraft carried Neil Armstrong and Buzz Aldrin, the first humans to stand on the lunar surface in 1969. The lower section of the spacecraft was left behind on the Moon.

⑪ The largest human-made object in space, at 109 m (357 ft) across, this machine is home to up to six astronauts, who live and conduct experiments on board.

Smaller modules are built on Earth and joined together in space.

⑫ This 52-m- (170- ft-) tall Chinese rocket was built to launch communication satellites. It also launched China's first mission to the Moon in 2007.

The elements

Everything around us is made up of simple substances called elements. Each one is made up of tiny particles called atoms, which are unique for every element. When two or more elements combine, they form a compound. For example, sodium and chlorine combine to form sodium chloride, or common salt.

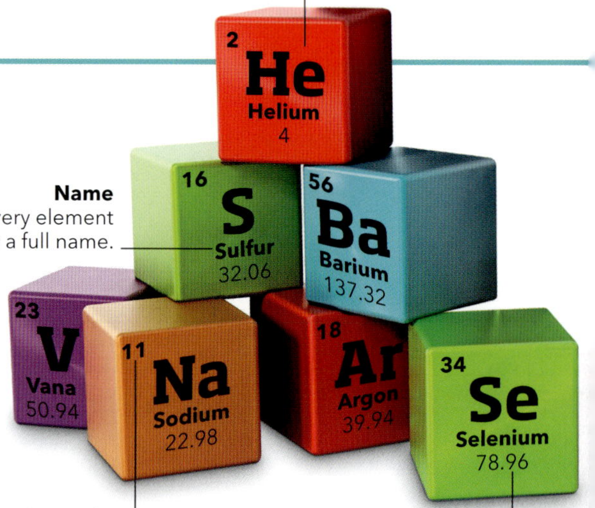

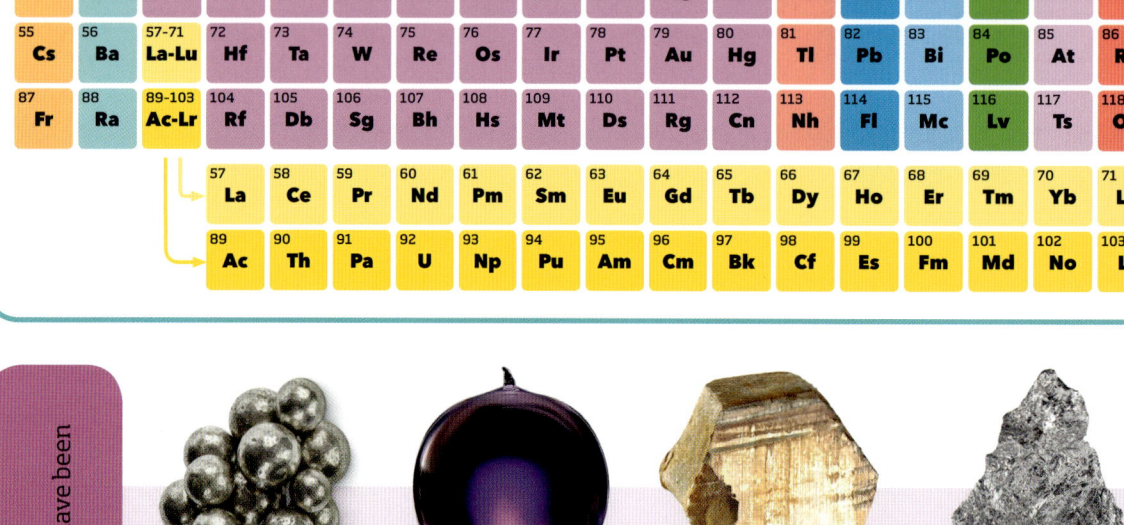

Chemical symbol
A unique one- or two-letter code for the element.
2 He Helium 4
16 S Sulfur 32.06
56 Ba Barium 137.32
23 V Vana 50.94
11 Na Sodium 22.98
18 Ar Argon 39.94
34 Se Selenium 78.96
Name
Every element has a full name.
Atomic number
The number of protons (positive particles) in one atom.
Atomic mass
The average mass of all the atoms of the element.

What is the periodic table?

There are 118 elements in the periodic table - 92 are found in nature, while others have been created in laboratories. They are arranged in a special order in a table developed by the Russian chemist Dmitri Mendeleev. The lightest elements are found at the top of the grid and those with similar properties are grouped together in columns.

1 H																	2 He
3 Li	4 Be											5 B	6 C	7 N	8 O	9 F	10 Ne
11 Na	12 Mg											13 Al	14 Si	15 P	16 S	17 Cl	18 Ar
19 K	20 Ca	21 Sc	22 Ti	23 V	24 Cr	25 Mn	26 Fe	27 Co	28 Ni	29 Cu	30 Zn	31 Ga	32 Ge	33 As	34 Se	35 Br	36 Kr
37 Rb	38 Sr	39 Y	40 Zr	41 Nb	42 Mo	43 Tc	44 Ru	45 Rh	46 Pd	47 Ag	48 Cd	49 In	50 Sn	51 Sb	52 Te	53 I	54 Xe
55 Cs	56 Ba	57-71 La-Lu	72 Hf	73 Ta	74 W	75 Re	76 Os	77 Ir	78 Pt	79 Au	80 Hg	81 Tl	82 Pb	83 Bi	84 Po	85 At	86 Rn
87 Fr	88 Ra	89-103 Ac-Lr	104 Rf	105 Db	106 Sg	107 Bh	108 Hs	109 Mt	110 Ds	111 Rg	112 Cn	113 Nh	114 Fl	115 Mc	116 Lv	117 Ts	118 Og
			57 La	58 Ce	59 Pr	60 Nd	61 Pm	62 Sm	63 Eu	64 Gd	65 Tb	66 Dy	67 Ho	68 Er	69 Tm	70 Yb	71 Lu
			89 Ac	90 Th	91 Pa	92 U	93 Np	94 Pu	95 Am	96 Cm	97 Bk	98 Cf	99 Es	100 Fm	101 Md	102 No	103 Lr

Key

- Hydrogen
- Alkali metals
- Alkaline Earth metals
- Transition metals
- Lanthanides
- Actinides
- The Boron Group
- The Carbon Group
- The Nitrogen Group
- The Oxygen Group
- The Halogen Group
- Noble gases

Timeline

Since the 1700s, scientists have been discovering new elements.

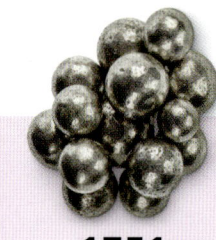

1751
Axel Fredrik Cronstedt discovers nickel while working as a Swedish mining expert.

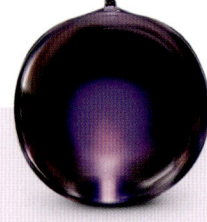

1772
At just 22 years of age, Scottish chemist Daniel Rutherford identifies nitrogen gas.

1807-08
English chemist Humphry Davy discovers potassium, sodium (above), calcium, strontium, barium, and magnesium.

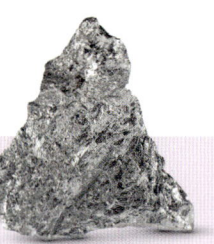

1823
Swedish chemist Jöns Jacob Berzelius discovers silicon while experimenting in his laboratory.

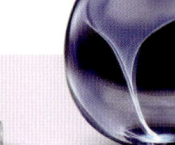

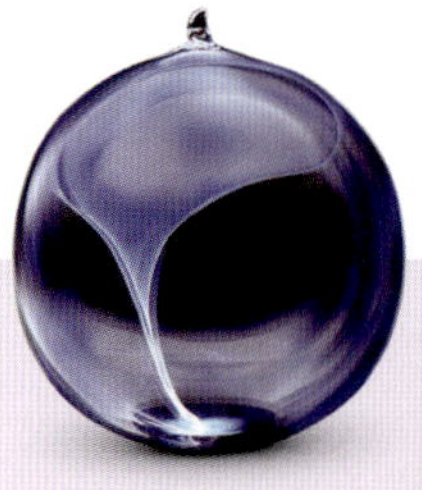

1896
Xenon gas is discovered by the British chemists Sir William Ramsay and Morris William Travers.

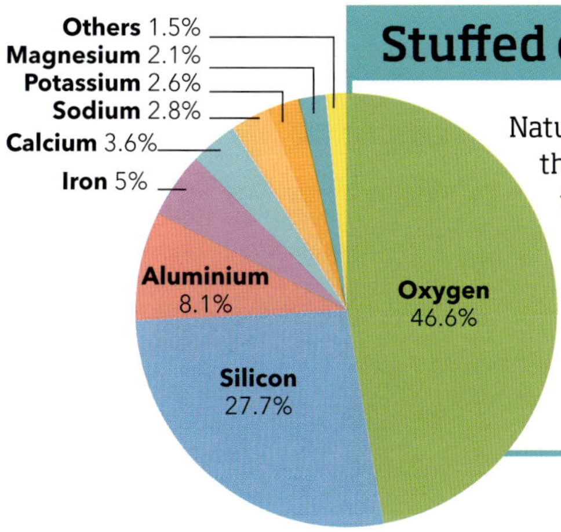

Stuffed crust

Natural elements are found in the minerals and rocks that form Earth's outer layer – its crust. Only a few are found in pure form – most of them combine with others to form compounds.

Pie chart:
- Oxygen 46.6%
- Silicon 27.7%
- Aluminium 8.1%
- Iron 5%
- Calcium 3.6%
- Sodium 2.8%
- Potassium 2.6%
- Magnesium 2.1%
- Others 1.5%

100,000,000
The approximate number of atoms that can fit in a row measuring 1 cm (½ in).

9,000
The approximate number of graphite pencils that could be made from all the carbon found in a human body.

3,414°C
(6,177°F) The temperature at which tungsten melts – the highest melting point of any naturally occurring element.

91
The percentage of the Sun made up of one element – hydrogen.

4
The number of elements that make up 96 per cent of the human body. Those are oxygen, carbon, hydrogen, and nitrogen.

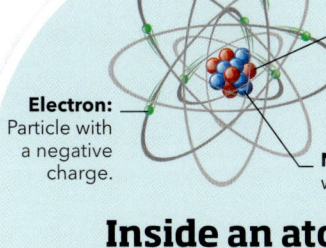

Inside an atom
There are three types of tiny particles in an atom. Neutrons and protons form the central nucleus, around which electrons are arranged in layers called shells.

Electron: Particle with a negative charge.
Proton: Particle with a positive charge.
Neutron: Particle with no charge.

I don't believe it
A piece of gold the size of a grain of rice can be hammered into a thin layer covering 10,000 sq cm (1,550 sq in).

Radium paint makes the numbers glow in the dark.

1898
French chemists Marie and Pierre Curie discover two new elements – radium and polonium.

1940
Plutonium is discovered by Glenn Seaborg and his team in the US. It is radioactive and used for nuclear power and weapons.

2016
Four elements are officially named, including Oganesson after one of the discoverers Yuri Oganessian (above).

It's chemical!

- Fireworks get their colours from different elements. Red sparks come from lithium and strontium.
- A lump of the element gallium melts just by clasping it in a hand.
- Carbon combines with other elements to form more than nine million different compounds.
- Platinum is highly ductile, which means it can be drawn into really thin wires – as thin as 0.00006 mm.
- Only two elements naturally exist in a liquid state – mercury and bromine.

SCIENCE GEEK

Simply elementary

Most of the 118 elements that make up the Universe are solids, but 11 are gases at room temperature, and two are liquids. Here are 18 elements for you to name. Alongside each picture, look out for the unique chemical symbol – one or two letters – that scientists across the world use to identify each element.

1 In 1669, a German alchemist accidentally discovered this element when he was boiling a large pot of his urine in search of the mythical Philosopher's Stone.

This element is highly flammable and is used on the strips on the side of safety match boxes.

P

2 Named after the Greek word for violet, this element does not melt on heating – it turns directly into vapour. It is used to make antiseptics and in food dyes.

The glass sphere traps the purple-black vapour.

I

When cooled to −183°C (−297°F) this colourless gas becomes a clear, blue liquid.

3 Life on Earth depends on this element for survival. All living things need to breathe in this gas to convert food into energy.

O

4 This shiny precious metal is a popular choice for making jewellery. It also conducts electricity well and is used in electronics.

Ag

Pure form of the element tarnishes when exposed to air.

Al

5 This lightweight metal is used to make all sorts of objects – from drinks cans to aircraft.

6 A small amount of this element is added to water in swimming pools to kill off harmful bacteria.

The glass sphere stops the gas from reacting with air.

Cl

7 When mixed with other elements, this metal forms strong but lightweight materials – it is used with other metals to make cars and aircraft. It also burns with a bright white flame and is found in flares and fireworks.

Mg

ANSWERS: 1. Phosphorus 2. Iodine 3. Oxygen 4. Silver 5. Aluminium 6. Chlorine 7. Magnesium 8. Neon 9. Iron 10. Bismuth 11. Gold 12. Krypton 13. Copper 14. Hydrogen 15. Osmium 16. Sulfur 17. Carbon 18. Mercury

Ne

⑧ Lighter than air, this gas is used in colourful lights and signs.

This colourless gas gives off a red-orange glow when electrified.

Fe

⑨ Used to make steel, this element rusts in its pure form. It is also found inside our bodies and in some types of food.

Bi

⑩ This brittle, heavy metal has been used in cosmetics for centuries to give a shiny glow.

In its pure form, this metal reacts with air to produce rainbow-coloured crystals.

Au

⑪ For thousands of years, this easy-to-work precious metal has been used to make jewellery. It was also forged into coins in the past.

Kr

A blue-white glow is produced when this colourless gas is electrified.

⑫ One of the rarest gases on Earth, this element was discovered in 1898.

Cu

⑬ Soft and flexible in its pure form, this metal conducts heat and electricity extremely well. For this reason it is used to make electrical wires and saucepans.

Unique reddish-orange colour

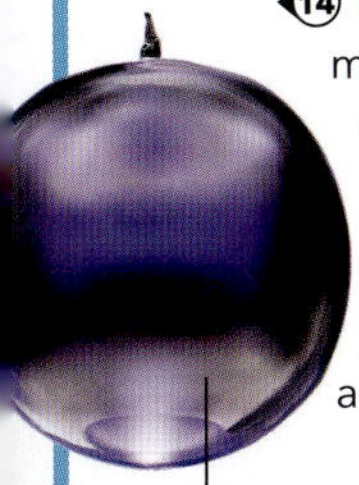

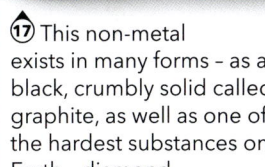

H

⑭ The lightest and most abundant element in the Universe, this gas is used as fuel by stars to generate heat and light.

Pure gas glows purple when electrified

Os

⑮ Shiny and hard wearing, this rare metal is the densest of all naturally occuring elements and has a very high melting point at 3,033°C (5,491°F).

S

⑯ Also known as "brimstone", this pale yellow element is found near volcanoes. Many compounds containing this element give off a foul rotten-egg smell.

C

⑰ This non-metal exists in many forms – as a black, crumbly solid called graphite, as well as one of the hardest substances on Earth – diamond.

Crystals of this element are often found attached to volcanic mud.

Hg

⑱ Known as quicksilver in the past, this metal is quite poisonous, but is still found in some thermometers.

This is the only metal that is liquid at room temperature.

TEST YOURSELF

STARTER	CHALLENGER	GENIUS!
Gold	Aluminium	Krypton
Silver	Oxygen	Osmium
Copper	Neon	Chlorine
Iron	Magnesium	Phosphorus
Carbon	Mercury	Bismuth
Sulfur	Hydrogen	Iodine

The human body

The human body is a miracle of nature. It is packed full of parts – from 206 bones and 2 sq m (21 sq ft) of skin, to hundreds of thousands of hairs and billions of blood cells. The body is organized into various systems which all perform vital tasks to keep you alive.

Building a body

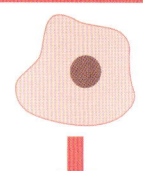

Cells: These are the smallest building blocks of the human body and come in lots of different types.

Tissue: Cells of the same type group together to form a tissue which performs a particular function.

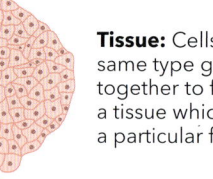

Organ: A group of different tissues make up an organ, such as the heart (left).

In numbers

250,000
The number of new brain cells a developing baby typically grows every minute.

25,000
The typical number of breaths you take every day.

106
The number of bones found in your hands and feet – more than half the number of bones in the body.

65
The percentage of your body made of oxygen.

Body systems

Organs that are linked together are called systems. Here are four body systems.

Skeletal system
Over 200 bones meet at joints to form your body's strong, movable frame.

Muscular system
Some 640 muscles make up 20 per cent of your weight and enable you to move your body.

Circulatory system
Blood carries oxygen and nutrients around your body through tubes called blood vessels.

Nervous system
A network of nerves runs throughout your body carrying electric signals to and from your brain.

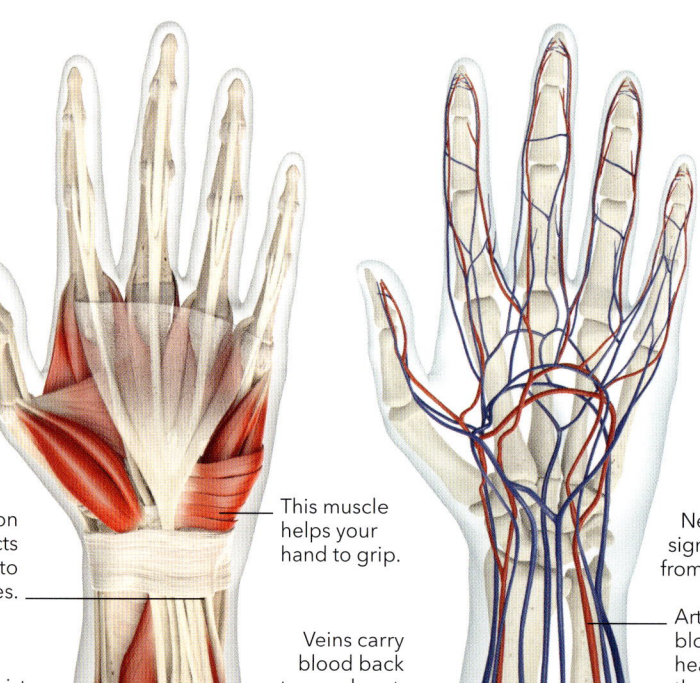

Tendon connects muscles to bones.

Ulna bone runs from elbow to wrist.

This muscle helps your hand to grip.

Veins carry blood back to your heart.

Nerves carry signals to and from the brain.

Arteries carry blood from your heart to parts of the body.

Looking inside

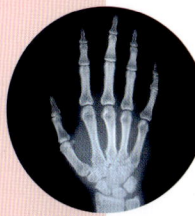
X-ray: X-rays are high energy waves that can pass through soft tissue in your body to reveal hard material such as teeth, joints, and bones.

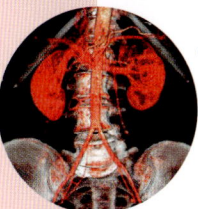
CT scans: Patients lie in a doughnut-shaped machine which takes X-ray images from all directions to give a detailed 3D view of the body.

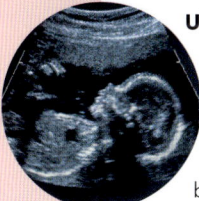
Ultrasound: High-pitched sounds are bounced around inside the body and the echoes are put together to build up a picture of internal organs, or an unborn baby in the womb.

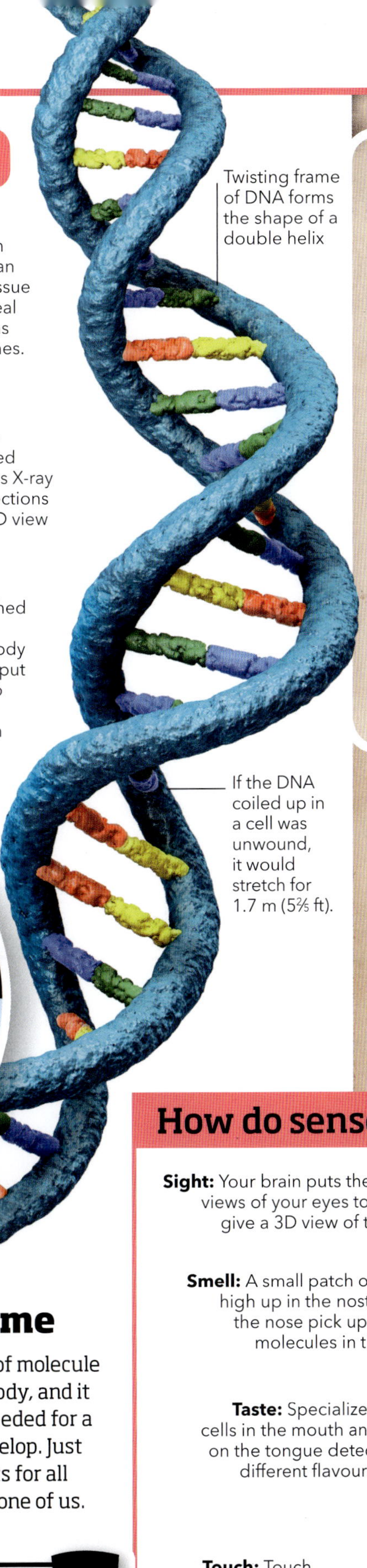

Twisting frame of DNA forms the shape of a double helix

If the DNA coiled up in a cell was unwound, it would stretch for 1.7 m (5⅔ ft).

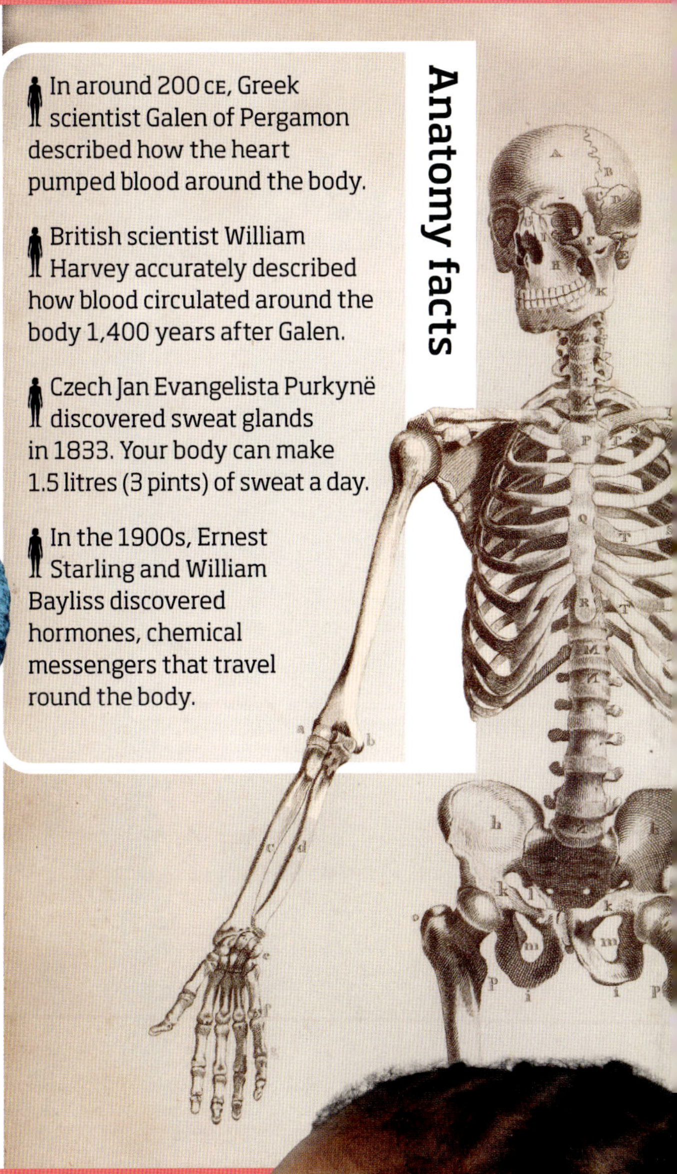

Anatomy facts

👤 In around 200 CE, Greek scientist Galen of Pergamon described how the heart pumped blood around the body.

👤 British scientist William Harvey accurately described how blood circulated around the body 1,400 years after Galen.

👤 Czech Jan Evangelista Purkyně discovered sweat glands in 1833. Your body can make 1.5 litres (3 pints) of sweat a day.

👤 In the 1900s, Ernest Starling and William Bayliss discovered hormones, chemical messengers that travel round the body.

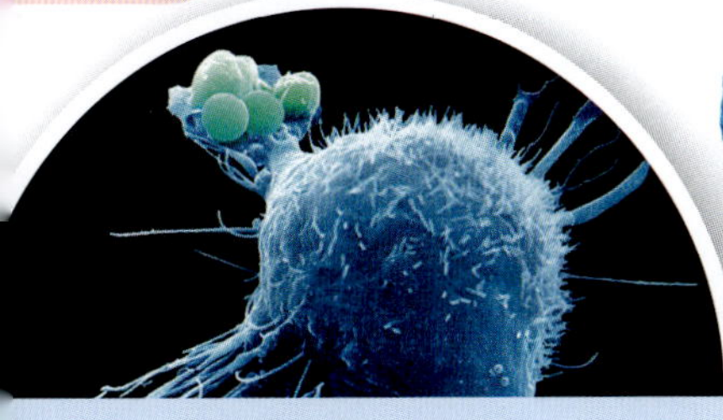

Soldier cell
This hungry hunter is a white blood cell, which seeks out germs and infected cells and gobbles them up to prevent infections.

Making me
DNA is a special kind of molecule inside every cell of our body, and it holds all the instructions needed for a human being to grow and develop. Just 0.1 per cent of all DNA accounts for all the differences between each one of us.

How do senses work?

Sight: Your brain puts the different views of your eyes together to give a 3D view of the world.

Smell: A small patch of cells high up in the nostrils of the nose pick up smell molecules in the air.

Taste: Specialized cells in the mouth and on the tongue detect different flavours.

Touch: Touch receptor cells in your skin tell you what objects feel like.

Hearing: Sound travels through the ears as vibrations.

I don't believe it
You shed around 10 billion dead skin cells from your body every day.

SCIENCE GEEK

Know your bones

The human skeleton is a fantastic framework of bones that gives us shape, provides anchoring points for muscles, and protects our inner organs. Without it, your body would just crumple on the floor! The average adult usually has 206 bones, more than half of them in the hands and feet. Pick the bones of this sporty skeleton to prove you are on the ball.

① Good for gripping, these bones form the fingers and thumbs. You have similar ones with the same name in your feet!

② Each finger and thumb is connected to the wrist by one of these long bones in the hand.

③ Eight small bones help to form the wrist and give it flexibility, so you can turn it this way and that.

④ The long, thin calf bone runs parallel to the shinbone and helps to support the ankle.

⑤ Longer and heavier than any other bone, the thighbone extends from hip to knee.

⑥ The shinbone is the larger of the bones of the lower leg. Run a finger down the front to feel its sharp edge.

⑦ This is your kneecap, a small thick bone that sits over the knee joint to protect it.

⑧ Seven small, movable bones form the ankle. The knobbly bits that you can see on either side are the ends of the bones in the lower leg!

⑨ Five long bones give the foot its arched shape – point your toes and take a look!

Inside the ear

The three smallest bones in the body are found in the ear. They pass on sound vibrations from the eardrum to the inner ear.

⑩ The tiniest of the ear bones is shaped like the ankle supports attached to a horse's saddle.

⑪ This flat-topped bone is the middle of the three linked ear bones.

⑫ This bone, which looks like a miniature DIY tool, is attached to the eardrum.

ANSWERS: 1. Phalanges 2. Metacarpals 3. Carpals 4. Fibula 5. Femur 6. Tibia 7. Patella 8. Tarsals 9. Metatarsals 10. Stirrup 11. Anvil 12. Hammer 13. Radius 14. Skull 15. Ulna 16. Mandible 17. Clavicle 18. Scapula 19. Ribs 20. Humerus 21. Sternum 22. Vertebrae 23. Sacrum 24. Pelvis

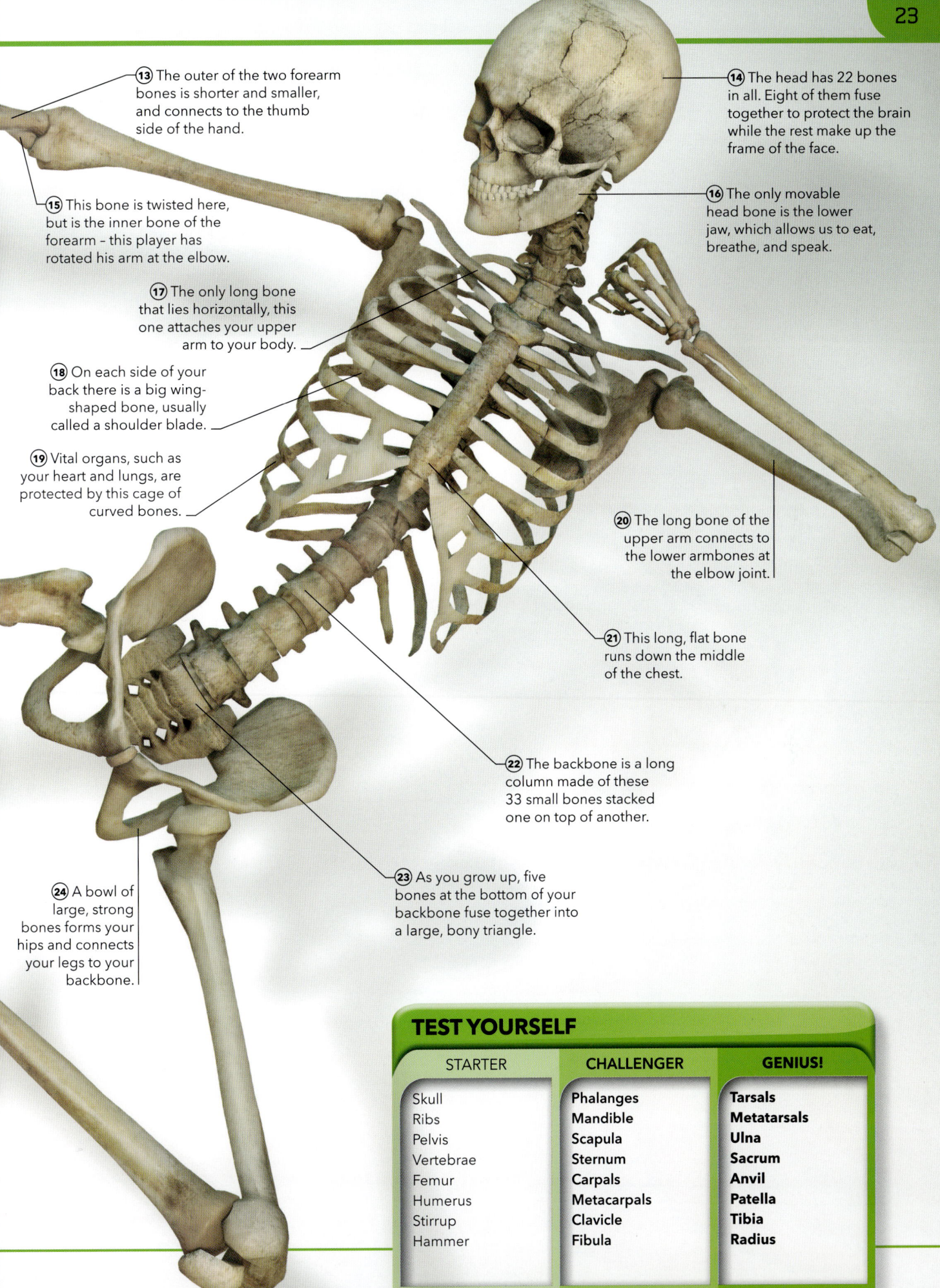

13 The outer of the two forearm bones is shorter and smaller, and connects to the thumb side of the hand.

14 The head has 22 bones in all. Eight of them fuse together to protect the brain while the rest make up the frame of the face.

15 This bone is twisted here, but is the inner bone of the forearm – this player has rotated his arm at the elbow.

16 The only movable head bone is the lower jaw, which allows us to eat, breathe, and speak.

17 The only long bone that lies horizontally, this one attaches your upper arm to your body.

18 On each side of your back there is a big wing-shaped bone, usually called a shoulder blade.

19 Vital organs, such as your heart and lungs, are protected by this cage of curved bones.

20 The long bone of the upper arm connects to the lower armbones at the elbow joint.

21 This long, flat bone runs down the middle of the chest.

22 The backbone is a long column made of these 33 small bones stacked one on top of another.

23 As you grow up, five bones at the bottom of your backbone fuse together into a large, bony triangle.

24 A bowl of large, strong bones forms your hips and connects your legs to your backbone.

TEST YOURSELF

STARTER	CHALLENGER	GENIUS!
Skull	Phalanges	Tarsals
Ribs	Mandible	Metatarsals
Pelvis	Scapula	Ulna
Vertebrae	Sternum	Sacrum
Femur	Carpals	Anvil
Humerus	Metacarpals	Patella
Stirrup	Clavicle	Tibia
Hammer	Fibula	Radius

SCIENCE GEEK

This open framework keeps things light and actually increases its strength!

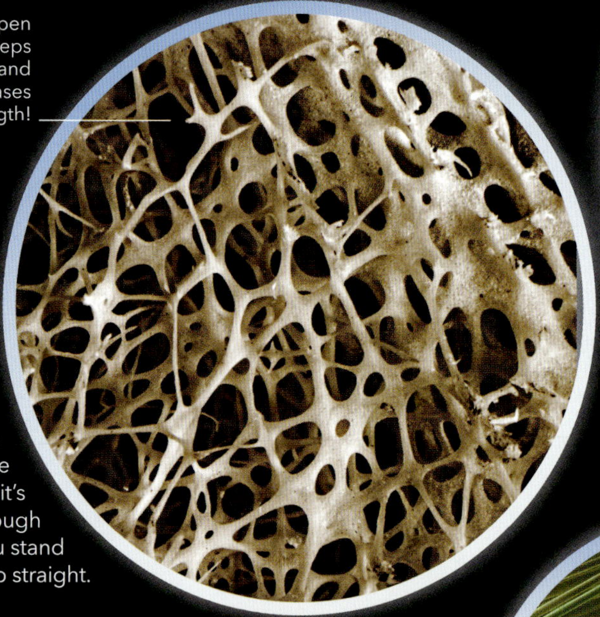

1 This may look like delicate lace – but it's strong enough to help you stand up straight.

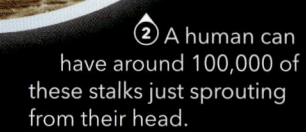

2 A human can have around 100,000 of these stalks just sprouting from their head.

3 Naming this creepy creature could have you scratching your head.

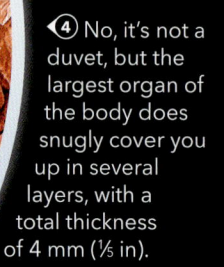

4 No, it's not a duvet, but the largest organ of the body does snugly cover you up in several layers, with a total thickness of 4 mm (⅕ in).

5 Hands up! Do you know where to find this unique body pattern?

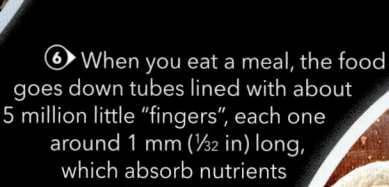

6 When you eat a meal, the food goes down tubes lined with about 5 million little "fingers", each one around 1 mm (¹⁄₃₂ in) long, which absorb nutrients into your body.

TEST YOURSELF

STARTER	CHALLENGER	GENIUS!
Eyelash mite	Sweat pore	Fingerprint
Head louse	Tooth enamel	Bone tissue
Hair	Blood cells	Intestinal lining
Skin	Lip skin	Muscle fibres

Under the microscope

Take a really close-up look at yourself! These jaw-dropping images, magnified many times through a powerful microscope, reveal the human body – and some of the things that live with us – in incredible detail. Can you recognize which bit of you is which?

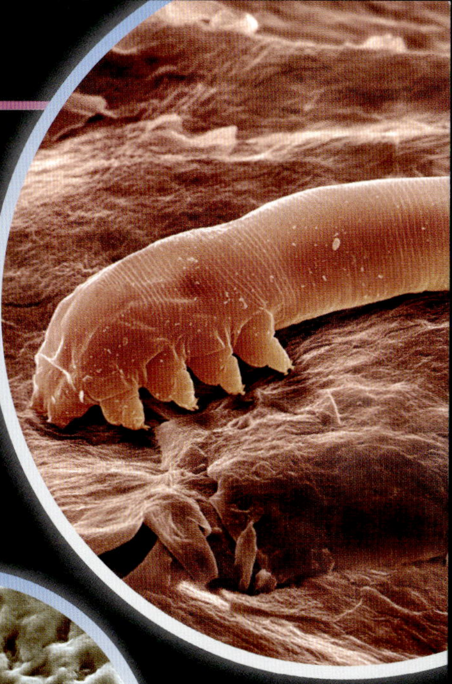

7 Watch out, there's a creepy crawly about, but at 0.4 mm (1/100 in) long, you won't see it, however hard you look!

Individual bundles of tissue

8 You need the hardest substance in the body for all that chomping!

9 Ready to run? These tightly packed bundles of tissues will get you on the move.

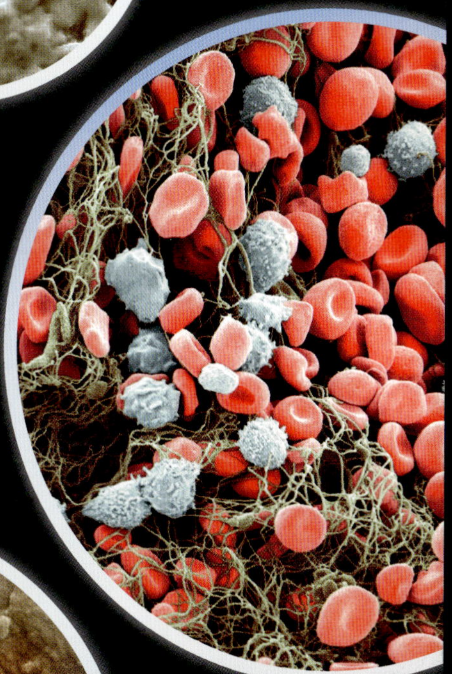

Sweat droplets

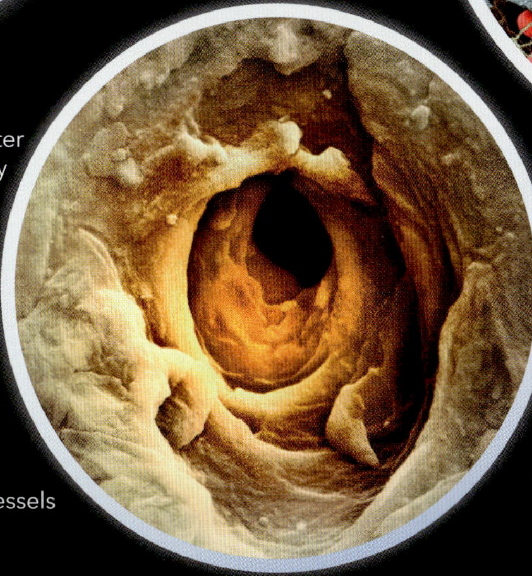

10 Stay cool! Salty water runs through this tiny tunnel, making it part of the body's temperature control system.

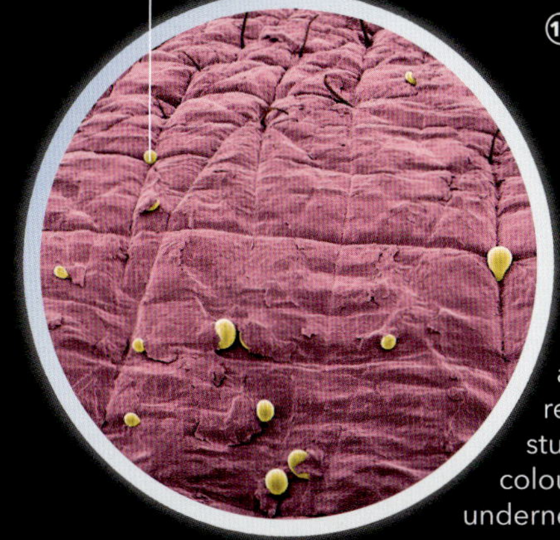

11 Allow yourself a big smile if you recognize this stretchy stuff. It is usually red in colour due to the blood vessels underneath the thin skin.

12 Every day, we produce hundreds of billions of these. Above you can see two types – the red ones transport oxygen around the body and the white ones fight germs.

Maths

Maths is the study of numbers and how they relate to each other and the world. We need maths for many things – for science, for building everything from houses to bridges, and for powering the computers and smartphones we use in our everyday lives.

Perfectly packed
Bees make their honeycomb out of hexagons (six-sided shapes) because they fit together perfectly.

I don't believe it
Although equations existed in ancient times, the equals sign was only invented in 1557, by Welsh mathematician Robert Recorde.

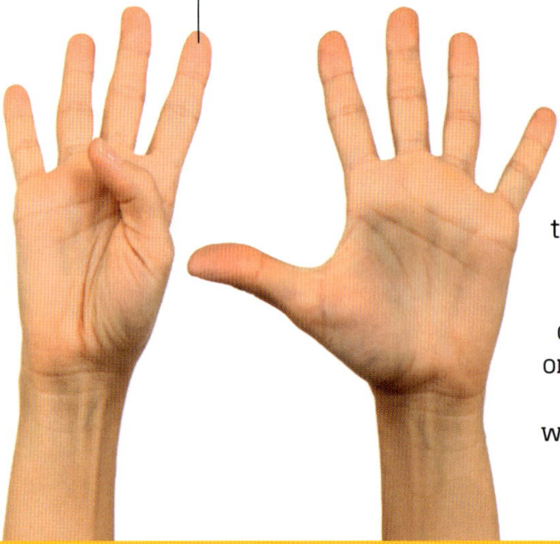

Using your fingers is also a handy way to communicate numbers without using words.

Counting in tens
The first people to count almost certainly used their hands and ten fingers to help them, like children today. As a result, our modern counting system, the decimal system, is based on tens. If we only had six fingers and thumbs, we would probably be using a system based on six.

Petal pattern
Next time you see a flower, count the number of petals it has – it is often a Fibonacci number.

Nature's numbers
Mathematical patterns can be found in nature. One number series, known as the Fibonacci sequence, turns up in all sorts of places. It begins: 1, 1, 2, 3, 5, 8, 13 and continues as the last two numbers are added together to give the next. Mathematical patterns can also be found in nature's shapes.

Early number systems
The Babylonians were the first to devise a number system and symbols, 4,000 years ago. Other ancient civilizations developed their own digits.

1	2	3	4	5	6	
1	2	3	4	5	6	Modern Hindu-Arabic
•	••	•••	••••	—	•̣	Mayan
一	二	三	四	五	六	Ancient Chinese
I	II	III	IV	V	VI	Ancient Roman
	||	|||	||||	|||||	||||||	Ancient Egyptian
𒐕	𒐖	𒐗	𒐘	𒐙	𒐚	Babylonian

Early mathematicians

Pythagoras: An ancient Greek mathematician, he is best known for working out the relationship between the sides and angles of a triangle.

Archimedes: This Greek thinker found ways to calculate the area of circles and other shapes as well as using maths to create many inventions.

Natural symmetry
If an object has two halves that look like reflections, we say it has lateral symmetry. Most animals have lateral symmetry, including you!

A snowflake has lots of lines of symmetry. You have only one – down the middle.

Measuring Earth

Greek scientist Eratosthenes was one of the first people to use maths to measure Earth's size, around 2,200 years ago. He worked this out using the angles cast by shadows at two different places in Egypt. He got the answer 40,000 km (25,000 miles) - almost exactly right!

The distance around Earth is called its circumference.

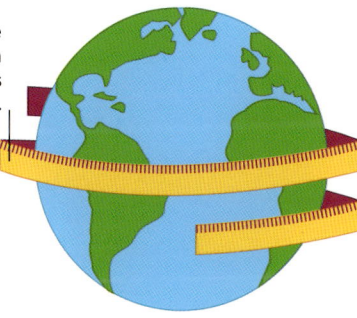

Naming numbers

Infinity
This is the word used by mathematicians to define an endless amount. The symbol for infinity is an eight on its side: ∞.

Zero
Number systems had no number for nothing until Indian mathematicians invented it around 650 CE.

Googol
The name of the number 1 followed by 100 zeros. It was named by a 9-year-old US schoolboy in 1920.

Super spiral
This plant is made up of five spirals – another Fibonacci number! Look out for spirals on pine cones and pineapples, too.

Hypatia: The first known female mathematician, Hypatia lived in Egypt more than 2,300 years ago and had her own school of maths.

Al-Khwarizmi: Born in 780 CE, this Arabic mathematician described equations and algebra and introduced Hindu-Arabic numbers (1–9) to Europe.

Maths magic
Impress a friend with your mind-reading maths.

1. Write the number 9 on a piece of paper, fold it, and give it to your friend telling them not to look at it.

2. Give your friend a calculator and ask them to:
• Put in their age and add the number of their house
• Add the last four digits of their phone number
• Multiply the result by 18
• Add the digits of the answer together. If the answer has more than one digit, keep adding the digits until they only have one left.

3. Tell your friend to look at the piece of paper and watch their amazement. The answer is always 9.

SCIENCE GEEK

Shape up!

Everything has a shape. Some things, such as a piece of paper, are flat, or 2D (two-dimensional) – they have height and width. Other objects, like a book, are 3D (three-dimensional) – they have height, width, and depth. So while paper is rectangular, a book is cuboid.

There are three sloping faces.

① Perfect for rolling, basketballs and marbles are this shape.

② This shape has four sides, only two of which are parallel to each other.

③ This 3D shape has five faces, including a triangle at each end.

① Every point on the surface of this 3D solid is the same distance away from its centre.

④ The opposite sides of this shape are equal and run parallel with each other.

The inner angles of all the corners of this shape add up to 360°.

⑤ This seven-sided shape gets its name from the Greek word for seven.

⑥ Count up! This shape has nine sides, all of equal length.

⑦ Each of the six faces of this shape is a rectangle, and the faces opposite each other are the same size.

⑧ Like a can of drink, this shape is round with two identical and circular flat ends.

⑨ There are four main types of this shape. The others are isosceles, right-angled, and scalene. The name of this one comes from the fact its three sides are the same length.

⑩ The giant building that is home to the US Department of Defense takes this five-sided shape.

The angle at each corner is 60°.

ANSWERS: 1. Sphere 2. Trapezium 3. Triangular prism 4. Parallelogram 5. Heptagon 6. Nonagon 7. Cuboid 8. Cylinder 9. Equilateral triangle 10. Pentagon 11. Decagon 12. Rhombus 13. Square-based pyramid 14. Kite 15. Hexagonal prism 16. Hexagon 17. Rectangle 18. Square 19. Octagon 20. Cube 21. Cone

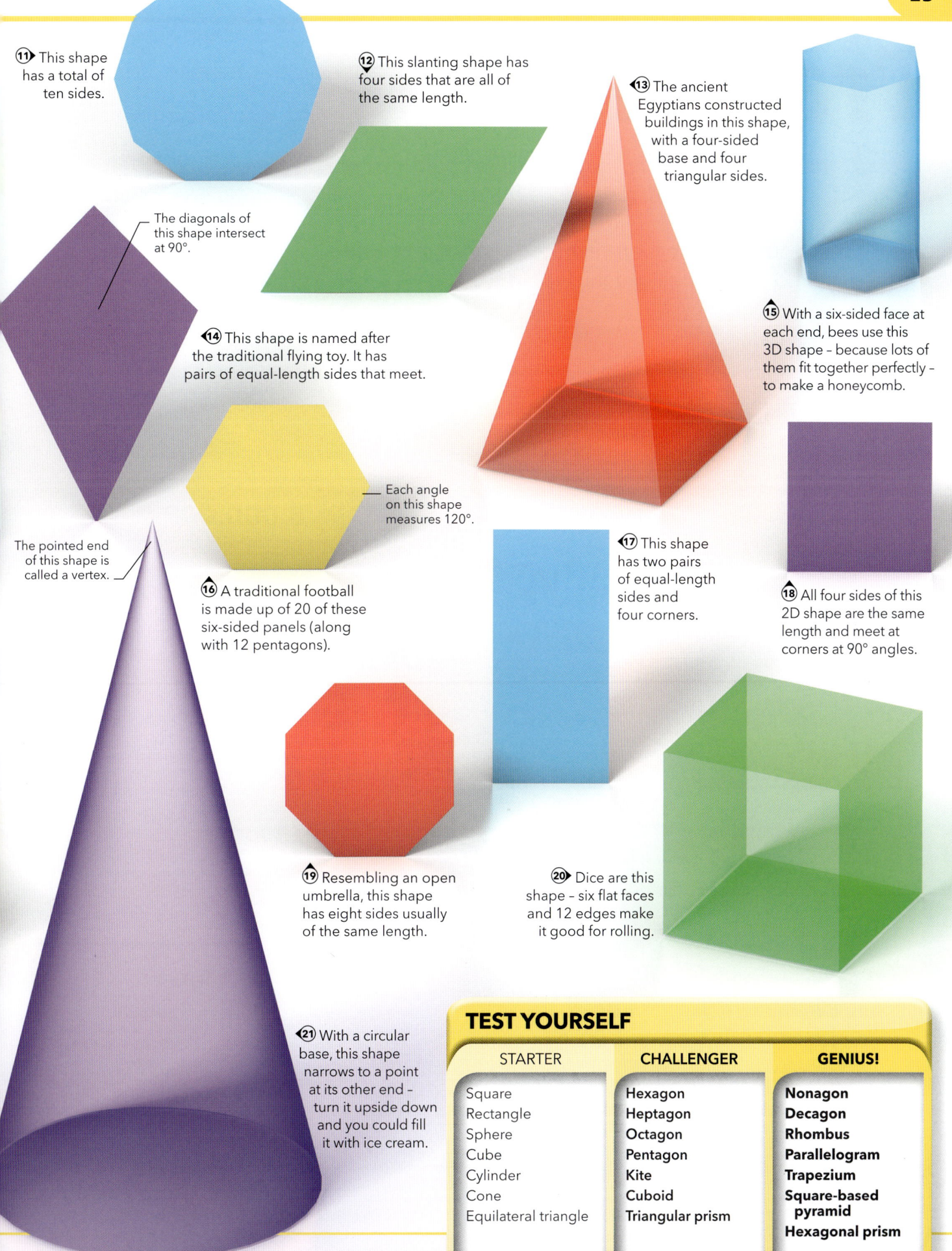

Science Geek

Transport

Before planes, trains, and cars, long journeys could take months. People walked, rode, used horsedrawn carriages, or sailed with the wind. Now we fly around the world in hours, cross oceans in hi-tech liners, and speed overland in all types of vehicles.

Steaming ahead

Invented over 200 years ago, the steam train would revolutionize travel, connecting cities and countries as never before. Steam trains burn wood or coal to heat water, which turns into steam. The steam pushes rods that turn wheels round, propelling the train and the carriages it pulls along the track.

How to fly a plane

01. Start the engine and release the brakes. The engine produces thrust – a force that pushes the plane forward.

Chimney Smoke leaves the engine through this outlet.

Boiler Water is heated in this large metal container, turning into steam.

Driver's cab The driver and fireman (who keeps the furnace going) stand here.

Driving wheels These are driven round by the steam.

In numbers

6,000,000 The number of parts used to build a Boeing 747 jet airliner.

458.45 m (1,505 ft) The length of the world's longest ship, the *Seawise Giant* supertanker.

36 The number of wheels on the world's longest stretch limo, which is 30.5 m (100 ft) long and contains a swimming pool and a double bed.

13 km/h (8 mph) The top speed of the Benz Motorwagen, the first car, made in 1888.

Speed machines

The first cars, planes, ships, and trains were slow, but modern advances in technology have really speeded things up!

 Vestas Sailrocket 2: The world's fastest sailing ship travels at 121.06 km/h (75.22 mph).

Westland Lynx AH.1: Reaching 400.87 km/h (249.09 mph), this is the fastest helicopter ever made to date.

Spirit of Australia: In 1978, this boat set the water speed record of 511.11 km/h (317.59 mph).

 **SR-71 Blackbird:** This military jet plane can fly at high levels, at a speed of 3,529.56 km/h (2,193.1 mph).

 **A4 Mallard:** The fastest-ever steam locomotive reached 203 km/h (126 mph) in 1936.

 **Bugatti Veyron 16.4 Super Sport:** This supercar has a top speed of 431.07 km/h (267.86 mph).

SCMaglev L0 train: In 2015, this experimental train reached 603 km/h (375 mph).

 **Thrust SSC:** The world land speed record holder achieved 1,227.9 km/h (763 mph) in 1997.

02. Use the throttle to increase the engine's speed along the runway. Air moving under and over the wings produces lift.

03. Pull back on the control column (the steering device) to lift the nose of the plane up off the ground.

04. As the plane climbs up into the air, activate the controls, which pull the wheels up into the plane's body.

05. Flaps on the wing and tail can be moved using the control column and rudder bar to steer the plane in the sky.

The Hawk T1A jet plane is flown by the British Royal Air Force's Red Arrows aerobatics team.

Weird watercraft

The *Seabreacher*, a two-person underwater craft, can leap out of the water like a dolphin.

This *Quadrofoil* Q2S electric boat skims above the water at 40 km/h (25 mph) using four wing-like hydrofoils.

This *Tredalo* paddleboat looks like a giant hamster wheel. In 2012, it carried Chris Todd 37 km (23 miles) across the Irish Sea.

Giant carrier
The body of the giant Airbus *Beluga* stands 17.2 m (56⅔ ft) tall and can carry entire aircraft, helicopters, and space station modules.

Get moving!

🚗 At only 1.37 m (4 ½ ft) long, the Peel P50 is the smallest drivable car in the world.

🚗 In 1999, a Mi-26 helicopter carried a 23,000-year-old woolly mammoth encased in an ice block across Russia.

🚗 A train line crosses right over the plane runway at New Zealand's Gisborne Airport.

🚗 The Rinspeed sQuba car can be driven both on land and up to 10 m (33 ft) under water.

Space Shuttle This craft raced through space at 28,000 km/h (17,500 mph).

I don't believe it
The first aircraft flight, by the Wright brothers' *Flyer 1* plane in 1903, lifted off the ground for just 36 m (118 ft).

SCIENCE GEEK

On the road

There are more than one billion motor vehicles on the world's roads and most of these are cars! Powered by electric motors or internal combustion engines, they come in all shapes and sizes.

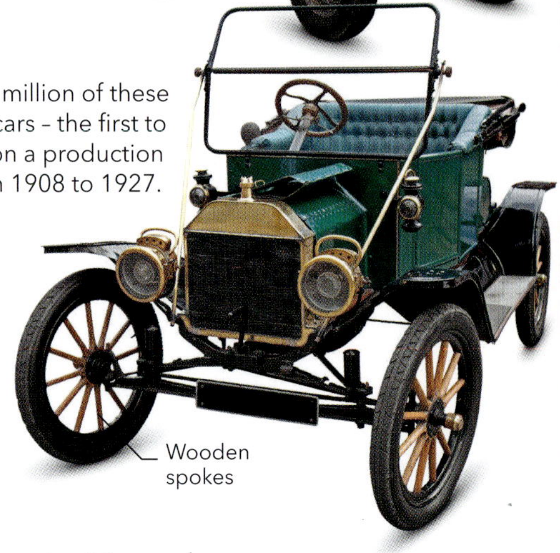

1. This extra-long luxury car can carry eight or more passengers in comfort and style!

2. This 1958 model was the first car made by a famous Japanese car company. Its engine is in the back, with room for storage in the front.

3. Fifteen million of these affordable US cars – the first to be mass-produced on a production line – were built from 1908 to 1927.

   Wooden spokes

4. This sleek, electric car was built in 2010 and can travel up to 393 km (244 miles) before its batteries need recharging.

5. This super small, two-seater car is ideal for driving around crowded city streets.

   Just 2.5 m (8⅕ ft) long

6. Known for its rocket-shaped tail fins, this iconic 1950s American convertible was very heavy at more than 2 tonnes.

7. This four-wheel drive vehicle from the 1940s was sturdy enough for driving over rough ground.

   No doors – making it easy for people to hop in and out

8. Small and zippy, this British car was first launched in 1959. Its design was later improved by a Formula 1 car designer.

   To keep the car small, the engine sits sideways under the bonnet.

TEST YOURSELF

STARTER
- Volkswagen Beetle
- Mini Cooper
- Smart Car
- Willys Jeep
- Stretch limousine

CHALLENGER
- Ford Model T
- Rolls Royce Phantom
- Bugatti Veyron
- Cadillac Eldorado
- DeLorean DMC-12

GENIUS!
- Aston Martin DB2/4
- Ford GT40
- Subaru 360
- Benz Patent-Motorwagen
- Tesla Roadster

ANSWERS: 1. Stretch limousine 2. Subaru 360 3. Ford Model T 4. Tesla Roadster 5. Smart Car 6. Cadillac Eldorado 7. Willys Jeep 8. Mini Cooper 9. DeLorean DMC-12 10. Aston Martin DB2/4 11. Ford GT40 12. Rolls Royce Phantom 13. Volkswagen Beetle 14. Bugatti Veyron 15. Benz Patent-Motorwagen

Gull-wing doors open upwards

⑨ Famous for featuring in the 1980s *Back To The Future* movie series, this unusual car had a stainless steel body.

⑩ This 1950s British sports car is known for its speed, and the manufacturer is James Bond's car producer of choice!

⑪ In 1960s, this powerful American car won the Le Mans 24-hour endurance race four times in a row.

The car was just 1.03 m (3⅖ ft) tall.

Figurehead is called the "Spirit of Ecstasy"

⑫ The manufacturer of this luxury car, with a ghostly name, is known for its quality production.

Distinctive bug-shaped body

⑬ First built in the 1930s, this German vehicle is the most popular car ever, with more than 21.5 million models built.

Folding roof for rainy days

Steering handle

At 5.7 m (18¾ ft), the car was very long for a two-door vehicle.

⑮ Made in 1886, this German vehicle was the first car to be built for sale. It was steered using a handle rather than a steering wheel.

⑭ This powerful supercar has a record-breaking top speed of 431 km/h (268 mph).

SCIENCE GEEK

1 This fast, French electric train whisks passengers along at speeds of up to 320 km/h (199 mph).

2 This American carriage had its own electric motors so it could run on rails, without an engine to pull it.

The coaches provide the look and feel of royal rail cars.

3 The world's fastest train service reached 431 km/h (268 mph) on a record-breaking run in China.

4 There are sleeping cabins, two restaurants, and even a spa on this luxury train that carries passengers around India.

All aboard!

Trains run on rails, or track, and carry millions of people every day to work, school, or on exciting adventures! The first trains were powered by steam engines and hauled small numbers of wagons or small carriages. Now, modern trains use diesel engines or electric motors to speed along their routes. Can you name the train?

5 A powerful, sturdy train is just right for hauling sightseers through the hilly wilderness of northwestern Canada and USA.

7 This train travels on the world's oldest below-ground railway system, which opened in 1863. Just please mind the gap!

The nose is streamlined for travel at high speeds.

6 In Japan, sleek electric trains, such as this one, pull 10 carriages at speeds of up to 320 km/h (199 mph) – getting passengers where they need to be fast!

8 The first British steam train to race at 160 km/h (100 mph), this train had travelled 3.35 million km (2½ million miles) by 1963 when it retired from service.

ANSWERS: 1. Train à Grande Vitesse (TGV) 2. Budd Metroliner 3. Shanghai Maglev 4. Palace on Wheels 5. Rocky Mountaineer 6. JRN Shinkansen bullet train 7. London Underground 8. The Flying Scotsman 9. The Fairy Queen 10. H-Bahn Sky-Train 11. GM Aerotrain 12. Osaka monorail 13. A4 Mallard 14. The Ghan 15. Stephenson's Rocket

Each end could be connected to another carriage to make a long train.

⑨ Built in 1855, this East Indian Railways train is the oldest steam locomotive still running full-steam ahead.

⑩ This driverless train hangs below its rail, carrying passengers around Germany's Düsseldorf airport.

⑪ This 1950s American train had a streamlined nose, like a plane, and carriages that were half the size of usual ones, which made the train so light that people complained about their rough journey!

Smoke leaves the train's boiler through this chimney.

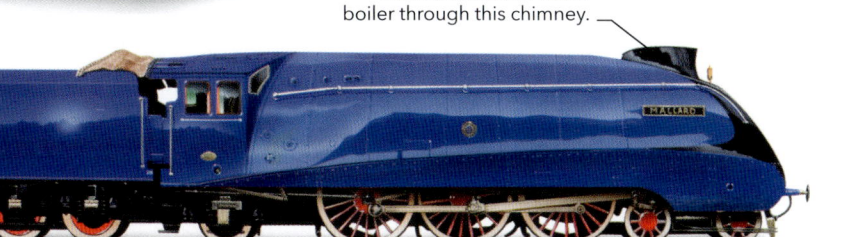

⑬ Named after a bird, the world's fastest steam locomotive reached 203 km/h (126 mph) in 1938.

⑭ Powerful engines in this train haul up to 44 passenger carriages on a 54-hour journey across Australia.

⑫ Most trains run on two rails, but this electric train runs through a Japanese city on just one!

The horn signals that the train is approaching.

⑮ A pioneering steam locomotive, this vehicle ran on the world's first intercity train line between Liverpool and Manchester, in the UK, in 1830.

TEST YOURSELF

STARTER	CHALLENGER	GENIUS!
London Underground	A4 *Mallard*	Budd Metroliner
Rocky Mountaineer	*Palace on Wheels*	Shanghai Maglev
Train à Grande Vitesse (TGV)	JRN Shinkansen bullet train	GM Aerotrain
The Flying Scotsman	H-Bahn Sky-Train	Stephenson's *Rocket*
The Ghan	Osaka monorail	*The Fairy Queen*

35

SCIENCE GEEK

These propellers tilt upwards to help the plane take off vertically.

①> The first powered, heavier-than-air plane was built and flown by two brothers in 1903.

Pilot lay across the wing.

②> This unusual military aircraft can take off and land like a helicopter and travel at speeds of up to 500 km/h (310 mph), like an airplane.

③> With floats underneath its body instead of wheels, this sturdy plane can take off and land on rivers and lakes.

Inflatable bags stored here for landing on water

④> This military helicopter once battled submarines but is now used for search-and-rescue missions.

The windshield is made of armoured glass.

Taking to the skies

For thousands of years people dreamed of flying through the air like birds. With the invention of aircraft in the early 20th century, they finally could! While some aircraft use spinning rotors or propeller blades to fly, others use powerful jet engines to zip through the air.

⑤> Known for its top speed of up to 720 km/h (447 mph), this iconic British fighter plane was flown in World War II.

37

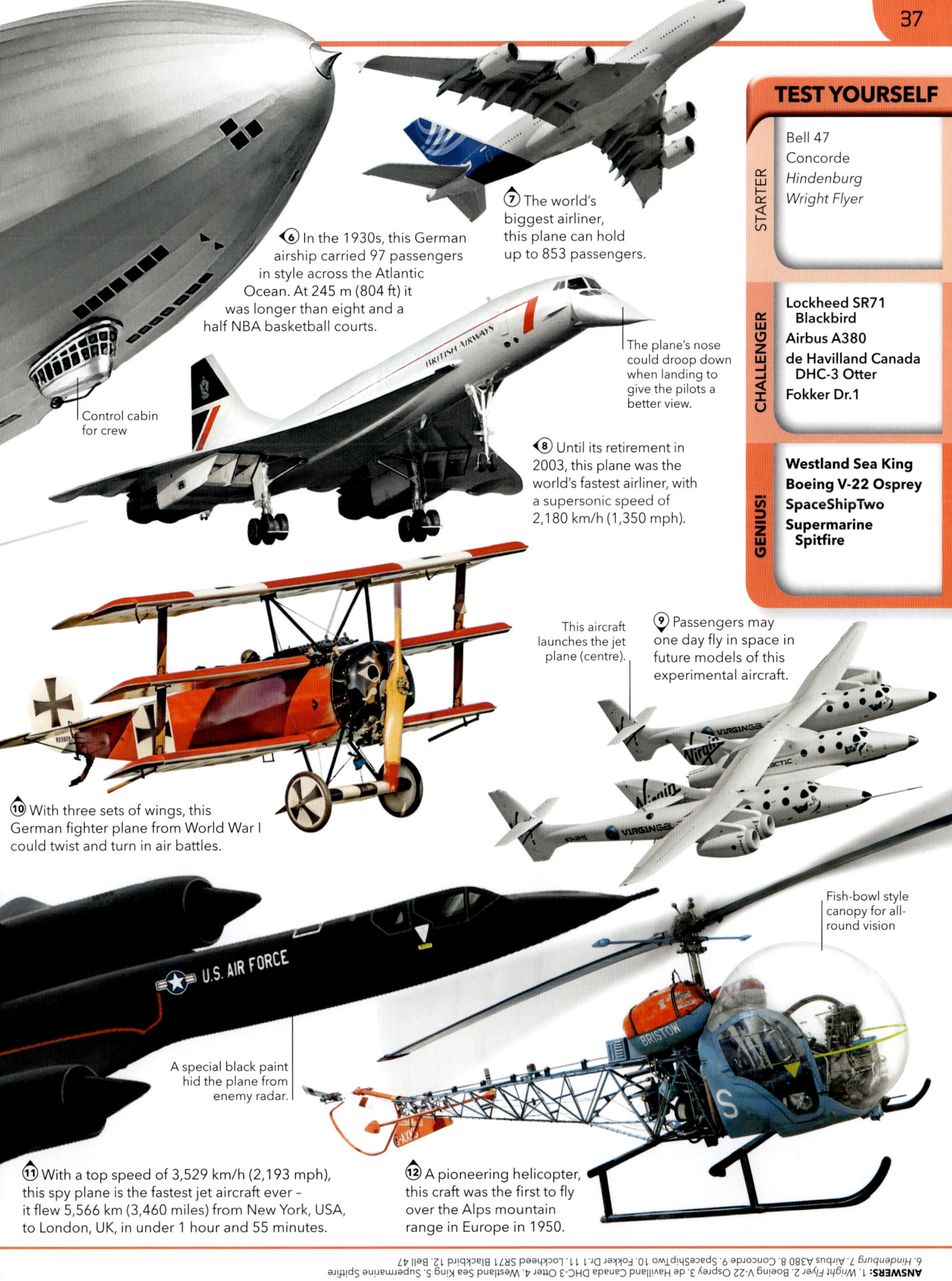

TEST YOURSELF

STARTER
Bell 47
Concorde
Hindenburg
Wright Flyer

CHALLENGER
Lockheed SR71 Blackbird
Airbus A380
de Havilland Canada DHC-3 Otter
Fokker Dr.1

GENIUS!
Westland Sea King
Boeing V-22 Osprey
SpaceShipTwo
Supermarine Spitfire

6 In the 1930s, this German airship carried 97 passengers in style across the Atlantic Ocean. At 245 m (804 ft) it was longer than eight and a half NBA basketball courts.

Control cabin for crew

7 The world's biggest airliner, this plane can hold up to 853 passengers.

The plane's nose could droop down when landing to give the pilots a better view.

8 Until its retirement in 2003, this plane was the world's fastest airliner, with a supersonic speed of 2,180 km/h (1,350 mph).

This aircraft launches the jet plane (centre).

9 Passengers may one day fly in space in future models of this experimental aircraft.

10 With three sets of wings, this German fighter plane from World War I could twist and turn in air battles.

Fish-bowl style canopy for all-round vision

A special black paint hid the plane from enemy radar.

11 With a top speed of 3,529 km/h (2,193 mph), this spy plane is the fastest jet aircraft ever – it flew 5,566 km (3,460 miles) from New York, USA, to London, UK, in under 1 hour and 55 minutes.

12 A pioneering helicopter, this craft was the first to fly over the Alps mountain range in Europe in 1950.

ANSWERS: 1. Wright Flyer 2. Boeing V-22 Osprey 3. de Havilland Canada DHC-3 Otter 4. Westland Sea King 5. Supermarine Spitfire 6. Hindenburg 7. Airbus A380 8. Concorde 9. SpaceShipTwo 10. Fokker Dr.1 11. Lockheed SR71 Blackbird 12. Bell 47

SCIENCE GEEK

All at sea

Early boats were hollowed-out tree-trunk canoes or simple rafts, used for short, local journeys. As their design developed, and ships and boats grew bigger, people were able to sail further, to trade and explore new lands. Today, cargo ships are so huge you need a bicycle to get from one end to the other!

① Shops, restaurants, and even swimming pools can be found in this floating hotel.

② Ancient Greek ships, such as this one, were rowed using three banks of oars on each side.

Sail was raised for long journeys

Ram was used to smash into enemy ships.

Large gun is used to fire at targets

③ Small, rapid military boats carry cannons or other weapons for patrolling coastal waters.

④ Fishermen and merchants use vessels like these to sail the Indian Ocean and the Red Sea.

Distinctive triangular sail

⑤ The huge, steel, dome-shaped tanks on this ship transport super-cooled fuel in liquid form across the world.

⑥ First used as warships more than 500 years ago, these three- or four-masted ships were later sailed by explorers.

⑧ This large, armoured military ship from World War II is one of the biggest and most heavily armed type of ship in large navies.

⑦ This 285-m- (935-ft-) long ship carries cargo in thousands of truck-sized boxes, which can be then handled at ports.

ANSWERS: 1. Cruise liner 2. Trireme 3. Gunboat 4. Dhow 5. Gas tanker 6. Galleon 7. Container ship 8. Battleship 9. River steamboat 10. Viking longship 11. Merchant junk 12. Sampan 13. Aircraft carrier 14. Car ferry 15. Icebreaker

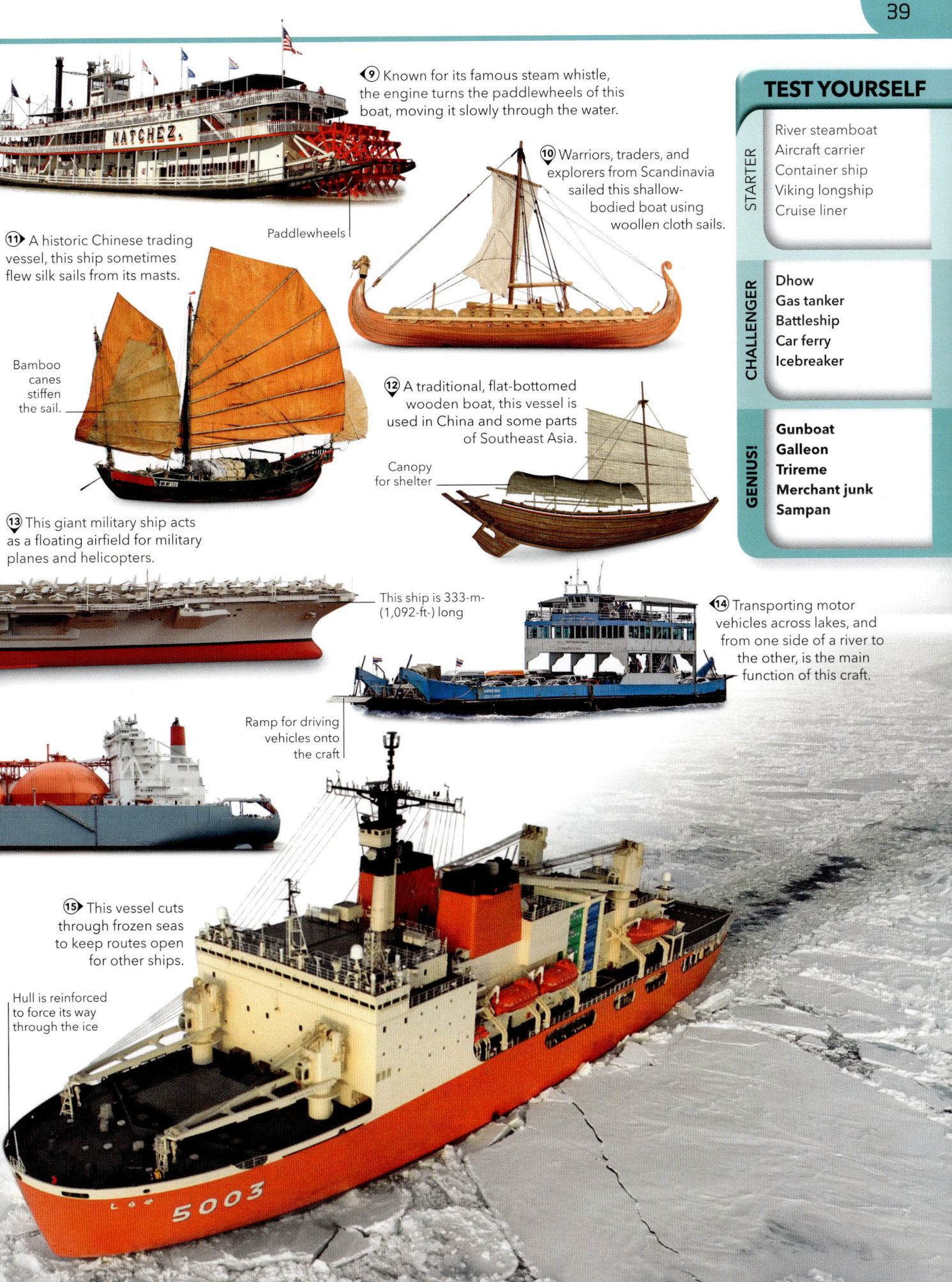

9 Known for its famous steam whistle, the engine turns the paddlewheels of this boat, moving it slowly through the water.

10 Warriors, traders, and explorers from Scandinavia sailed this shallow-bodied boat using woollen cloth sails.

Paddlewheels

11 A historic Chinese trading vessel, this ship sometimes flew silk sails from its masts.

Bamboo canes stiffen the sail.

12 A traditional, flat-bottomed wooden boat, this vessel is used in China and some parts of Southeast Asia.

Canopy for shelter

13 This giant military ship acts as a floating airfield for military planes and helicopters.

This ship is 333-m- (1,092-ft-) long

14 Transporting motor vehicles across lakes, and from one side of a river to the other, is the main function of this craft.

Ramp for driving vehicles onto the craft

15 This vessel cuts through frozen seas to keep routes open for other ships.

Hull is reinforced to force its way through the ice

TEST YOURSELF

STARTER
- River steamboat
- Aircraft carrier
- Container ship
- Viking longship
- Cruise liner

CHALLENGER
- Dhow
- Gas tanker
- Battleship
- Car ferry
- Icebreaker

GENIUS!
- Gunboat
- Galleon
- Trireme
- Merchant junk
- Sampan

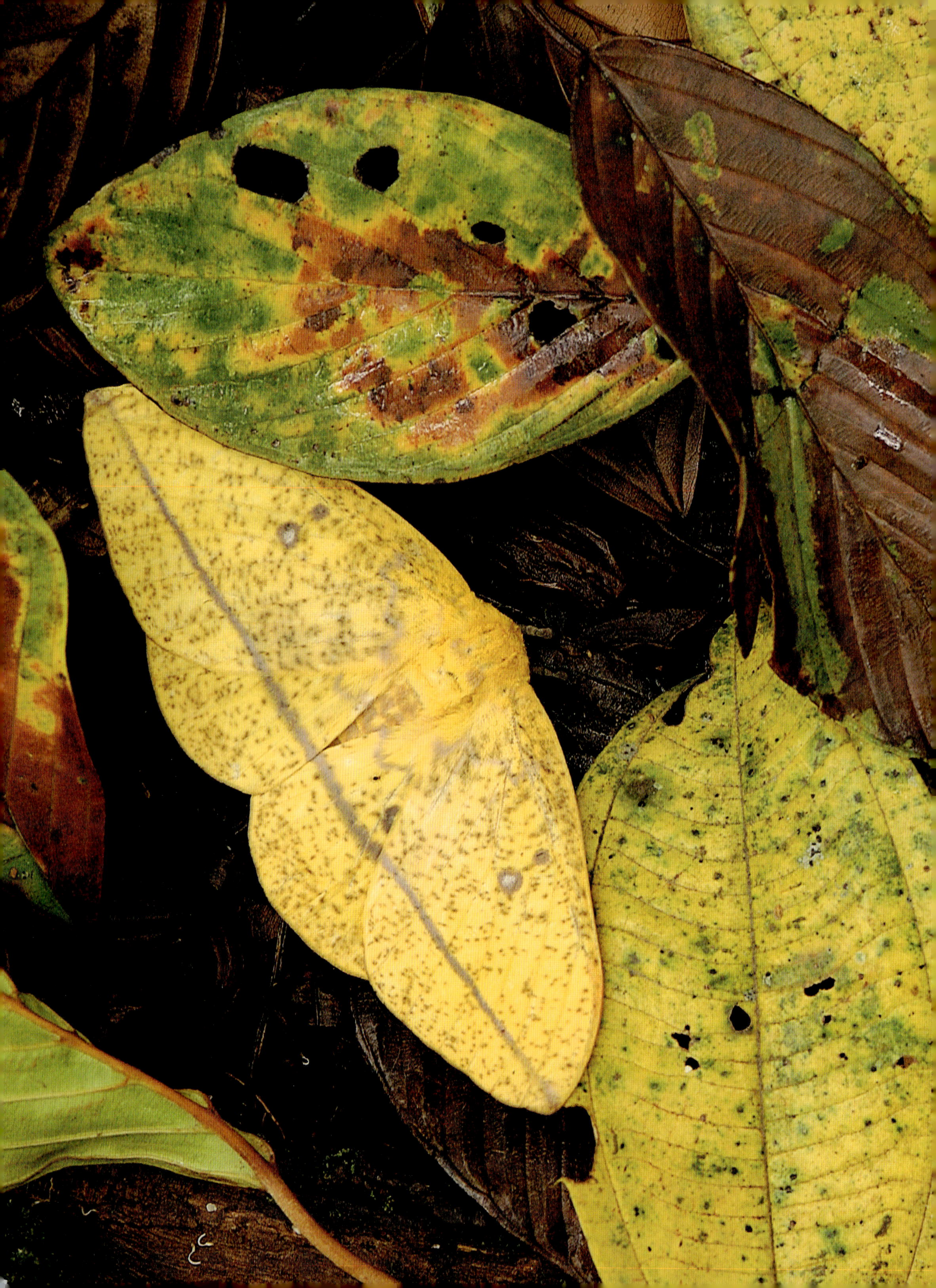

2 NATURE KNOW-IT-ALL

Camouflage challenge
The world's plants come in a variety of extraordinary colours and patterns. But there is more than just foliage in this picture – these leaves are the perfect hiding place for the imperial moth. Can you see past its clever camouflage and spot it?

NATURE KNOW-IT-ALL

How fossils are formed

01. To become a fossil, a dinosaur body needs to be quickly buried, for example, by being covered by volcanic ash.

02. Once the soft parts rot away, the hard bones end up under deeper layers of sediment.

03. Over millions of years, minerals fill spaces in the bones, which turn the sediment into rock and bones into fossils.

04. Over millions more years, wind and rain wear the rocks away, exposing the fossil so it can be found.

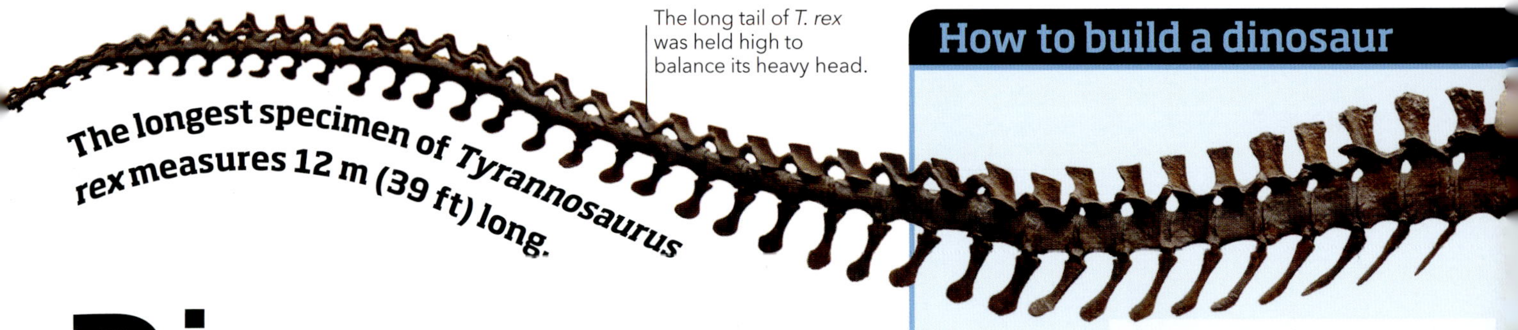

The long tail of *T. rex* was held high to balance its heavy head.

The longest specimen of Tyrannosaurus rex measures 12 m (39 ft) long.

Dinosaurs

Prehistoric reptiles called dinosaurs walked the Earth for 180 million years, long before humans were around. Scientists are able to tell how the dinosaurs lived by studying their remains, preserved in rock as fossils.

How to build a dinosaur

01. Fossil bones are very heavy and fragile so take 3D scans of them to create casts and then make copies of them using lighter materials.

Extinction event
Many dinosaurs were wiped out when an asteroid collided with Earth and destroyed their habitats.

What was a dinosaur?

Dinosaurs were giant scaly reptiles, some with feathers, that lived on land. They shared their world with many other kinds of giant reptiles that were not dinosaurs, for example, flying reptiles such as the pterosaurs and marine reptiles such as the plesiosaurs.

Flying reptile   **Dinosaur**   **Marine reptile**

Types of fossil

Body fossil: Hard body parts, such as skeletons, are replaced by minerals that turn them to rock.

Egg fossil: Dino eggs are usually found as fossil shell fragments, but are sometimes intact if buried and preserved quickly.

243 million
The age, in years, of the fossils of *Nyasasaurus*, the oldest dinosaur.

700
The number of dinosaur species discovered and named by 2018.

60 cm
(2 ft) The length of the biggest fossilized dinosaur eggs.

18 m
(60 ft) The height of the tallest known dinosaur, *Sauroposeidon*.

Dino birds

Some dinosaur fossils, such as this *Archaeopteryx* specimen (right), show the impressions of feathers – these dinosaurs were the first birds. By comparing body structures, scientists have worked out that birds evolved from ancestors that were upright-walking dinosaurs closely related to *T. rex*.

Fine sediment reveals the details of the *Archaeopteryx*'s feathered wing.

T. rex walked with its body roughly parallel to the ground.

Holes for large nostrils for sniffing out prey.

I don't believe it
The longest and heaviest dinosaur discovered to date is *Argentinosaurus*. It was the length of four fire engines and would have weighed as much as 17 African elephants!

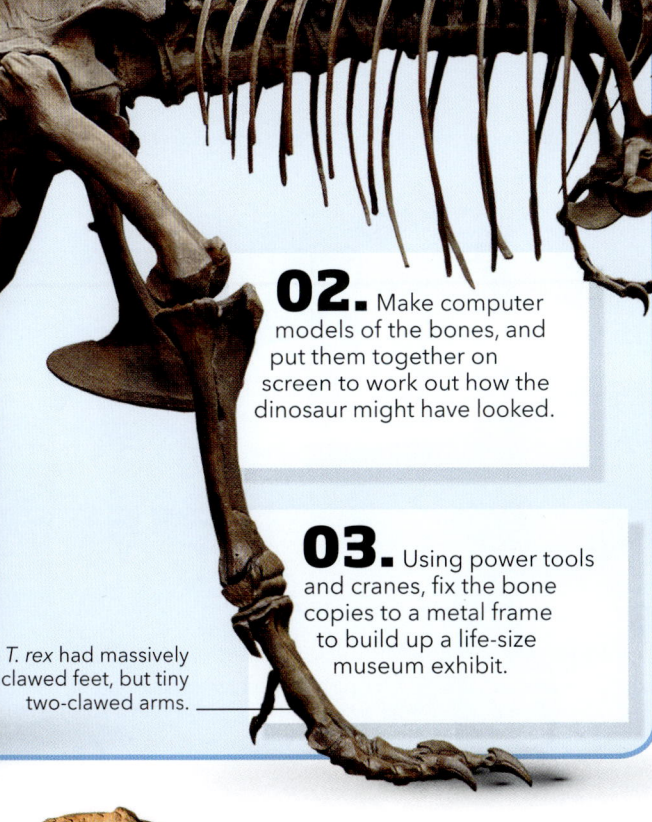

02. Make computer models of the bones, and put them together on screen to work out how the dinosaur might have looked.

03. Using power tools and cranes, fix the bone copies to a metal frame to build up a life-size museum exhibit.

T. rex had massively clawed feet, but tiny two-clawed arms.

Fossil finds

- Dinosaur fossils have been found on every continent, including Antarctica.
- Scientists can often work out the height of a dinosaur from its fossilized footprint. Roughly, its leg length is four times the length of its footprint.
- Certain fossil sites, such as some lake beds, have preserved tissue, ranging from skin to even the outlines of muscles.
- Small stones found in the stomach cavities of plant-eating dinosaurs probably helped them grind up tough leaves.

Mould and cast: Moulds are formed when impressions of something, such as this dinosaur skin, turn to stone. Later mud fills the mould to create a cast fossil.

Trace fossil: Preserved signs of animal life, such as footprints or poo (called coprolites) are known as trace fossils.

NATURE KNOW-IT-ALL

Clawed carnivores

Dinosaurs have ruled the Earth for millions of years. These extraordinary beasts came in all shapes and sizes – the biggest were the plant-eaters but the most formidable were the meat-eaters. Some grew as tall as a three-storey building, while other smaller ones were the ancestors of modern-day birds.

1 This creature had feathery, clawed wings that enabled it to fly for short bursts – but it also had a toothy dino-like jaw!

2 The most famous meat-eating dinosaur had banana-shaped teeth that delivered a bone-crushing bite. Its tiny, but strong forelimbs may have helped to grip prey.

3 This dinosaur had powerful, muscular legs and may have run as fast as an ostrich, at up to 60 km/h (37 mph).

4 Found in Asia, this large species had a bumpy crest along the middle of its snout.

Three strong toes, each with a blunt claw

5 One of the earliest known dinosaurs was scarcely bigger than an adult human at 3 m (10 ft). Its sharp, angled teeth were ideal for catching small prey.

6 Although small, this feathered dinosaur had enormous claws – up to 6.5 cm (2½ in) long – for gripping prey.

7 This is one of the few meat-eaters with horns on its head and a ridge of bony scales down its back.

8 With lots of tiny backward-facing teeth for seizing slippery fish, this dinosaur also had front limbs armed with claws up to 30 cm (12 in) long.

ANSWERS: 1. Archaeopteryx 2. Tyrannosaurus 3. Gallimimus 4. Monolophosaurus 5. Coelophysis 6. Velociraptor 7. Ceratosaurus 8. Baryonyx 9. Spinosaurus 10. Allosaurus 11. Dilophosaurus 12. Cryolophosaurus

9 Measuring 14 m (46 ft) long, the biggest meat-eating dinosaur had a giant "sail" on its back and crocodile-like jaws for catching fish.

The spiny "sail" was supported by bones as long as 1.8 m (6 ft).

TEST YOURSELF

STARTER
- Spinosaurus
- Archaeopteryx
- Tyrannosaurus
- Velociraptor

CHALLENGER
- Gallimimus
- Allosaurus
- Coelophysis
- Cryolophosaurus

GENIUS!
- Dilophosaurus
- Monolophosaurus
- Baryonyx
- Ceratosaurus

The double crests may have been used in courting displays.

11 Unusual skull crests set this dinosaur apart from other meat-eaters.

Powerful, three-clawed hand

10 This Jurassic dinosaur had more than 70 knife-like teeth, perfect for eating big plant-eating dinosaurs.

Three-clawed hand

Powerful legs for chasing prey

12 Found in Antarctica, this top predator is known for its strange bony crest, which was probably used for display.

45

NATURE KNOW-IT-ALL

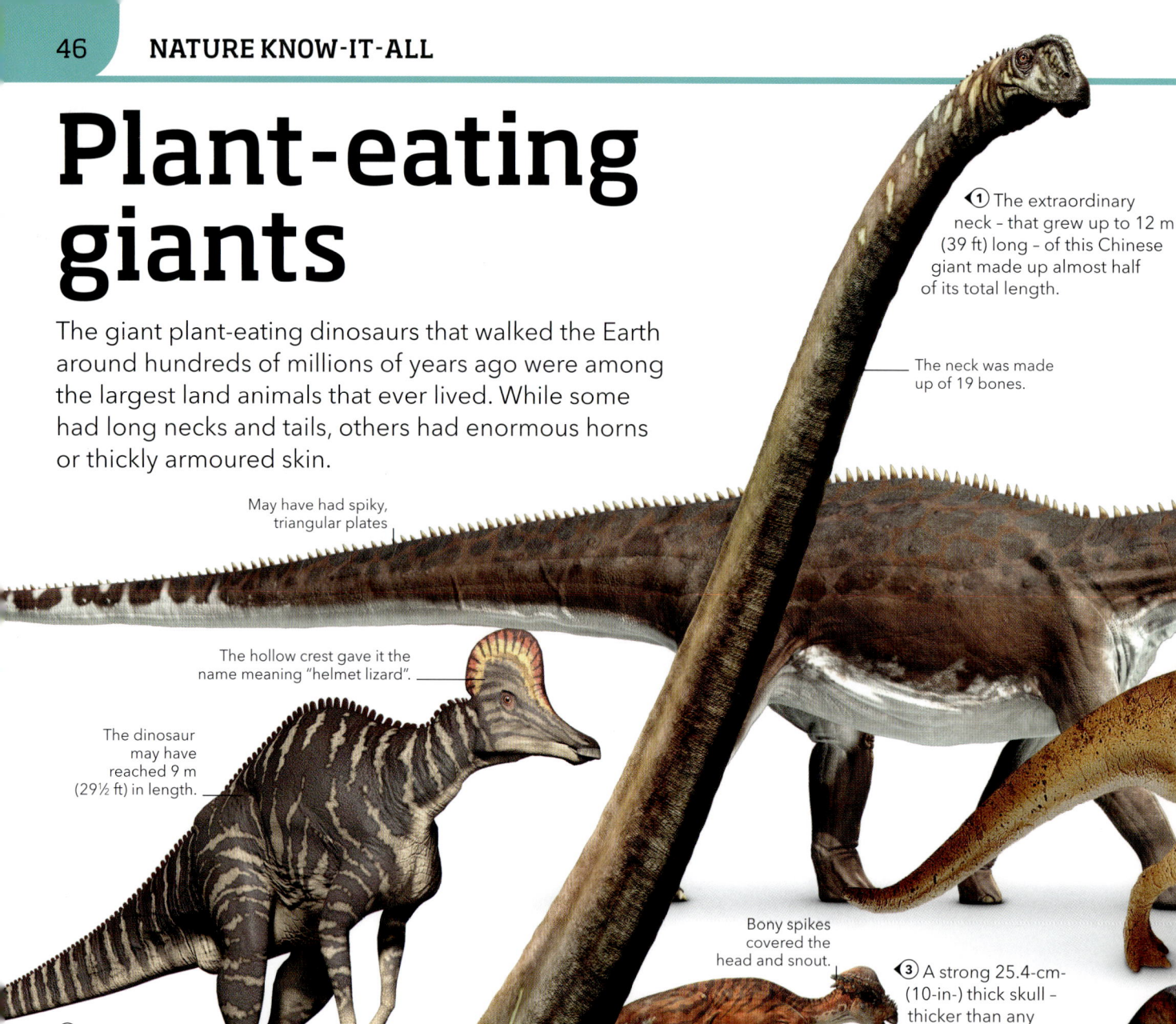

Plant-eating giants

The giant plant-eating dinosaurs that walked the Earth around hundreds of millions of years ago were among the largest land animals that ever lived. While some had long necks and tails, others had enormous horns or thickly armoured skin.

1 The extraordinary neck – that grew up to 12 m (39 ft) long – of this Chinese giant made up almost half of its total length.

The neck was made up of 19 bones.

May have had spiky, triangular plates

The hollow crest gave it the name meaning "helmet lizard".

The dinosaur may have reached 9 m (29½ ft) in length.

2 This North American plant-eater had a narrow, sharp beak, which it used to rip leaves from plants.

Bony spikes covered the head and snout.

3 A strong 25.4-cm- (10-in-) thick skull – thicker than any other dinosaur skull – may have been used for head-butting contests.

The 1-m- (3-ft-) long crest was the longest crest of any dinosaur.

Heavy tail helped to balance the long neck.

4 The unusual, hollow head crest may have been used to attract mates.

47

- The tiny brain inside the skull weighed only about 110 g (4 oz).

6 Unlike most dinosaurs, the front limbs of this plant-eater were longer than its hind limbs, which allowed it to browse tall vegetation.

5 One of the longest land animals ever, at 33 m (108 ft), this dinosaur could gather leaves from the top of tall trees. Its vast body contained a huge digestive system to process the tough plant food.

- Flat, bony plates were as long as 60 cm (2 ft).

TEST YOURSELF

STARTER
- Diplodocus
- Ankylosaurus
- Triceratops
- Stegosaurus

CHALLENGER
- Iguanodon
- Brachiosaurus
- Corythosaurus
- Parasaurolophus

GENIUS!
- *Maiasaura*
- *Mamenchisaurus*
- *Scelidosaurus*
- *Pachycephalosaurus*

7 Evidence suggests this dinosaur looked after its young, with babies staying in the nest for several weeks.

8 The big, distinctive plates on this dinosaur's back were possibly used for show.

9 This dinosaur had a sharp thumb spike, possibly used for defence or for ripping plants.

- Bony neck frill was a useful defensive shield but may also have been used for display to attract mates or put-off rivals.

- Narrow head with strong beak
- Thumb spike

10 Rows of bony knobs gave this dinosaur a tough armour against predators.

11 The two horns, each 1.3 m (4 ft) long, were probably used in combat with rivals of the same species.

- Bony knobs
- Bony plates

12 This dinosaur was protected by an armoured back and a tail club that could be swung at its foe.

- Club-like lump of bone

ANSWERS: 1. Mamenchisaurus 2. Corythosaurus 3. Pachycephalosaurus 4. Parasaurolophus 5. Diplodocus 6. Brachiosaurus 7. Maiasaura 8. Stegosaurus 9. Iguanodon 10. Scelidosaurus 11. Triceratops 12. Ankylosaurus

NATURE KNOW-IT-ALL

Prehistoric creatures

After the age of the dinosaurs, some extraordinary animals walked the Earth. Some grew into giant beasts, while others remained as small as rats. Though they may look similar to some modern-day animals, the creatures shown here, many with truly tricky names, are now all extinct.

Curved tusks may have been used to scrape ice and snow.

① The shaggy coat of this elephant cousin was necessary to survive the bitterly cold Ice Age. It measured 3.4 m (11 1/10 ft) at the shoulder.

A thick layer of fat helped to keep it warm.

② A giant mammal, this animal could gather and digest large amounts of plant food.

Hair could grow up to 90 cm (3 ft) long.

③ Unlike its slow-moving modern-day relatives, this giant beast, at 6 m (20 ft), was too heavy to climb trees and lived on the ground – but used its large claws to pull branches within reach.

④ Possibly the largest meat-eating land mammal ever, at up to 4 m (13 ft) long, this predator is probably a relative of modern-day whales.

5 One of the earliest known bats, this insect-eater may have been able to use echolocation to locate its prey, just like present-day bats.

Skin stretched over four long finger bones

6 About the size of a white rhinoceros, which can weigh up to 2.5 tonnes, this Ice Age grazer used its large cheek teeth to grind tough vegetation.

The front horn was flat rather than conical.

The short snout looked like a trunk.

7 This strange-looking mammal roamed the grasslands of South America, feeding on leaves and grass.

8 Flightless, like the modern-day ostrich, this big bird had a long neck and large beak, possibly for cracking nuts.

Hooked beak

Long, powerful legs

9 The long, curved, canine teeth of this fearsome predator were used to kill large prey.

10 This mammal had strange one-toed feet that looked like a single, large claw. It could be 3 m (10 ft) tall.

The upper canines could grow up to 18 cm (7 in) long.

Like kangaroos, mothers carried the baby in a pouch.

11 Weighing as much as a small car, this armadillo-like herbivore had tough armour made up of hundreds of bony plates.

TEST YOURSELF

STARTER
Woolly mammoth
Smilodon
Woolly rhinoceros
Giant ground sloth

CHALLENGER
Uintatherium
Glyptodon
Gastornis

GENIUS!
Procoptodon
Icaronycteris
Andrewsarchus
Macrauchenia

ANSWERS: 1. Woolly mammoth 2. Uintatherium 3. Giant ground sloth 4. Andrewsarchus 5. Icaronycteris 6. Woolly rhinoceros 7. Macrauchenia 8. Gastornis 9. Smilodon 10. Procoptodon 11. Glyptodon

Mammals

From the tiniest shrews and bats to the blue whale, the biggest animal ever, mammals thrive in many habitats across the planet. Most live on land, but some can even hold their breath long enough to survive in the deep ocean.

01. In the freezing Arctic you need a large skeleton – the bigger the body the more heat generated.

02. A thick fur coat and a layer of fat – up to 10 cm (4 in) thick – traps body heat, keeping you even warmer!

How to survive in the Arctic

Like nearly all mammals, polar bear cubs are born live and feed on their mother's milk.

03. Take care of your cubs – for up to two to three years.

A polar bear's hairs are actually transparent, but the way they scatter light makes them appear white.

04. As a warm-blooded mammal you can generate your own body heat, even in cold climates.

Small ears keep heat loss to a minimum.

A polar bear can sniff a seal over 30 km (18½ miles) away.

Large, padded, and hairy feet help the polar bear walk across slippery ice. Its sharp claws give it extra grip.

Flapping about!

A few kinds of tree-living mammals – such as squirrels – can glide through the air, but bats are the only mammals that can truly fly. Their wings are made up of skin stretched over very long finger bones.

Thin wings help bats move easily through the air.

7.7 billion
The world population of the most abundant large mammal ever – humans!

120 km/h
(75 mph) Top speed of the cheetah, the fastest land mammal.

40
The percentage of mammal species that are rodents.

2
The number of hours an elephant seal can hold its breath while diving for food.

Hairless wonders!
Many ocean mammals, such as dolphins, don't have hairy skin. Instead they have a thick layer of fat, called blubber, to keep their body warm.

I don't believe it!
The pangolin is the only mammal with scaly skin. It has huge scales, which form a protective armour.

A giraffe has an extra-strong heart to pump blood up to its head!

Tallest to the smallest

- The giraffe is the tallest mammal, reaching up to 6 m (20 ft). It grasps higher leaves by extending its tongue an extra 50 cm (20 in).

- African elephants are the heaviest land mammals, weighing up to 10 tonnes. Males also have the tallest shoulder height – up to 4 m (13 ft).

- The Etruscan shrew is the smallest mammal by weight, averaging just 1.8 g (0.06 oz). The bumblebee bat has a smaller body length, but weighs more.

Types of mammals

Monotremes: The only egg-laying mammals are echidnas and the duck-billed platypus.

Marsupials: These mammals give birth to tiny young that are usually protected in a mother's pouch.

Placentals: Most mammals fall into this group. Mothers nourish their babies inside their womb.

Know your cats

Cats are more than teeth and claws – although these sharp weapons are certainly a big part of their lives. They are sleek, nimble-footed predators. For the smallest, a mouse makes a decent meal, but others are big enough to tackle full-grown cattle.

① The tail of this solitary American cat is nearly as long as the rest of its body!

The long tail balances the cat when it turns at speed.

② The fastest animal on legs would easily beat the speediest human sprinter – it can reach speeds of 115 km/h (70 mph).

③ Look closer and you'll be able to see the tell-tale spots of this African-Asian cat. It's best known for its orange coat, but comes in black, too!

④ This cat moves its long, tufted ears to signal other members of its kind.

⑤ The biggest of all cats, weighing up to 363 kg (800 lb), has giant paws for swiping prey.

Distinctive rosette-patterned fur

⑥ A tropical cat from the Americas, this hunter is the emblem of a famous luxury car.

⑦ Out on the Asian plains, this short-legged cat ambushes prey from behind large rocks.

White cheek with black stripes

⑧ This small cat lives in the Americas. Each one has a coat with a unique pattern of stripes and spots.

TEST YOURSELF

STARTER
Cheetah
Jaguar
Lion
Tiger

CHALLENGER
Puma
Snow Leopard
Ocelot
Leopard

GENIUS!
Marbled cat
Caracal
Pallas's cat
Eurasian lynx

Long, pointed ears help hearing.

⑨ Found high in the mountains, this Asian cat can leap effortlessly from ledge to ledge, using its super strong legs.

⑩ At up to 1.1 m (3½ ft) this cat may be small, but it has the strength to kill reindeer and wild boar.

⑪ The distinctive patterned coat that gives this cat its name is a good camouflage when hunting in the forests of Southeast Asia.

The mane makes the male look bigger than it really is.

⑫ Found in Africa, the males of this fierce species have such loud roars, they can sometimes be heard 8 km (5 miles) away!

ANSWERS: 1. Puma 2. Cheetah 3. Leopard 4. Caracal 5. Tiger 6. Jaguar 7. Pallas's cat 8. Ocelot 9. Snow Leopard 10. Eurasian lynx 11. Marbled cat 12. Lion

① After gnawing through tree bark, this primate from Madagascar uses its long middle finger to scoop out the insect larvae lurking beneath.

② This relative of the lemurs is the only primate to produce venom.

③ This monkey from Borneo has the biggest nose and is also the best primate swimmer.

Primate party

Our closest relatives certainly make a cheeky, noisy bunch. Monkeys and apes, lemurs, and lorises use brains and brawn to survive in the wild. Some – like us – are more at home on the ground, while others prefer to be up in the trees.

This gibbon's throat sac helps project his call across 2 km (1 1/5 miles).

④ The largest gibbon at up to 90 cm (35½ in), it is found across forests in Southeast Asia.

⑤ Found in Africa, the world's biggest primate thumps his chest to intimidate others.

⑥ The tail is more than a good clue. This primate covers it in a smelly substance, produced by scent glands, to waft at a territorial opponent!

⑦ This African ape uses sticks to probe for tasty termites.

9. Golden lion tamarin 10. Orangutan 11. Japanese macaque 12. Geoffroy's spider monkey 13. Verreaux's sifaka 14. Angolan colobus 15. Mandrill

55

8 ▶ A face that is flushed red signals this primate's good health, not embarrassment. It is usually found in the Amazon forest treetops.

Prehensile (meaning it can grip) tail acts like a fifth limb, supporting weight.

Glossy mane of fur

10 ▶ One of the best climbers, this primate, found in Southeast Asia, has arms longer than its legs – its armspan can be around 2.25 m (7½ ft).

A thick coat helps it survive the cold northern winters.

9 ▶ This beautiful tiny monkey, at 33 cm (13 in), is the colour of a precious metal.

11 ▶ This primate from Japan is known to take hot spring baths to survive in cold weather.

12 ▶ A grasping tail is enough to match any climbing superhero – especially one that lives in high rainforest canopies.

13 ▶ Bouncing on two legs across the ground gets this Madagascan primate from tree to tree.

Tail helps to balance while climbing.

14 ▶ A white, warm mane is perfect for this primate's home – the cool mountain forests of Central and East Africa.

15 ▶ These primates, with their red and blue faces (and bums!), live in groups called "troops" in African rainforests. They can reach 1.1 m (3½ ft) in length, making them the largest monkey.

TEST YOURSELF

STARTER	CHALLENGER	GENIUS!
Ring-tailed lemur	Aye-aye	Verreaux's sifaka
Gorilla	Slow loris	Angolan colobus
Orangutan	Siamang	Japanese macaque
Chimpanzee	Proboscis monkey	Bald uakari
Mandrill	Golden lion tamarin	Geoffroy's spider monkey

ANSWERS: 1. Aye-aye 2. Slow loris 3. Proboscis monkey 4. Siamang 5. Gorilla 6. Ring-tailed lemur 7. Chimpanzee 8. Bald uakari

NATURE KNOW-IT-ALL

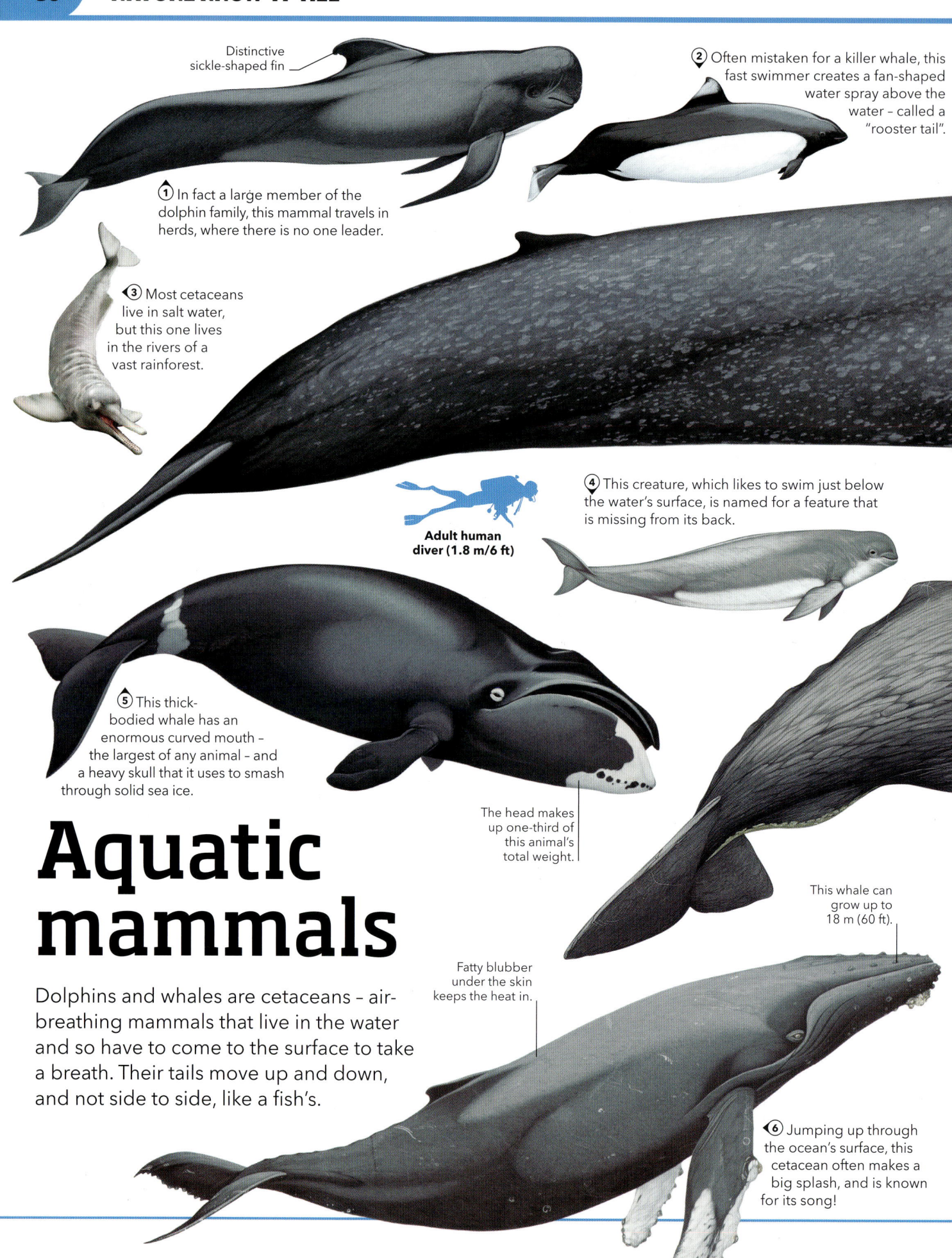

Distinctive sickle-shaped fin

2 Often mistaken for a killer whale, this fast swimmer creates a fan-shaped water spray above the water – called a "rooster tail".

1 In fact a large member of the dolphin family, this mammal travels in herds, where there is no one leader.

3 Most cetaceans live in salt water, but this one lives in the rivers of a vast rainforest.

Adult human diver (1.8 m/6 ft)

4 This creature, which likes to swim just below the water's surface, is named for a feature that is missing from its back.

5 This thick-bodied whale has an enormous curved mouth – the largest of any animal – and a heavy skull that it uses to smash through solid sea ice.

The head makes up one-third of this animal's total weight.

This whale can grow up to 18 m (60 ft).

Aquatic mammals

Fatty blubber under the skin keeps the heat in.

Dolphins and whales are cetaceans – air-breathing mammals that live in the water and so have to come to the surface to take a breath. Their tails move up and down, and not side to side, like a fish's.

6 Jumping up through the ocean's surface, this cetacean often makes a big splash, and is known for its song!

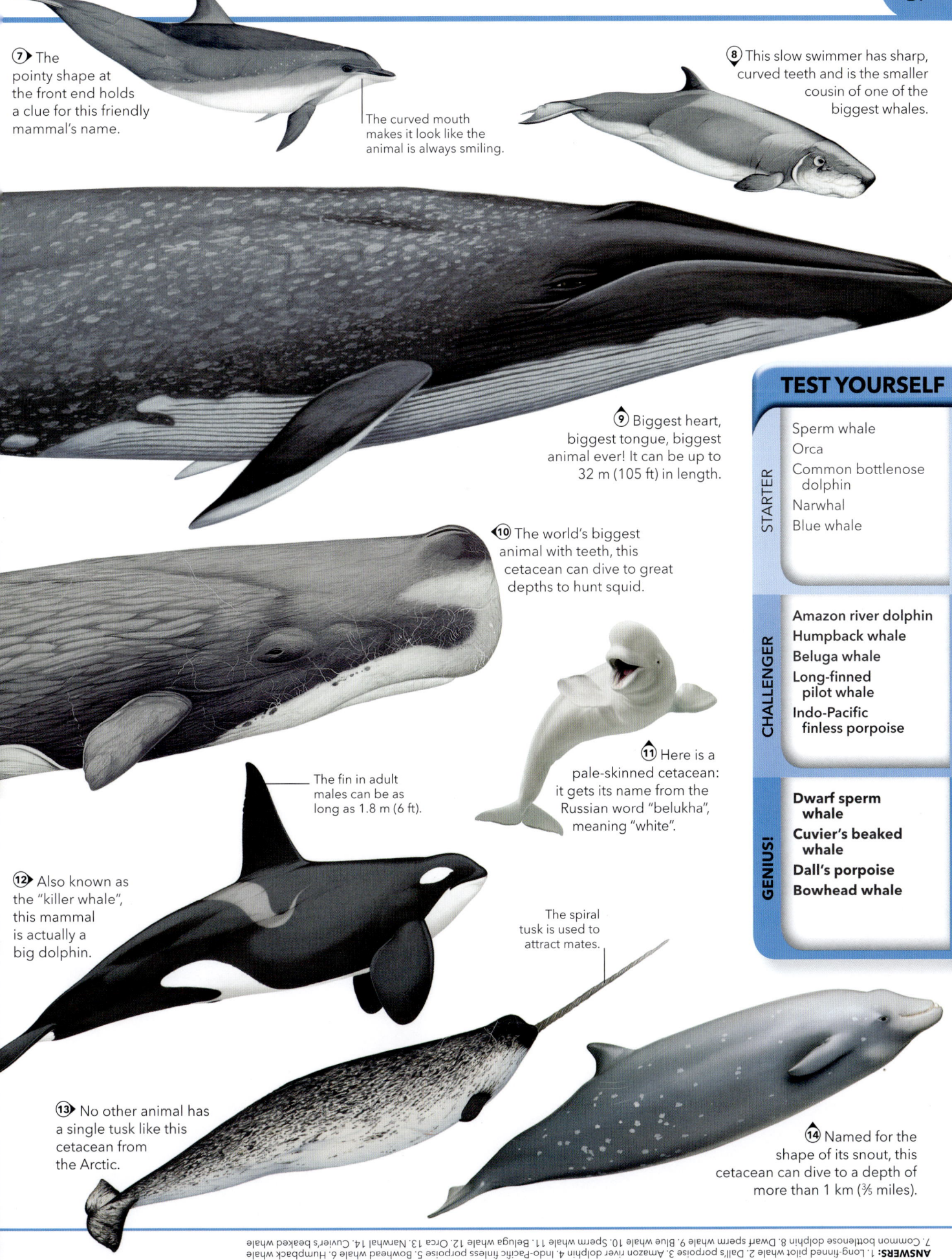

7 The pointy shape at the front end holds a clue for this friendly mammal's name.

The curved mouth makes it look like the animal is always smiling.

8 This slow swimmer has sharp, curved teeth and is the smaller cousin of one of the biggest whales.

9 Biggest heart, biggest tongue, biggest animal ever! It can be up to 32 m (105 ft) in length.

10 The world's biggest animal with teeth, this cetacean can dive to great depths to hunt squid.

The fin in adult males can be as long as 1.8 m (6 ft).

11 Here is a pale-skinned cetacean: it gets its name from the Russian word "belukha", meaning "white".

12 Also known as the "killer whale", this mammal is actually a big dolphin.

The spiral tusk is used to attract mates.

13 No other animal has a single tusk like this cetacean from the Arctic.

14 Named for the shape of its snout, this cetacean can dive to a depth of more than 1 km (⅗ miles).

TEST YOURSELF

STARTER
- Sperm whale
- Orca
- Common bottlenose dolphin
- Narwhal
- Blue whale

CHALLENGER
- Amazon river dolphin
- Humpback whale
- Beluga whale
- Long-finned pilot whale
- Indo-Pacific finless porpoise

GENIUS!
- Dwarf sperm whale
- Cuvier's beaked whale
- Dall's porpoise
- Bowhead whale

ANSWERS: 1. Long-finned pilot whale 2. Dall's porpoise 3. Amazon river dolphin 4. Indo-Pacific finless porpoise 5. Bowhead whale 6. Humpback whale 7. Common bottlenose dolphin 8. Dwarf sperm whale 9. Blue whale 10. Sperm whale 11. Beluga whale 12. Orca 13. Narwhal 14. Cuvier's beaked whale

Invertebrates

Animals without a backbone are known as invertebrates. They make up more than 80 per cent of all types of animal and are incredibly varied. Invertebrates include some with hard outer cases, such as insects and shellfish, and soft-bodied animals such as jellyfish and worms.

01. As a giant centipede, you have more than 20 pairs of jointed legs on your segmented body. As some pairs step forward, the rest will follow.

How to move like a centipede

02. Let your body wriggle from side to side. This will help you pick up speed.

Antennae
Long, jointed antennae, or "feelers", sense surroundings.

Leg muscles
Each leg has muscles to bend or straighten the joints.

03. Use the claws at the ends of your legs to help you run along, grip prey, and even climb.

I don't believe it!
When a pistol shrimp snaps its claws, the sound is so loud that it sends out shock waves strong enough to kill the shrimp's prey.

Octopus suckers grasp prey.

Types of invertebrates

Cnidarians: This is a group of simple invertebrates with tentacles, such as jellyfish and corals.

Worms: There are different kinds of long-bodied worms. Some can burrow and others swim.

Molluscs: This group includes slugs and snails. Molluscs are soft and fleshy and often have a shell.

Arthropods: These include spiders and relatives. They have an outer skeleton and jointed legs.

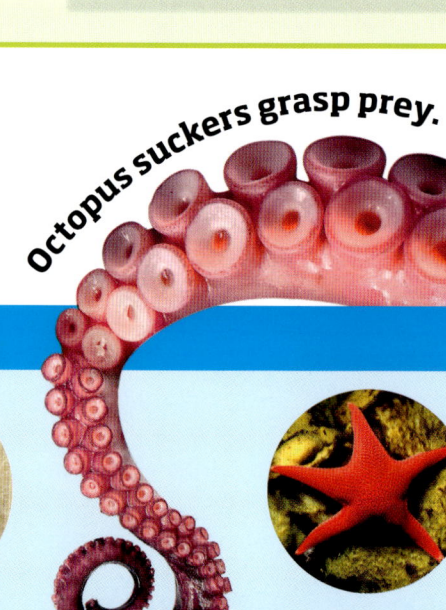

Echinoderms: These include sea urchins and starfish, which are shaped like discs or stars.

12.5 trillion
Estimated size of the biggest insect swarm: a plague of Rocky Mountain locusts.

400,000
Number of known beetle species, the largest group of insects. Very many more await discovery.

50 g
(1⅘ oz) Weight of a goliath beetle, one of the heaviest flying insects – that's more than a golf ball.

0.139 mm
(0.0055 in) Length of the smallest known insect, a fairy fly.

Extreme living
An invertebrate holds the animal record for high-altitude living. A type of jumping spider lives at heights of up to 6,700 m (22,000 ft) on the slopes of Mount Everest. This little predator feeds on tiny insects that get blown high onto the mountain by the gales of the Himalayas.

Biggest and smallest

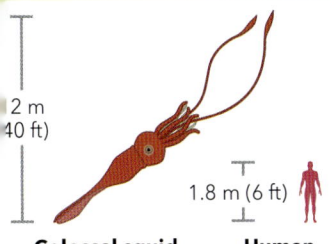

12 m (40 ft)
Colossal squid

1.8 m (6 ft)
Human

0.05 mm (0.002 in)
Rotifer

0.07 mm (0.003 in)
Width of human hair

The giant of all invertebrates is the colossal squid that lives in the deep ocean. It snags fish with its hooked tentacles.

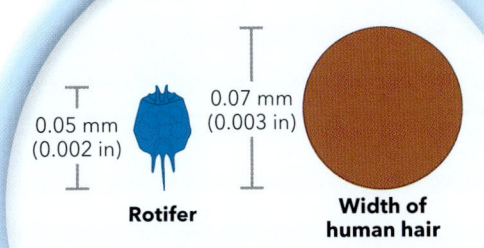

Some invertebrates, such as rotifers, are so tiny you need a microscope to see them. Thousands could swim in one drop of water.

Invertebrate facts

- A jellyfish has no brain. Its simple nervous system carries electrical messages for moving but cannot control complex behaviour.

- Microscopic animals called tardigrades are great survivors. They can dry out into husks that have lost 95 per cent of their body water and still recover, and they have survived being sent into space without any oxygen.

- The deep-sea Pompeii worm that lives in tubes near volcanic vents can bear temperatures of 80°C (176°F).

Smart octopus
Although most invertebrates have tiny brains, a few, such as octopuses, are quite intelligent. A super-smart octopus is able to extract lobsters from lobster traps, or even make its escape from public aquariums.

Living fossils
Horseshoe crabs (more related to spiders than shellfish) have been around for more than 400 million years.

NATURE KNOW-IT-ALL

Insects everywhere

There are more species of insects on Earth than any other living animal, so it's no wonder they turn up in practically every place you look. Insects have six legs for crawling and most of them also have wings for flying – and that's clearly a winning combination in their fight for survival.

① This tropical American butterfly has see-through wings, so it's difficult to spot when perched on a leaf.

Coloured scales at the edges are the only way to spot this insect.

② Sunlight bouncing off this Central American beetle makes it shine like a precious metal and helps disguise it in the rainforest.

③ It's a busy life for this insect collecting nectar, which will be turned into honey back at the hive.

Hair traps pollen

④ Despite its name, this jewel-like insect does not sting, but it does lay its eggs in other insects' nests.

The pattern on the wings helps it to camouflage in forests.

⑤ With its strong legs, this insect can jump 70 cm (27½ in) into the air – giving it its name.

⑥ This flying insect lives for only 1–2 days, and starts its life as a nymph that lives underwater in ponds and lakes.

Wings are covered with tiny scales.

⑦ One of the biggest and most colourful of its kind, this Asian insect has a wingspan of 25 cm (10 in).

Three tails

⑧ Billions of these insects, which can be 7.5 cm (3 in) long, form hungry swarms that can quickly strip crops of all their leaves.

Ridged wings are longer than the body.

⑨ The long "snout" on this insect's head was once thought to glow in the dark – which gave it its name.

Pattern on the wings reflects light

Broad fore legs

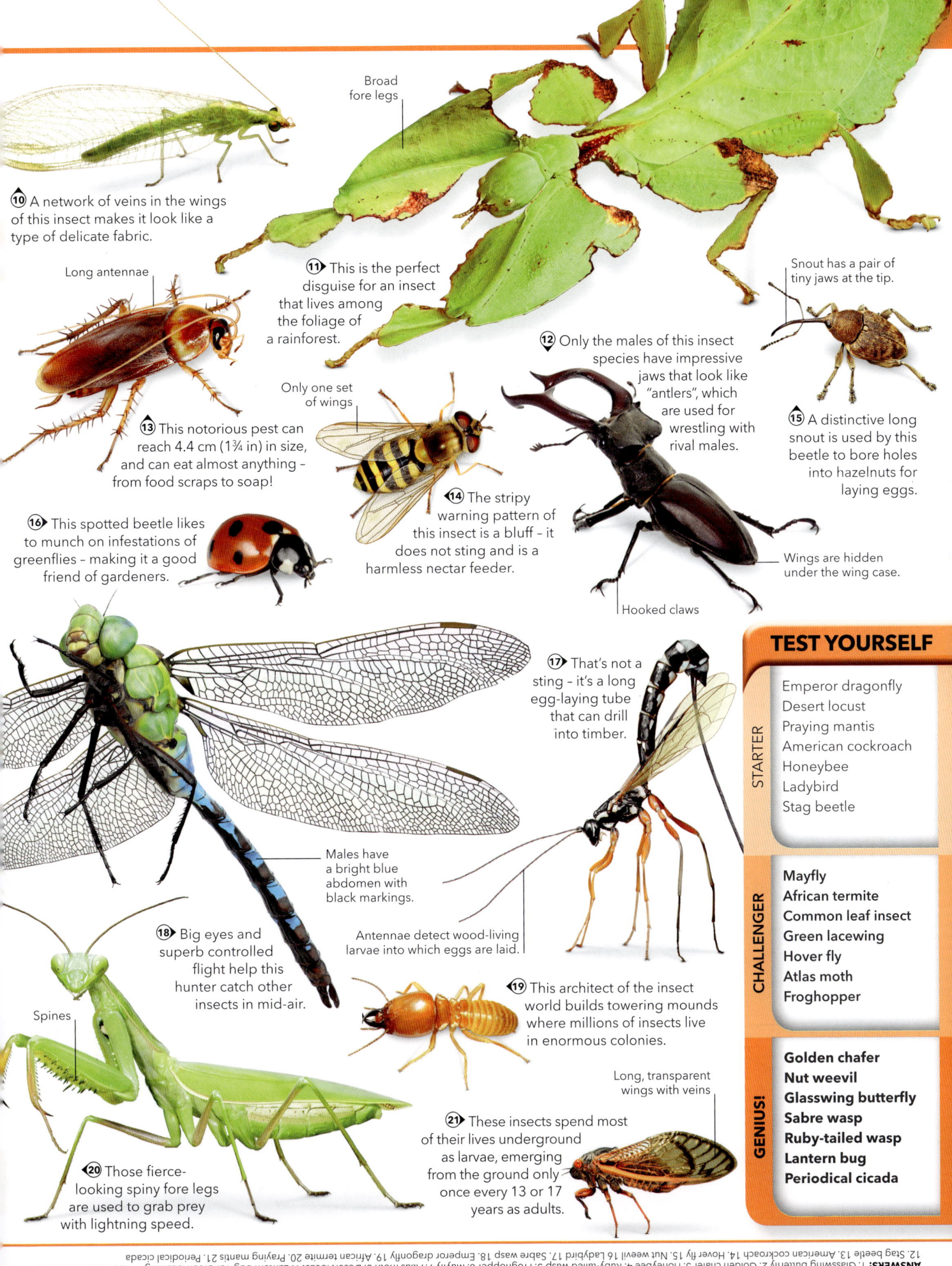

10 A network of veins in the wings of this insect makes it look like a type of delicate fabric.

11 This is the perfect disguise for an insect that lives among the foliage of a rainforest.

Snout has a pair of tiny jaws at the tip.

Long antennae

Only one set of wings

12 Only the males of this insect species have impressive jaws that look like "antlers", which are used for wrestling with rival males.

15 A distinctive long snout is used by this beetle to bore holes into hazelnuts for laying eggs.

13 This notorious pest can reach 4.4 cm (1¾ in) in size, and can eat almost anything – from food scraps to soap!

14 The stripy warning pattern of this insect is a bluff – it does not sting and is a harmless nectar feeder.

16 This spotted beetle likes to munch on infestations of greenflies – making it a good friend of gardeners.

Wings are hidden under the wing case.

Hooked claws

17 That's not a sting – it's a long egg-laying tube that can drill into timber.

TEST YOURSELF

STARTER
Emperor dragonfly
Desert locust
Praying mantis
American cockroach
Honeybee
Ladybird
Stag beetle

Males have a bright blue abdomen with black markings.

18 Big eyes and superb controlled flight help this hunter catch other insects in mid-air.

Antennae detect wood-living larvae into which eggs are laid.

19 This architect of the insect world builds towering mounds where millions of insects live in enormous colonies.

CHALLENGER
Mayfly
African termite
Common leaf insect
Green lacewing
Hover fly
Atlas moth
Froghopper

Spines

Long, transparent wings with veins

20 Those fierce-looking spiny fore legs are used to grab prey with lightning speed.

21 These insects spend most of their lives underground as larvae, emerging from the ground only once every 13 or 17 years as adults.

GENIUS!
Golden chafer
Nut weevil
Glasswing butterfly
Sabre wasp
Ruby-tailed wasp
Lantern bug
Periodical cicada

ANSWERS: 1. Glasswing butterfly 2. Golden chafer 3. Honeybee 4. Ruby-tailed wasp 5. Froghopper 6. Mayfly 7. Atlas moth 8. Desert locust 9. Lantern bug 10. Green lacewing 11. Common leaf insect 12. Stag beetle 13. American cockroach 14. Hover fly 15. Nut weevil 16 Ladybird 17. Sabre wasp 18. Emperor dragonfly 19. African termite 20. Praying mantis 21. Periodical cicada

62   NATURE KNOW-IT-ALL

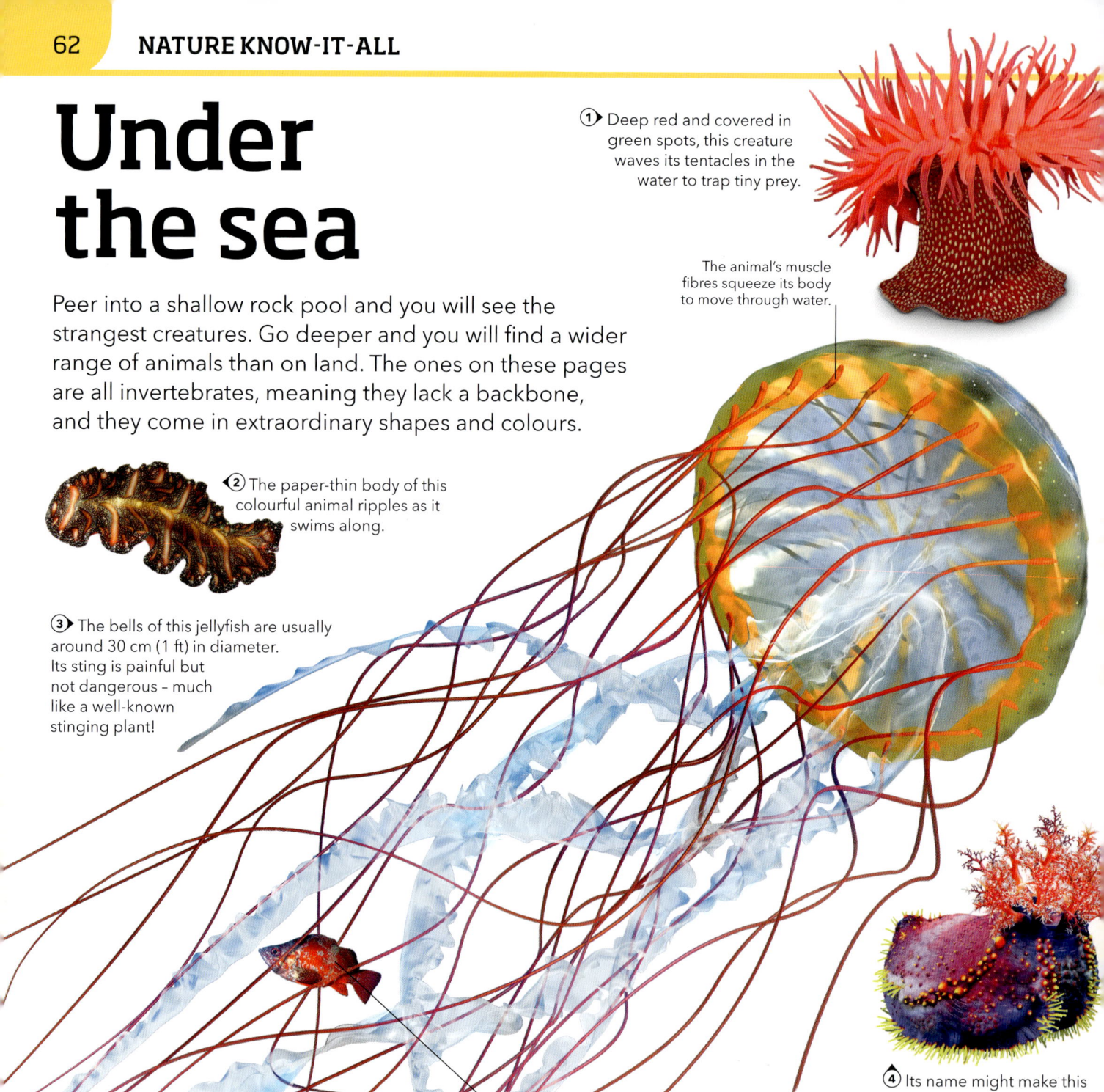

Under the sea

Peer into a shallow rock pool and you will see the strangest creatures. Go deeper and you will find a wider range of animals than on land. The ones on these pages are all invertebrates, meaning they lack a backbone, and they come in extraordinary shapes and colours.

1 Deep red and covered in green spots, this creature waves its tentacles in the water to trap tiny prey.

The animal's muscle fibres squeeze its body to move through water.

2 The paper-thin body of this colourful animal ripples as it swims along.

3 The bells of this jellyfish are usually around 30 cm (1 ft) in diameter. Its sting is painful but not dangerous – much like a well-known stinging plant!

4 Its name might make this creature sound edible, but it's a relative of starfishes and is actually poisonous to eat – a good defence!

Prey is paralysed by venom.

5 This animal lives attached to the rocks, and is a bivalve, which means it has two shell parts hinged together.

Big eyes help to see clearly while moving at high speeds.

6 A pale shell is a good disguise for scurrying on a sandy beach.

Fibrous threads attach to rocks.

ANSWERS: 1. Strawberry anemone 2. Polyclad flatworm 3. Pacific sea nettle 4. Sea apple 5. Common mussel 6. Horned ghost crab 7. Blue-ringed octopus 8. Christmas tree tube worm 9. Chambered nautilus 10. Purple sea pen 11. Spanish shawl nudibranch 12. Lined chiton 13. Mushroom coral 14. Red general starfish 15. Peacock mantis shrimp

7 One of the deadliest animals on Earth, the colour pattern is a warning that its bite is deadly venomous.

The rings flash vividly when the animal feels threatened.

8 The feathery tentacles might look festive – but they are used for catching food.

The whorls of tentacles also help to take in oxygen.

9 Unlike its relatives, the squid and octopus, this swimming creature lives in a mobile shell.

10 This is really a branching colony of tiny animals that are like miniature anemones.

It has up to 90 sticky tentacles.

11 This sea slug is the enemy of anemones – not only does it eat them, but it steals their stingers and stores them on its back!

12 The flexible shell of this snail-relative can help it roll up for protection.

The shell is made of 8 plates.

13 Although it might look rather fungus-like, this creature moves, and slides across soft sand.

Tube feet help the animal to move and grip.

14 The shape is a give-away! Each of this animal's arms can grow back after injury.

15 This crustacean has two swinging clubs that are used to smash prey to pieces.

Prey is swallowed through a central mouth on the underside.

Clubs

TEST YOURSELF

STARTER
Common mussel
Red general starfish
Blue-ringed octopus
Horned ghost crab
Strawberry anemone

CHALLENGER
Mushroom coral
Chambered nautilus
Polyclad flatworm
Pacific sea nettle
Peacock mantis shrimp

GENIUS!
Lined chiton
Christmas tree tube worm
Purple sea pen
Sea apple
Spanish shawl nudibranch

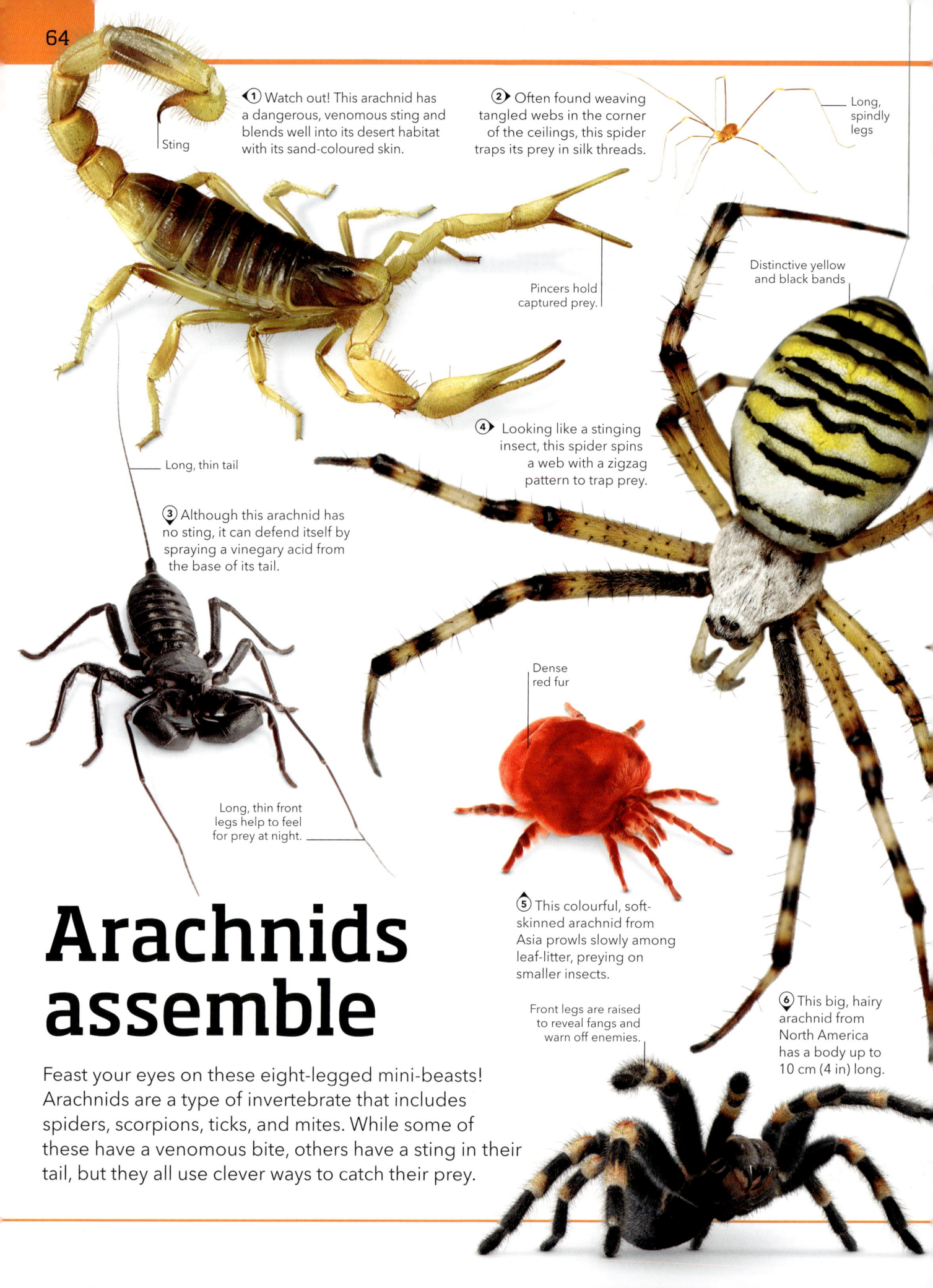

1. Watch out! This arachnid has a dangerous, venomous sting and blends well into its desert habitat with its sand-coloured skin.
— Sting

2. Often found weaving tangled webs in the corner of the ceilings, this spider traps its prey in silk threads.
— Long, spindly legs
— Pincers hold captured prey.

— Distinctive yellow and black bands

3. Although this arachnid has no sting, it can defend itself by spraying a vinegary acid from the base of its tail.
— Long, thin tail
— Long, thin front legs help to feel for prey at night.

4. Looking like a stinging insect, this spider spins a web with a zigzag pattern to trap prey.

— Dense red fur

5. This colourful, soft-skinned arachnid from Asia prowls slowly among leaf-litter, preying on smaller insects.

— Front legs are raised to reveal fangs and warn off enemies.

6. This big, hairy arachnid from North America has a body up to 10 cm (4 in) long.

Arachnids assemble

Feast your eyes on these eight-legged mini-beasts! Arachnids are a type of invertebrate that includes spiders, scorpions, ticks, and mites. While some of these have a venomous bite, others have a sting in their tail, but they all use clever ways to catch their prey.

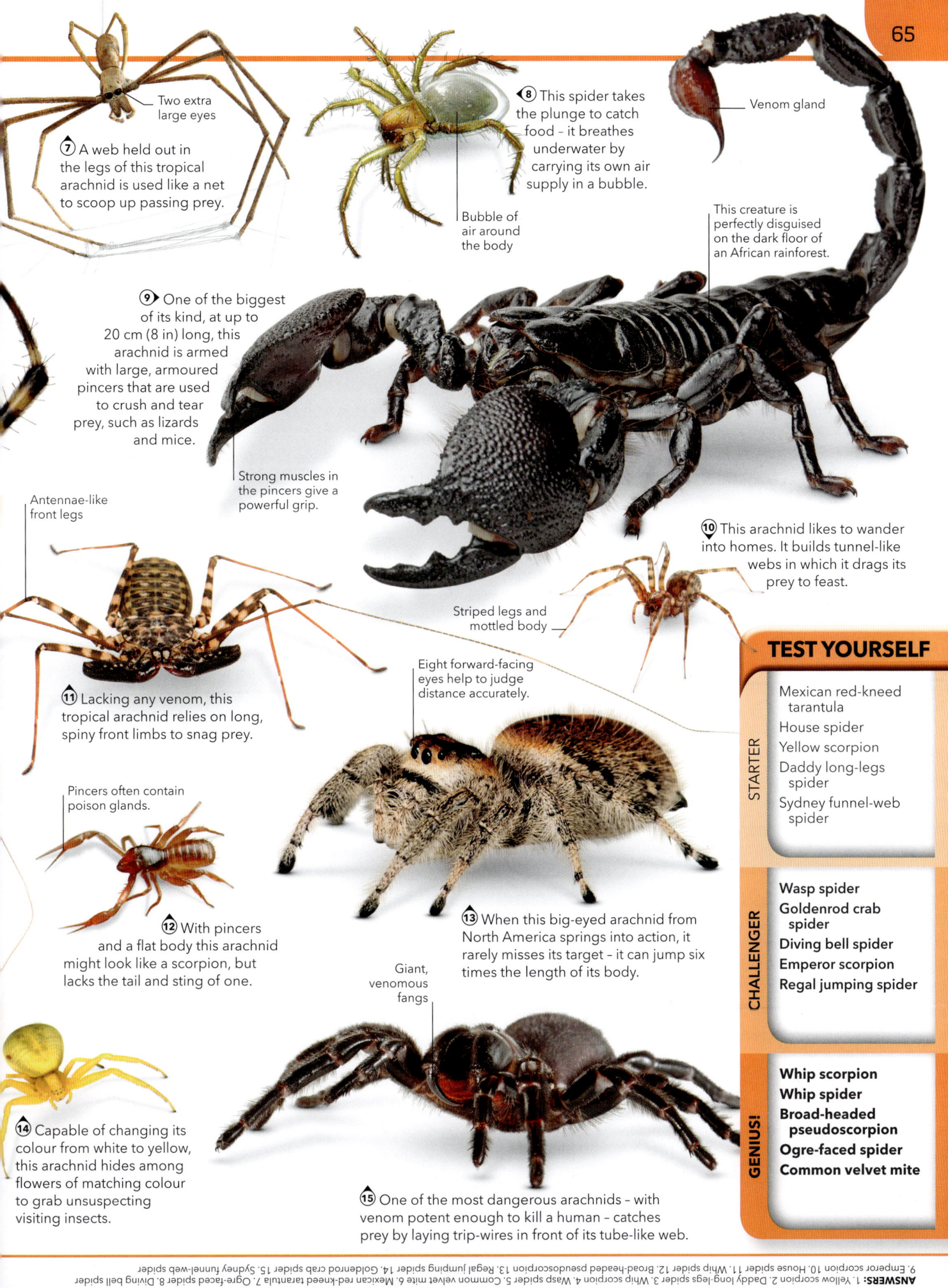

7 A web held out in the legs of this tropical arachnid is used like a net to scoop up passing prey.

Two extra large eyes

8 This spider takes the plunge to catch food – it breathes underwater by carrying its own air supply in a bubble.

Bubble of air around the body

Venom gland

This creature is perfectly disguised on the dark floor of an African rainforest.

9 One of the biggest of its kind, at up to 20 cm (8 in) long, this arachnid is armed with large, armoured pincers that are used to crush and tear prey, such as lizards and mice.

Strong muscles in the pincers give a powerful grip.

Antennae-like front legs

10 This arachnid likes to wander into homes. It builds tunnel-like webs in which it drags its prey to feast.

Striped legs and mottled body

11 Lacking any venom, this tropical arachnid relies on long, spiny front limbs to snag prey.

Eight forward-facing eyes help to judge distance accurately.

Pincers often contain poison glands.

12 With pincers and a flat body this arachnid might look like a scorpion, but lacks the tail and sting of one.

13 When this big-eyed arachnid from North America springs into action, it rarely misses its target – it can jump six times the length of its body.

Giant, venomous fangs

14 Capable of changing its colour from white to yellow, this arachnid hides among flowers of matching colour to grab unsuspecting visiting insects.

15 One of the most dangerous arachnids – with venom potent enough to kill a human – catches prey by laying trip-wires in front of its tube-like web.

TEST YOURSELF

STARTER
- Mexican red-kneed tarantula
- House spider
- Yellow scorpion
- Daddy long-legs spider
- Sydney funnel-web spider

CHALLENGER
- Wasp spider
- Goldenrod crab spider
- Diving bell spider
- Emperor scorpion
- Regal jumping spider

GENIUS!
- Whip scorpion
- Whip spider
- Broad-headed pseudoscorpion
- Ogre-faced spider
- Common velvet mite

ANSWERS: 1. Yellow scorpion 2. Daddy long-legs spider 3. Whip scorpion 4. Wasp spider 5. Common velvet mite 6. Mexican red-kneed tarantula 7. Ogre-faced spider 8. Diving bell spider 9. Emperor scorpion 10. House spider 11. Whip spider 12. Broad-headed pseudoscorpion 13. Regal jumping spider 14. Goldenrod crab spider 15. Sydney funnel-web spider

NATURE KNOW-IT-ALL

Birds

There are more than 10,000 different kinds of birds, living in habitats that vary from wetlands, moorlands, coasts, and forests to city streets. Being a bird means leading a busy life. Flying uses up a lot of energy, so birds need plenty of fuel in the form of food.

The kingfisher closes transparent eyelids as it hits the water.

What is a bird?

Plumage: All birds have body feathers and, usually, bare legs and feet.

Vertebrate: A bird is a vertebrate, but has more neck bones than most other animals with backbones.

Wings: The forelimbs of birds are in the form of wings, but not all birds can fly.

Lays eggs: Birds' eggs provide protection and food for growing chicks.

I don't believe it

In 1956, a five-year-old albatross called Wisdom was ringed so that her movements could be tracked. She was still alive in 2017, aged 66.

The smallest bird

The tiniest bird of all is the bee hummingbird, found only on the Caribbean island of Cuba. Males, which are smaller than females, measure on average just 5.5 cm (2 in) long and weigh 1.9 g (7/100 oz).

How to hunt like a kingfisher

Feathers

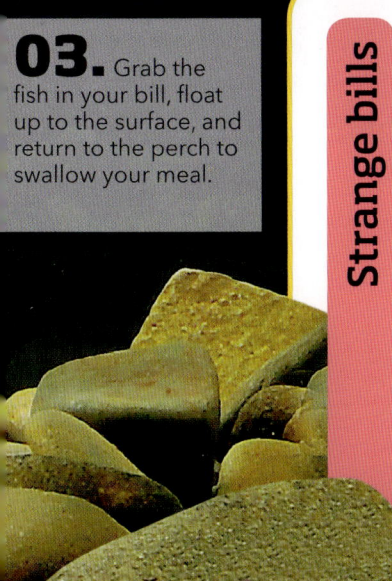

Feathers are made from keratin, a material also found in animal hair, nails, and reptile scales. Some feathers are fluffy for warmth, but most of the outer ones are flat and stiffened to improve streamlining and aid flight.

Quill Every feather has a hard central quill or shaft.

Vane The flat surface (vane) is made up of side branches (barbs), held together by tiny hooks.

Flying facts

- The oilbird from South America sleeps in caves during the day and flies at night, using bat-like echolocation.
- Birds' beaks contain a mineral that is sensitive to Earth's magnetic fields. This helps them to navigate on migration.
- The longest-known non-stop bird flight – of 11,500 km (7,146 miles) – was tracked during the migration of a wading bird called a bar-tailed godwit.
- The wandering albatross has the longest wingspan of any bird – 3.65 m (12 ft).

01. Find a perch above the water and watch for fish. Get ready to dive in a split second.

02. When a fish catches your eye, plunge into the water, pulling back your wings to streamline your body.

03. Grab the fish in your bill, float up to the surface, and return to the perch to swallow your meal.

Using tools

A few brainy birds use tools to find food. The New Caledonian crow can even bend twigs into hooks to get insect grubs from wood.

Strange bills

Shoebill: An enormous bill with a cutting edge helps this large wading bird of the African swamps catch and kill big fish by slicing off their heads.

Spoonbill: Sweeping its bill from side to side in the water, this bird feels for insects and shrimps with the touch-sensitive "spoon" at the tip.

Hummingbird: This tiny South American nectar-feeder has a long thin bill for probing flowers and a long grooved tongue to collect the liquid inside.

NATURE KNOW-IT-ALL

2 Showing off its spectacular plumage by dancing in the trees is how this bird attracts a mate.

3 In Central America the long green tail feathers of this bird, which can be around 1 m (3 ft) long, were used in ceremonial headdresses.

4 Known for its deep red colour, this water bird uses its long beak to probe for insects in the mud.

5 The biggest bill of any bird is just what you need to fish for your food.

1 The Amazon rainforest is the ideal habitat for a bird that only eats leaves of trees.

Birds of a feather

They are masters of land and water, and the champions of the sky – welcome to the wonderful world of birds! No other living animal has a coat of feathers, and this means it's easy to spot a bird. But can you tell one from another?

The tail was thought to resemble a harp-like instrument.

6 These birds are famous for mimicking sounds, from the calls of other birds to car alarms.

About 100-150 feathers make up this brilliant fan.

7 This giant flightless bird lives in the tropical rainforests of New Guinea.

8 By spreading its brilliant plumes, this male show-off likes to strut in front of the females.

9 The pink of this bird's feathers comes from eating shrimp and other tiny animals living in the water.

10 The hard, hollow projection on the upper bill helps make calls louder.

11 An enormous, colourful bill looks inconvenient, but helps this bird grab hard-to-reach fruit.

12 The claws of this colourful bird have an excellent grip, which helps with the everyday tasks of clasping onto branches and grasping food.

Wingspan is 104–114 cm (41–45 in)

13 Well known in Japan, a pair of these birds will dance and honk in a beautiful courtship display.

14 The second-largest bird in the world lives in the Australian outback.

15 A white parrot from Australia, this bird is a popular pet – if you don't mind the loud squawks.

16 The world's largest living bird is also the fastest animal on two legs – it can run at a speed of 70 km/h (43 mph).

17 A fan-like tuft of stiff golden head feathers gives this bird its name.

Red, inflatable throat pouch

Reddish-brown, spiky feathers

18 The national bird of New Zealand has nostrils at the tip of its beak to sniff out worms.

The big wings are too weak for flight.

TEST YOURSELF

STARTER
- Ostrich
- Pelican
- Sulfur-crested cockatoo
- Toucan
- Indian peacock
- Flamingo

CHALLENGER
- Emu
- Scarlet ibis
- Kiwi
- Blue-and-yellow macaw
- Lesser bird of paradise
- Southern cassowary

GENIUS!
- Hoatzin
- Resplendent quetzal
- Superb lyrebird
- Red-crowned crane
- Great hornbill
- Grey-crowned crane

ANSWERS: 1. Hoatzin 2. Lesser bird of paradise 3. Resplendent quetzal 4. Scarlet ibis 5. Pelican 6. Superb lyrebird 7. Southern cassowary 8. Indian peacock 9. Flamingo 10. Great hornbill 11. Toucan 12. Blue-and-yellow macaw 13. Red-crowned crane 14. Emu 15. Sulfur-crested cockatoo 16. Ostrich 17. Grey-crowned crane 18. Kiwi

Deadly hunters

Watch out! There's a bird of prey overhead. These feathered hunters all have a taste for meat. Some prefer rotting, dead animals (known as carrion) but most need fresh prey, and use their deadly talons and sharp beaks to make a kill.

① A wedge-shaped tail allows this bird to turn while in flight, and also helps to identify it.

② Found in icy coniferous forests, this bird has pointed wings, much like a hawk's, and can hunt in thick snow.

The wings can measure 1.8 m (6 ft) across from tip to tip.

③ A tiny hunter, this Asian bird targets small prey, such as insects and birds.

④ Fishes can be slippery prey, but this bird has spiky, clawed talons for keeping a firm grip.

⑤ One of the biggest flying birds, this species is found soaring over the longest mountain range of South America.

⑥ This bird's massive and powerful talons are used for killing sloths and monkeys in the Amazon rainforest.

Wingspan can be more than 3 m (10 ft)!

71

TEST YOURSELF

STARTER
Rüppell's vulture
Bald eagle
Peregrine falcon
Barn owl

CHALLENGER
Andean condor
Secretary bird
Harpy eagle
Osprey

GENIUS!
Red kite
Pied falconet
Eurasian eagle owl
Northern hawk owl

⑦ Faster than any other animal, this hunter can reach up to 320 km/h (199 mph) when dive-bombing through the air.

Long, feathery tufts

⑧ One of the biggest of its kind at around 75 cm (29½ in), this hunter's favourite prey are rabbits and hares. Its huge orange eyes are three times more sensitive than the human eye.

Striking white head feathers

Strong talons snatch fish near the water's surface.

⑨ The national emblem of the USA also appears on the country's coat of arms.

Heart-shaped face

⑩ Super-sensitive hearing helps this pale night-time predator track down mice and voles in the dark.

A powerful hooked beak makes it easy for the bird to tear off flesh and break bones.

⑪ A bare neck is perfect for reaching right inside a dead animal to feast without getting dirty feathers.

This long-legged bird stands up to 120 cm (47 in) tall.

⑫ How do you catch a snake? By stomping it to death with strong, clawed feet like this African bird.

ANSWERS: 1. Red kite 2. Northern hawk owl 3. Pied falconet 4. Osprey 5. Andean condor 6. Harpy eagle 7. Peregrine falcon 8. Eurasian eagle owl 9. Bald eagle 10. Barn owl 11. Rüppell's vulture 12. Secretary bird

Reptiles

With hard, scaly skins and body heat controlled by outside temperatures, reptiles are unique animals. Most of them live in tropical forests and warm deserts, but some can cope with cooler habitats. A few, such as sea turtles and sea snakes, are perfectly at home in the oceans.

Types of reptile

Crocodilians
These predatory crocodiles and alligators with long toothy jaws include the largest reptiles.

Lizards and snakes
This is the biggest reptile group and includes lizards - with or without legs - and snakes.

Turtles and tortoises
Both aquatic turtles and land-living tortoises have protective shield-like shells.

Tuatara
This New Zealand reptile is the only survivor of a group that lived at the time of the dinosaurs.

What is a reptile?

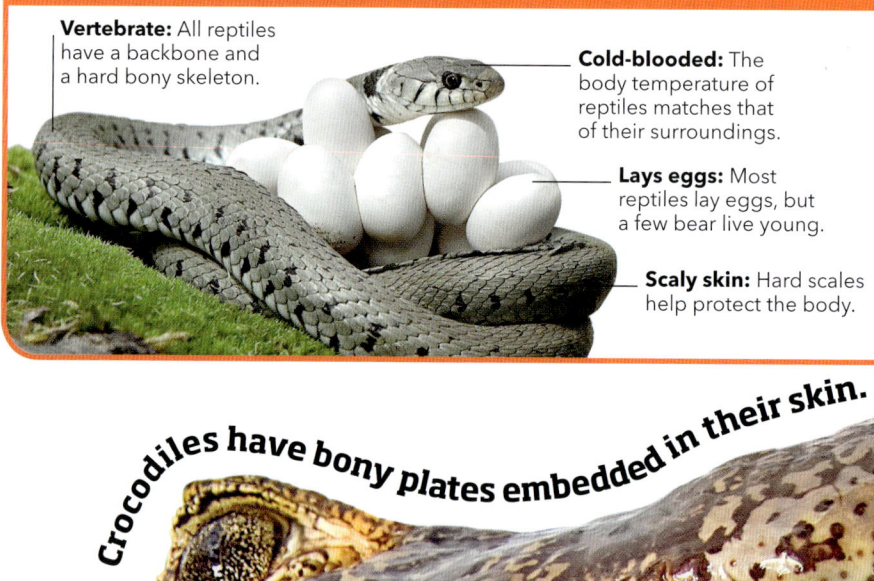

Vertebrate: All reptiles have a backbone and a hard bony skeleton.

Cold-blooded: The body temperature of reptiles matches that of their surroundings.

Lays eggs: Most reptiles lay eggs, but a few bear live young.

Scaly skin: Hard scales help protect the body.

Crocodiles have bony plates embedded in their skin.

How to hunt like a crocodile

01. Lurk in the water, with just your eyes above the surface of the water and wait.

02. When prey moves close, spring out of the water and grip it with your teeth.

03. If your prey needs air to breathe, hold it underwater until it drowns.

Defence tactics

Many reptiles run or crawl away from danger, but the frilled lizard from Australia has an extra trick. It opens a wide neck frill to make itself look bigger. If that doesn't scare the intruder, the lizard rises up on its back legs and sprints away on two legs!

Shedding skin

The outer skin of reptiles wears down over time and has to be replaced. As new skin grows underneath, so the old skin peels away. In lizards this usually happens in small patches, but in most snakes the skin comes off in one piece like a sleeve.

Crocodilian teeth are shaped to stab and hold prey, rather than slice like knives.

A snake can slither out of its skin in one piece by rubbing against a hard surface.

Waterproofing
A reptile's scales protect the skin from injury and help to stop the body losing water in dry habitats.

I don't believe it
Some species of skinks (a type of lizard) have green blood, which gives them green hearts, bones, and tongues too.

Venom flows from the gland down a channel in the tooth.

A special gland produces and stores venom.

Hollow fangs

Venom is injected through a tiny hole in the tooth tip.

04. Keeping hold of your prey, spin round and round like a log, to pull off a lump of flesh.

In numbers

16,000
The power in Newtons (units of force) of the bite of a saltwater crocodile – enough to crush a human skull.

1,000 m
(3,280 ft) Depth of the deepest recorded dive by a leatherback turtle.

9.5 km
(6 miles) Distance over which a Komodo dragon lizard can smell food.

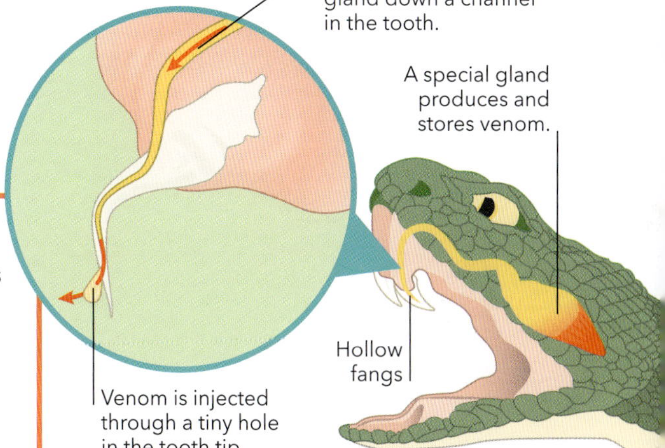

How do snakes produce venom?

All snakes are predators of other living animals and many kinds kill with venom, a poison they inject into their prey with a bite. Venomous snakes store their poison in glands (sacs that release a fluid) that lie behind their eyes and deliver it through hollow fangs.

Muscular tail can grip branches.

1 Although slow-moving by nature, this lizard can catch an insect with a flick of its long tongue.

Long claws for climbing trees

2 Green skin is perfect for a climbing lizard that wants to stay hidden in the forests of South America.

3 A worm-like lure on the tongue of this patient predator attracts fishes into its open mouth, which then snaps shut with a powerful bite.

Pink lure

4 By biting its tail, and rolling into a spiky ball, this armoured lizard fends off predators.

5 The world's largest lizard, reaching lengths of 3 m (10 ft), lives on tiny islands in Indonesia, where it is the top predator, hunting prey up to the size of deer.

Reptile room

Scaly skin may make a reptile look like it belongs to a prehistoric age, but these animals are still found in most places on Earth! As cold-blooded creatures, they rely on the warmth of the Sun's rays to get them moving, and live on both land and water.

6 This lizard has an excellent grip. It has splayed-out toes with pads covered in sticky "hairs", which help it climb and cling to anything – even ceilings!

7 This beast's long jaws are filled with up to 110 sharp teeth – perfect for snatching fish in the rivers of northern Asia.

The tail helps this reptile to move in water.

8 One of only two kinds of venomous lizard, this one is found in the United States and Mexico. It has a strong bite and doesn't let go.

9 In a dry Australian desert, spiky skin is a good defence against predators for this ant-eating lizard.

10 Found in New Zealand, this lizard looks prehistoric with its spiny crest.

11 A snorkel-like tube on its nose helps this turtle breathe while it's under the water of South American rivers.

Sharp claws help to dig burrows for shelter.

Up to 68 teeth line the jaws.

12 Brute strength helps this African reptile pull large prey the size of a zebra under water.

13 At home on the volcanic Galápagos Islands, this is the only lizard that feeds on seaweed. Usually black, the males turn a vibrant green or pink during breeding season.

A forked tongue allows this lizard to detect the scent of potential prey.

Tail will drop off if the lizard is cornered, to distract predators.

14 This plant-eating animal eats algae, which gives its body fat a unique colour. It also has flipper-like legs – perfect for ocean swimming!

15 Native to Madagascar, the distinctive star-like pattern on its shell gives this reptile its name.

TEST YOURSELF

STARTER
- Radiated tortoise
- Green turtle
- Nile crocodile
- Tokay gecko
- Komodo dragon

CHALLENGER
- Gila monster
- Common green iguana
- Marine iguana
- Panther chameleon
- Alligator snapping turtle

GENIUS!
- Gharial
- Matamata
- Thorny devil
- Tuatara
- Armadillo girdled lizard

ANSWERS: 1. Panther chameleon 2. Common green iguana 3. Alligator snapping turtle 4. Armadillo girdled lizard 5. Komodo dragon 6. Tokay gecko 7. Gharial 8. Gila monster 9. Thorny devil 10. Tuatara 11. Matamata 12. Nile crocodile 13. Marine iguana 14. Green turtle 15. Radiated tortoise

NATURE KNOW-IT-ALL

Scaly serpents

Being legless is no big deal for snakes: they get around just as well as any other reptile. Their body is packed with muscle for gripping the ground, climbing trees, or even swimming at times. They eat other living animals, using either constricting coils or venom to kill. How many can you identify?

1 ▶ Most snakes lay eggs, but this gloriously green climbing species from South America gives birth to live young.

An upturned nose helps this snake rummage through soil for prey.

2 ▶ Flipping onto its back, keeping still, and being smelly, make predators think this snake is long dead – a clever trick!

Large jaw muscles clamp down on prey, such as small mammals and birds, with great force.

Mottled markings help this snake disguise itself amongst rainforest vegetation.

A scaled hood helps the snake look bigger, warding off predators.

3 ▶ Watch out! When this snake spreads its hood, it means it is ready to strike.

4 ▶ In the Amazon basin, the world's heaviest snake – weighing up to 246 kg (542 lb) – spends most of its time in water.

5 ▶ The only venomous snake in many European countries, this species can fold away its fangs when not in use.

Distinctive zigzag pattern

ANSWERS: 1. Emerald tree boa 2. Eastern hog-nosed snake 3. Indian cobra 4. Green anaconda 5. Common adder 6. Gaboon viper 7. Spiny bush viper 8. Western diamondback rattlesnake 9. Elephant-trunk snake 10. Black mamba 11. Eastern coral snake 12. Common egg-eating snake

6 Found in Africa, this scary serpent has the longest fangs – up to 5 cm (2 in) long – and produces the most venom of any snake.

The distinctive patterns on this snake's skin help it blend in amongst leaf litter.

7 Spiky scales cover the head and neck of this venomous snake from Central Africa.

The scales might help the snake to climb reeds and stalks.

Wrinkly skin

The loose, scaly rings make a buzzing noise.

8 By shaking the tip of its tail, this venomous snake warns everyone to stay away.

9 The wrinkly skin of this aquatic snake makes it look like the nose of a land mammal!

This snake's name comes from the colour of its mouth.

10 Possibly the fastest snake, this speedy striker from Africa is lethally venomous.

By wriggling, it punctures the shell of its meal to reach the yolky goodness.

11 The brilliant colour bands of this American snake are a warning that its venom can be deadly.

12 This African snake swallows its meal whole and digests it in its stomach.

TEST YOURSELF

STARTER	CHALLENGER	GENIUS!
Indian cobra	Eastern coral snake	Gaboon viper
Common adder	Black mamba	Emerald tree boa
Western diamondback rattlesnake	Green anaconda	Eastern hog-nosed snake
Common egg-eating snake	Elephant-trunk snake	Spiny bush viper

NATURE KNOW-IT-ALL

Amphibians

The word "amphibian" means "leading two kinds of life". Many of these animals start their lives underwater as tadpoles and grow into adults that are as much at home on land as in water. Most amphibians prefer damp places with enough water in which to lay their eggs.

Frog or toad: what's the difference?

Frogs
Most kinds of frogs around the world have a smooth, moist skin and very long back legs, which makes them the best jumpers.

Toads
Toads usually have rough, warty skins and squat bodies. Most have shorter legs than frogs, and prefer to walk rather than hop.

Types of amphibian

Frogs and toads
Most kinds of amphibians are frogs or toads. They usually have long back legs for swimming, hopping, or burrowing.

Salamanders and newts
These have lizard-like bodies. They waddle or run over the ground, and some even climb trees.

Caecilians
The wormlike shape of the tropical legless caecilians is ideal for burrowing in soil or leaf litter.

How to hunt like a tree frog

01. Look out for a juicy insect, then use your strong back legs to leap towards it.

02. Open your mouth wide and stick out your long tongue to reach your prey.

Long legs give extra propulsion power!

I don't believe it
Some American salamanders have no lungs and breathe entirely through their skin.

Keep away!
Many amphibians have brightly coloured skin. This is a warning that they are poisonous and may be deadly to eat.

Life-cycle of a frog

In Europe and North America, most amphibians lay their eggs in water, where the tadpoles can swim. Amphibians native to tropical rainforests often lay eggs on wet ground.

Adult frog → Eggs → Tadpoles → Legs develop → Froglet → Young frog → Adult frog

Tadpole tales

- The tadpoles of amphibians that breed in fast-flowing streams have special suckers so they can cling to rocks and not get washed away.

- The tadpoles of the paradoxical frog from South America are much bigger than the adults they grow into. They shrink as they develop.

- The parents of some kinds of poison dart frogs carry their tadpoles on their backs.

- Some tree frogs build a foam nest for their eggs among the branches, using froth beaten up with their legs. Once hatched, the tadpoles drop into a pool below.

Regrowing limbs

In the same way as lizards often do, salamanders may grow back tails lost through injury – but they go a stage further. Some salamanders can regrow lost limbs, producing perfect new feet and toes in the process.

Stump where tail has been lost

03. A sticky pad on your tongue grips the prey. Pull back your tongue, with dinner attached!

Glass frog

Some kinds of frogs from tropical America, called glass frogs, have transparent skin on their underside. This means that their skeleton and even their beating heart is visible inside.

Red blood vessels can be seen through the clear skin on the frog's belly.

In numbers

20,000
The number of eggs that a common frog can lay in a single breeding season.

102
The number of cane toads that were introduced to Australia in 1935. There are now millions of them and they are major pests.

10
The number of months spent underground by the African bullfrog in very dry years.

NATURE KNOW-IT-ALL

Amazing amphibians

Amphibians are animals with soft, moist skin, which means they survive best in wet places – but they can also live on land. There are crawlers, jumpers, and swimmers. Can you tell frogs from toads, or newts from salamanders?

Webbed feet act like parachutes, slowing down the frog as it falls.

① Webbed feet aren't just good for swimming – this rainforest-dwelling frog uses them for gliding through the air.

Green on top with a yellow underside makes perfect rainforest camouflage.

A tiny amount of poison produced in the skin could kill a human.

② Vivid colours warn that there are deadly poisons in the skin of this South American amphibian.

Six feathery external gills

Knobbly back makes it look like a certain giant reptile.

③ This salamander can regrow its organs and limbs if damaged. It also never grows up, keeping its baby gills into adulthood.

⑤ Orange bumps on the back of this Asian amphibian show where its poison-producing glands are.

④ A safe place to store eggs is in the skin of your back, as this South American frog does.

Semi-webbed feet

A flash of its colourful eyes scares away predators.

Fertilized eggs embedded on female's back

⑥ This Central American frog likes to climb trees in rainforests, using suction cups on its toes to help grip.

81

8 In Northern European ponds, the male of this species dances and fans its tail to impress females.

The toes are not webbed, unlike those of a frog.

Yellow belly with black splotches

Only the males have this frill, which grows in breeding seasons.

7 This looks like an eel but is really an extra-long salamander with tiny legs – it can be 1.1 m (3½ ft) long.

Legs are around 2 cm (⅘ in) long

Pointy nose

9 A big mouth enables this aggressive amphibian to swallow big prey – including small mammals and birds.

Rough, warty skin is usually green, brown, or grey.

10 A spiky brown head is a good disguise on the leaflitter of a gloomy rainforest floor.

11 A quick flash of a red-and-black belly is a warning to predators that it is poisonous.

Dry, bumpy skin on top

Thick, blunt toes

12 Yellow spots mark the positions of poisonous glands on this European forest amphibian.

13 This amphibian is the second biggest in the world and can reach 1.4 m (4½ ft) in length – only its relative from China is bigger.

14 This amphibian not only looks like a colourful worm but also behaves like one – it burrows in soil.

Small tentacles help locate prey.

15 This North American blood-coloured amphibian lacks lungs, so it breathes entirely through its skin.

TEST YOURSELF

STARTER
Axolotl
Blue-and-black poison dart frog
Red-eyed tree frog
Japanese giant salamander
Wallace's flying frog

CHALLENGER
Red salamander
Great crested newt
Fire salamander
African bullfrog
Oriental fire-bellied toad

GENIUS!
Amphiuma
Long-nosed horned frog
Surinam toad
Caecilian
Crocodile newt

ANSWERS: 1. Wallace's flying frog 2. Blue-and-black poison dart frog 3. Axolotl 4. Surinam toad 5. Crocodile newt 6. Red-eyed tree frog 7. Amphiuma 8. Great crested newt 9. African bullfrog 10. Long-nosed horned frog 11. Oriental fire-bellied toad 12. Fire salamander 13. Japanese giant salamander 14. Caecilian 15. Red salamander

Fish

Streamlined bodies, fins, and gills – fish have all the adaptations needed to live in water. Some swim in mid-water, others prefer to lurk near the bottom, but each kind uses its own special tactics for surviving below the surface.

Types of fish

Jawless fish
With more than 120 species, these kinds of fish, including this hagfish, do not have a jaw, but have sucker discs with rows of small teeth.

Bony fish
Most fish, more than 33,000 species, including this catfish, have a bony skeleton and a gas-filled bladder, which helps them to keep afloat.

Many cartilaginous fish have a venomous spine.

Cartilaginous fish
Some types of fish have a skeleton made of cartilage – a substance softer than bone. This ratfish, along with sharks and rays, falls in this group of more than 1,200 species.

How to make a baitball

01. When threatened, stay close to and swim in the same direction as the other fish around.

02. Swim in tight formation, to form a big, swirling baitball. This will confuse the predators, who will find it tricky to pick out individual prey.

Bluefish and barracudas circle the baitball.

Deep-sea terror
In deep oceans, where food is scarce, the Sloane's viperfish makes sure that its prey doesn't escape by trapping the victim with its long fangs.

03. Keep moving and stay alert. The bluefish are determined, and may dive into the baitball at any time and snap at random.

In numbers

300
The number, in millions, of eggs laid in one go by an ocean sunfish.

110 km/h
(68 mph) The maximum recorded speed of the sailfish – the fastest fish in the ocean.

8 mm
(¼ in) The length of the *Paedocypris* – the world's smallest fish.

Eggs are held in the male's mouth for up to 30 days until they hatch.

Parenting

Most fish produce a large number of eggs and release them in water, providing no care. However, some species, such as this cardinalfish, protect their eggs by brooding them in their mouth.

Fish scales

Diamond-shaped: The garfish has closely-fitted, interlocking scales, which work like a suit of armour, and provide protection.

Spines: The spines of the porcupine fish are a perfect defence. When in danger, the fish inflates, pushing the spines out like tiny needles.

Tooth-like: Sharks are covered in tiny tooth-like scales, which makes the skin rough – like sandpaper.

04: The tail then swings back as before while the fins keep the fish level in the water.

03: The muscles on the left contract to swing the tail the other way.

02: The sweeping tail pushes against the water, helping to force the fish forwards.

How fish swim

Fish swim in a wave-like motion. Their bodies are packed with strong muscles that bend the spine one way and then the other – a motion that propels them through the water.

Tail swings back

01: Muscles on the right side of the body contract to pull the tail to the right.

I don't believe it

The deep-sea barrel-eye fish has a transparent head to maximize the amount of light that can reach its eyes.

NATURE KNOW-IT-ALL

① Its tall, flattened shape allows this South American fish to slip in between grassy weeds.

② This fish, recognizable by its trunk-like nose, can generate an electric field which works like radar to help the fish find its way through muddy rivers.

Sucker-like mouth

The clue to its name is in the tail.

Breathing holes

③ A taste for blood drives this long, eel-like European fish to attack its prey with a circular, sucker-like mouth.

④ This long South American fish has a scoop-like mouth. It can jump 2 m (6½ ft) out of the water to snatch prey such as birds and bugs.

⑤ Found in the mangrove swamps of Southeast Asia, this tiny fish is named after its black-and-yellow stripes.

Long dorsal fin

⑥ A perfect parent, this African fish protects her eggs by holding them in her mouth until they hatch.

⑦ First bred in China 2,000 years ago, this favourite pond fish comes in many different colours including red, white, and orange.

Just 4 cm (1½ in) in length.

Distinctive spots

⑧ The rippling fin running along the underside of this knife-shaped fish helps it move forwards.

Freshwater fishes

From rivers and streams, to lakes and ponds, freshwater is a habitat for many kinds of fish. Some like water to be flowing and churning, while others prefer it calm and still. Can you spot who's who under the surface?

Can grow 1.5 m (5 ft) long, from tail to the tip of its pointed nose

⑨ The deep-olive colour helps this stealthy predator to remain camouflaged among water reeds before it darts out to grab prey.

⑩ Armed with razor-sharp teeth, this South American fish bands together in shoals for safety – and sometimes to eat.

Long snout is covered with sensory pores

11 Found only in North America, this fish collects prey such as plankton by swimming with its mouth wide-open.

12 This South American fish uses its whisker-like barbels to feel its way around in cloudy waters.

Barbel

13 Known for its aggression, this fish has been bred in Asia for hundreds of years. It uses its colourful fins to attract mates and scare off enemies.

Grows up to 2.5 m (8 ft) long

14 Named for its blue-and-green colour, this North American fish can be identified by the pink line running along its length. It can weigh up to 25 kg (55 lb).

The bright underside gives the fish its name.

A single anal fin stretches to the tail.

15 Watch out! Lurking in the Amazonian swamps, this fish can fire a 500-volt electric shock to stun and capture prey – a shocking surprise.

16 This popular pet fish is easily recognized by its orange colour, which deepens with the amount of light it receives. It can live for more than 20 years!

Can grow up to 1.8 m (6 ft) long

Big eyes allow this fish to see in murky tropical waters.

17 By looking like a piece of floating foliage, this fish can creep up on its underwater prey.

Floats with its head down

18 Most fish breathe underwater with gills, but if the level of oxygen in the water drops, this fish can also breathe air on land.

TEST YOURSELF

STARTER
- Goldfish
- Koi carp
- Pike
- Freshwater angelfish
- Red-bellied piranha
- Siamese fighting fish

CHALLENGER
- Electric eel
- Rainbow trout
- Red-tailed catfish
- Bumblebee goby
- Australian lungfish
- Leaf fish

GENIUS!
- Arowana
- Elephant fish
- Nile tilapia
- River lamprey
- American paddlefish
- Clown featherback

ANSWERS: 1. Freshwater angelfish 2. Elephant fish 3. River lamprey 4. Arowana 5. Bumblebee goby 6. Nile tilapia 7. Koi carp 8. Clown featherback 9. Pike 10. Red-bellied piranha 11. American paddlefish 12. Red-tailed catfish 13. Siamese fighting fish 14. Rainbow trout 15. Electric eel 16. Goldfish 17. Leaf fish 18. Australian lungfish

NATURE KNOW-IT-ALL

Grows up to 2 m (6½ ft)

① Shaped like a torpedo, this top ocean predator can suddenly accelerate at speed to catch its prey in its dagger-like teeth.

Strange, glowing organ or "fishing rod"

② Food is hard to find in the deep, dark sea. But this hunter overcomes this obstacle by using a glowing lure to attract prey.

Long fang-like teeth

③ This scaly fish was believed to have become extinct more than 65 million years ago, but was found to be alive in 1938!

The bright colours and patterns give this fish its name.

④ A narrow mouth only nibbles tiny food, but is good for plucking morsels from rocky crevices.

Blue spots distort the fish's shape when viewed by predators from above.

⑤ A razor-sharp spine in the tail of this fish can inject venom into an attacker, giving an agonizing wound.

Mane of venomous spines

An expandable mouth helps it swallow large prey.

⑥ Keep back! The spectacular fins on this big-mouthed fish carry vicious stinging spines.

Dorsal fin

A fan-shaped dorsal fin is displayed in the mating season.

⑦ Using its strong fins, this fish is able to waddle up onto the shore.

⑧ Found near tropical coral reefs, this sharp-toothed predator can be identified by the colour of its skin.

ANSWERS: 1. Great barracuda 2. Humpback anglerfish 3. Coelacanth 4. Butterflyfish 5. Blue-spotted ribbontail ray 6. Red lionfish 7. Mudskipper 8. Grey reef shark 9. Clownfish 10. Spotted ribbontail ray 11. Mandarinfish 12. Hammerhead shark 13. Common remora 14. Porcupine fish 15. Zebra moray eel

Marine life

Most of the world's 33,500 or so different species of fish live in the oceans. Some live in the deep, where all is dark and cold. Others swim in the sunlit open seas, while many more live on colourful coral reefs. How many can you recognize?

The babies are known as fry.

10 In this species, it's the father who carries the eggs, in a pouch on his belly, and when they hatch, he gives birth!

Venomous barb

9 Home for this fish is among the tentacles of an anemone – a thick slimy layer on its skin protects it from stings.

11 This fish gets its name from its fantastic colours, which resemble those of the robes of a Chinese emperor.

12 The distinctively shaped head is packed with special sensors that can detect prey – even if they are buried in sand.

Flat dorsal fin acts as a sucker so the fish can attach itself to its host.

13 By sticking itself to the underside of whales and sharks, this fish gets a free ride and feeds on leftovers.

14 What better way to defend yourself than by swallowing water and swelling up like a spiky ball?

Round snout

15 This stripy, nocturnal fish can be around 1.5 m (5 ft) long. It has strong teeth and can bite through the hardest shellfish.

TEST YOURSELF

STARTER
Clownfish
Zebra moray eel
Spotted seahorse
Hammerhead shark
Porcupine fish

CHALLENGER
Humpback anglerfish
Mudskipper
Red lionfish
Coelacanth
Blue-spotted ribbontail ray

GENIUS!
Common remora
Mandarinfish
Butterflyfish
Great barracuda
Grey reef shark

NATURE KNOW-IT-ALL

Innate vs learned

Innate behaviour refers to skills animals are born with, which they don't have to learn as they grow up. For example, the praying mantis snatches prey using lightning-fast front legs instinctually – it was never taught this skill.

Learned behaviour develops as an animal gets older. Young lions are born with a hunting instinct, but have to watch and follow their parents to get better at it.

Defensive tactics

Animals use many tactics to defend themselves against attack from predators. Some animals use their body parts, such as horns or claws, as weapons. Others use very different techniques. The skunk, for example, squirts a smelly liquid from its bottom to deter hunters.

Black-and-white stripes warn attackers they might get a faceful of smelly liquid!

Animal behaviour

Whether they are getting food, avoiding danger, or raising a family, animals behave in lots of different ways. Sometimes they do things by instinct; other times they must learn what they have to do. Animal behaviour is driven mainly by one reason: the need to stay alive in the continual fight for survival.

The journey to the nest can sometimes be 30 m (100 ft) long.

A smooth curved edge is left where the ant's jaws have sliced through the leaf.

02. Smaller ants can sit on leaves, to guard them from predators and keep them clean on the journey back to the nest.

Working together

Sometimes different species help one another. Oxpeckers are birds that clean zebras of blood-sucking ticks – and get a meal in the process! This mutually beneficial relationship is called mutualism.

Using tools

The cleverest animals can use tools to help them get food – such as this young chimpanzee learning to "fish" for juicy termites with a stick.

How to work as a team

01. Medium-sized leafcutter ants head into the tropical forests of Central and South America to find some good leaves and bite off pieces they can carry, which can be up to 20 times their body weight.

03. At the nest, guarded by the biggest ants, the smallest ants add pieces of leaf to the "garden" of fungus they grow for food.

In numbers

6,000 km (3,728 miles) The length of a giant colony of Argentine ants in Europe.

100 The number of words learned by Alex, a famous African grey parrot.

20 The number of different alarm calls used by meerkats, to warn others in the group of different kinds of danger.

10 The number of seconds it takes for a European cuckoo to lay its egg in the nest of another bird, while the owner is not looking.

Tricksters

Cantil snake: Young snakes waggle a worm-like, coloured tail to help them attract prey.

Black heron: Opening its wings over the water like an umbrella, this bird creates shade to attract fish – making them easy pickings for the bird.

Flatfish: By changing colour to match the sea floor, fish such as the plaice disguise themselves from predators.

Portia spider: This spider pretends to be a wriggling fly stuck in a web so it can prey on other spiders.

Large ants carry leaf fragments in their strong jaws.

NATURE KNOW-IT-ALL

Tricky tracks

There's an animal about, but what is it? A lot of animals are very secretive and take care not to be seen. But if they wander over mud, sand, or snow, they can't help the tracks they leave behind them. Some might be obvious – but others are puzzling.

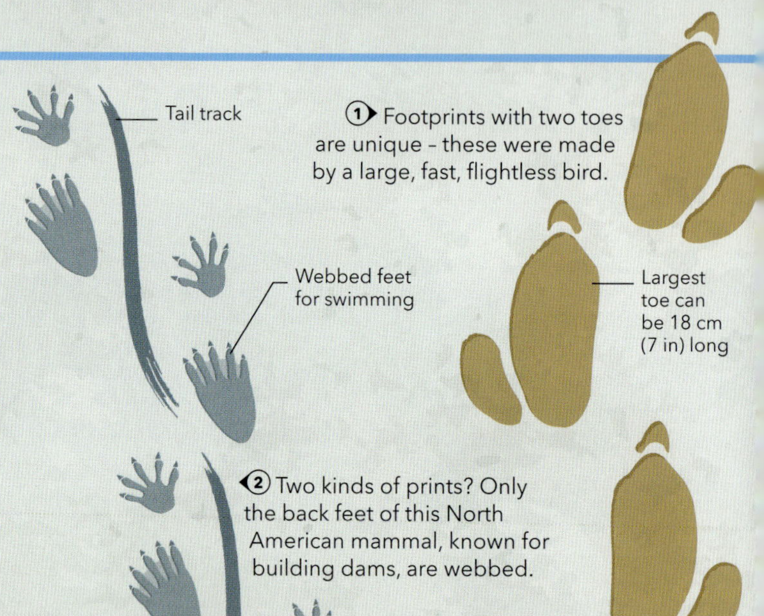

Tail track

① Footprints with two toes are unique – these were made by a large, fast, flightless bird.

Webbed feet for swimming

Largest toe can be 18 cm (7 in) long

② Two kinds of prints? Only the back feet of this North American mammal, known for building dams, are webbed.

Wide-spread toes help in walking

③ The hooves of this animal are clearly cloven – each one split down the middle to give two toes.

Hoof-shaped toenail of about 7 cm (2¾ in)

Glands between the toes leave a scent trail for others of its kind to follow.

④ This feathered friend, often seen in cities, has three toes at the front and one at the back – making its tracks easy to spot!

This mammal walks on the soles of it feet.

Forelimb feet are smaller than the hind feet

Hind feet can be twisted backwards while climbing down trees.

Its claws also make tracks.

⑥ A tree-dwelling rodent leaves behind these prints as it scurries around looking for nuts and seeds.

⑤ Who's been lumbering by? These giant flat-footed pawprints can only belong to one large, furry mammal, which can be found in the USA.

7 Although more at home in the sea, this mammal moves on land by using its flippers to drag its large body forwards.

Flipper tracks

Small hook at the end where the animal curls its tail

9 This furry little animal sprints at the first sign of danger. Its long, strong hind legs give it speed.

8 The winding body of this reptile leaves behind parallel, streaky tracks as it zigzags across its desert habitat.

When the chest, stomach, and tail are kept flat on the ground, they make a track of their own!

10 The tiny feet that have made these tracks belong to a common pest that has reached almost all of the world's continents as a stowaway on ships.

12 One of the most powerful reptiles, this animal drags its long, heavy tail as it prowls on the ground.

11 Webbed feet, seen in these tracks, help this black-and-white bird to steer when swimming underwater.

Most birds walk on tiptoes, but this one walks on the soles of its feet.

A dew claw at the back of the foot doesn't reach the ground.

Hind feet are webbed.

13 These paw prints have been left by a four-toed animal that is a popular pet.

TEST YOURSELF

STARTER
- Rabbit
- Dog
- Pigeon
- Rat

CHALLENGER
- Bear
- Sidewinder snake
- Deer
- Ostrich
- Squirrel

GENIUS!
- **Crocodile**
- **Seal**
- **Penguin**
- **Beaver**

ANSWERS: 1. Ostrich 2. Beaver 3. Deer 4. Pigeon 5. Bear 6. Squirrel 7. Seal 8. Sidewinder snake 9. Rabbit 10. Rat 11. Penguin 12. Crocodile 13. Dog

Get cracking

Inside an egg is a baby animal just waiting to hatch out. The eggs of birds must have a hard shell, to stop them breaking when the parent sits on them to keep them warm. Most fish, insects, and reptiles lay eggs too, and they all look very different.

1 This egg belongs to a giant jungle bird that cannot fly but will defend its eggs with huge clawed feet.

2 The world's biggest living bird lays the biggest egg – weighing up to 1.4 kg (3 lb).

Green-blue eggs can be up to 14 cm (5½ in) long.

3 These creatures lay eggs in huge colonies on islands around bitterly cold Antarctica.

The egg is incubated between the parents' belly and feet.

The eggs take 42–46 days to hatch.

4 The animal that lays this egg is known for its melodious call.

5 Almost all furry animals give birth to live young – but this egg was laid by a spiky mammal.

6 The nest for this egg is made of twigs, grass, and feathers by a bird with a brightly coloured breast.

The egg is known for its blue colour.

7 You'll find the egg of this fish-hunting raptor in a massive nest made from sticks, high in a tree.

Unlike other reptile eggs, this eggshell is hard, not leathery.

8 These eggs are laid in other birds' nests. They look like the other eggs already in the nest, so they go unnoticed.

9 Belonging to a South African animal, this egg hatches into a female at warmer temperatures; at cooler temperatures it produces a male.

TEST YOURSELF

STARTER
- Chicken
- Ostrich
- Cassowary
- Leopard tortoise
- Corn snake
- Frogspawn
- Dinosaur

CHALLENGER
- Rainbow trout
- Ladybird
- King penguin
- American robin
- Mute swan
- Japanese quail
- Cuckoo

GENIUS!
- Lesser spotted dogfish
- Elegant crested tinamou
- Common guillemot
- Leopard gecko
- Osprey
- Short-beaked echidna
- Garden snail
- Song thrush

11. Mute swan 12. Leopard gecko 13. Chicken 14. Elegant crested tinamou 15. Common guillemot 16. Corn snake 17. Ladybird 18. Garden snail 19. Japanese quail 20. Lesser spotted dogfish 21. Rainbow trout 22. Frogspawn

93

10 This egg certainly looks in very bad shape – but it is 75 million years old!

Eggs laid in water

Eggs that are laid by animals that live in water are very different from those that are laid on dry land.

20 Tassels help to anchor this egg case to seaweed so it is not washed away by ocean currents.

21 The female scatters thousands of these eggs over gravel in a pool – then leaves them to develop alone.

22 Masses of jelly-coated eggs laid in a pond will hatch into swimming larvae that develop into hopping land animals.

11 The animal that lays this egg will attack with big flapping wings if you get too close.

12 The baby that hatches from this egg has stripes – but will grow into a reptile with spots.

13 Eaten all over the world, this farmed egg is an important food source.

14 This beautiful, green egg of a South American bird has a glossy texture.

15 A pointy shape stops this sea bird's egg from rolling off the clifftop ledge where it is laid.

A leathery shell helps protect the young reptile inside.

The eggs are covered with soil.

17 On hatching, the young from these tiny eggs feed on greenflies. They later grow up to be greenfly-munching beetles.

16 A slimline egg is needed if you have a very slimline body to do the laying.

19 A mottled pattern helps to disguise this Asian bird's egg from predators.

18 These eggs were laid by a slow-moving invertebrate.

ANSWERS: 1. Cassowary 2. Ostrich 3. King penguin 4. Song thrush 5. Short-beaked echidna 6. American robin 7. Osprey 8. Cuckoo 9. Leopard tortoise 10. Dinosaur

94

Eye spy

What a sight! All animals have eyes that are just right for them. While some eyes work well underwater, others are designed for life on land, and some even see clearly in the dark. But all of them help animals take in the world around them.

1 In the warty skin just behind this amphibian's eye is a poison gland that is used for self-defence.

2 Enormous forward-facing eyes help this small primate see at night as it leaps through trees.

3 Unlike others of its kind, this spotted reptile has eyelids which can open and close.

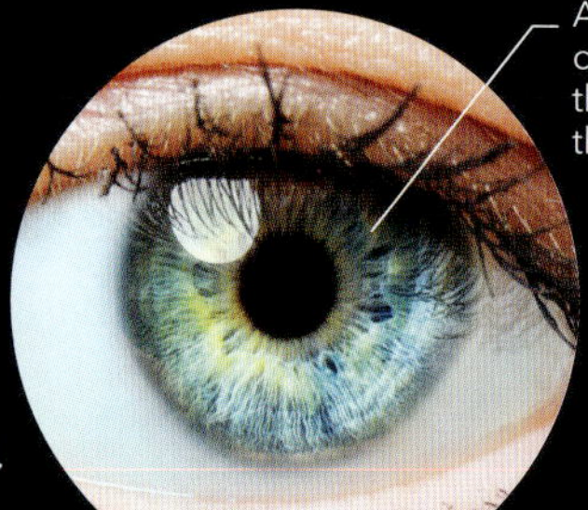

4 Is this like looking in a mirror? Thousands of years ago, all of these mammals had brown eyes, but now they can be blue and green as well.

A ring of muscles, called the iris, controls the amount of light that enters the eye.

5 With its luminous yellow eyes, this feathered night-time hunter cannot rotate its eyeballs, so it swivels its neck – up to 270 degrees – to look around.

6 A compound eye (made of many parts) helps this insect to see in all directions – enabling it to get close enough to bite animals for their blood.

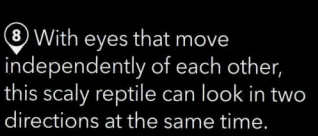

7 Lurking just under the water surface, this animal waits to snap up passing prey with the eyes on top of its head sticking out.

8 With eyes that move independently of each other, this scaly reptile can look in two directions at the same time.

The W-shaped pupil helps improve vision in dim water.

9 The vivid colour of its bulging eye helps this climbing amphibian startle potential enemies – giving it time to hop away.

10 With a "W"-shaped, slit-like pupil, this distinctive eye belongs to an underwater creature that can change colour.

11 The night-time eyeshine of this animal inspired the invention of a road safety feature that reflects the beam of car headlights.

95

12 An oversized eye helps this ocean-dwelling animal hunt for prey at night.

13 A vertical slit for a pupil helps this scaly, venomous animal focus on moving prey from its hiding place in trees and bushes.

14 Descended from wolves, this furry animal has icy blue eyes and is sometimes used to pull sledges over snow.

Multicoloured eye filters different colours

15 No, this eye does not belong to a dinosaur! It belongs to a rare, large tree-climbing lizard that lives on the Grand Cayman Island.

Golden iris

16 Extra-long lashes are needed to help stop sand being blown into the eye of this desert animal.

17 This soft-bodied invertebrate has multiple, skilful arms, a big brain, and excellent vision to match.

Horizontal pupil draws into a slit during the day

18 At only 3.8 cm (1½ in), this is a small eye for the world's biggest land animal, which can grow up to 7.5 m (24½ ft) long.

19 A horizontal, rectangular pupil gives this hoofed mammal a wider field of view, which increases its chances of spotting a predator.

20 The eyes of this dangerous, slithery reptile have no eyelids, meaning it cannot blink.

21 This sea animal moves its eyes independently of each other, and is known for swelling up like a balloon when threatened.

TEST YOURSELF

STARTER
- Human
- Red-eyed tree frog
- Domestic cat
- Husky dog
- Horsefly
- Camel
- Crocodile

CHALLENGER
- Elephant
- Goat
- Panther chameleon
- Giant Pacific octopus
- Cane toad
- Great horned owl
- Bushbaby

GENIUS!
- Cuttlefish
- Starry pufferfish
- Blue iguana
- Red big-eye fish
- Leaf viper
- Leopard gecko
- Boomslang snake

ANSWERS: 1. Cane toad 2. Bushbaby 3. Leopard gecko 4. Panther chameleon 5. Human 6. Great horned owl 7. Crocodile 8. Horsefly 9. Red-eyed tree frog 10. Cuttlefish 11. Domestic cat 12. Red big-eye fish 13. Leaf viper 14. Husky dog 15. Blue iguana 16. Camel 17. Giant Pacific octopus 18. Elephant 19. Goat 20. Boomslang snake 21. Starry pufferfish

Plants

A world without foliage and flowers would be a far less colourful place. The green leaves of plants make food using the energy in sunlight, and – as part of forests and grasslands – they provide habitats for animals that live on land. In one way or another, we all rely on plants.

Types of plants

Non-flowering: These plants scatter spores (dust-like cells), which grow into new plants on moist soil.

Flowering: After pollination, these plants form seeds inside fruits. The seeds scatter and develop into new plants.

Red tentacles produce sweet, glue-like droplets to attract the fly.

As the fly struggles, more tentacles stick to its body.

It takes about 30 minutes for the leaf to coil around the fly.

Nutrients from the fly's body seep into the plant to help it grow.

When the leaf curls, the fly dies by exhaustion or suffocation.

How to catch a fly

01. As a carnivorous (meat-eating) sundew, you are perfectly designed as a killer plant. First, attract a fly with the sugary drops on your leaf.

02. When the fly is totally trapped in the stickiness, slowly coil the leaf around it as it struggles to escape.

03. Once the fly is dead, trigger the leaf to produce chemicals that will break down the fly's body, and then absorb all its nutrients.

Parts of a plant

Leaves make food using energy from sunlight.

Flowers have pollen that is carried by insects or wind to other plants, fertilizing them so they can produce seeds.

Roots anchor the plant and take in water and minerals from the soil.

Fruits contain seeds which, when scattered, produce more plants.

Stem carries water and minerals into the leaves, fruits, and flowers.

Record-breaking trees

- The world's tallest tree is a coast redwood from California, nicknamed Hyperion, which reaches a height of 115.92 m (380$^{3}/_{10}$ ft).

- A bristlecone pine found in the mountains of western USA is the world's oldest tree, and also one of the oldest of all living things. Its seed first sprouted more than 5,000 years ago.

- The Guyana chestnut produces the widest flowers of any tree – growing up to 66 cm (26 in) across.

- The coco de mer Palm produces the largest seed of any kind of plant – each can weigh up to 30 kg (66 lb).

In number

6 million kg
(13 million lb) The estimated weight of a group of quaking aspen trees in Utah, USA, which are connected to form a giant superorganism.

32,000 years
The age of a seed of the Arctic Campion – a small flowering plant – that was planted and successfully grown.

2,000
The number of seeds that can form in a single sunflower.

Cheeky monkey
The *Dracula simia* is an orchid with a surprising feature – the inside of it looks like a monkey's face!

A scientist studies a giant sequoia, which is more than 75 m (247 ft) tall.

Strange plants

Titan arum: This plant has the tallest flowering spike, at 3 m (10 ft), which stinks of rotting meat to attract pollinating flies.

Spanish moss: Not technically a moss, this flowering plant blankets trees and absorbs moisture from the air.

Giant water lily: This aquatic plant has a giant leaf, which can measure more than 2 m (6½ ft) across.

Stone plant: This plant looks like a pebble to deter plant-eaters, until its flower gives the game away!

① Spots mimic aphids to attract predatory insects.

② Native to warm and tropical regions, the petals of this large, trumpet-shaped flower are used to make a type of tea.

① The flower's pouch may look like a piece of footwear – but is used to trap pollinating insects.

③ These bell-shaped flowers are narrow, but the perfect fit for bumblebees looking for nectar.

④ In South Asia, these bright, globe-shaped flowers are used to make garlands for many religious ceremonies.

The flowers begin opening from bottom to top.

Flower power

Flowers are the parts of plants from which fruits or seeds develop. We love them because they brighten our gardens and homes, but their main purpose is to help plants with pollination. Their showy colours and, sometimes, powerful perfumes attract insects and other animals, who then carry pollen from one plant to another.

⑤ The stigma of this flower is dried to make saffron, which is used to season or colour food and dye clothes.

⑥ Birds and butterflies are attracted to the nectar produced by these tall spikes of striking red flowerheads.

Sticky stigma traps pollen carried by insects

Can grow to 1.5 m (5 ft) tall

Each head is made up of many florets.

⑧ In many cultures, these fragrant blooms are symbols of purity. They produce a lot of orange pollen, which can stain fingers and clothes.

⑦ These flowers grow wild in Asia, where they are the symbol of wealth, and have large heads that come in many colours.

9 Prized for their bright colours, millions of these flowers are cultivated in the Netherlands each year.

10 Said to resemble the plumes of an exotic bird, this African flower blooms in warm countries.

11 Though more familiar in its red form, this garden favourite comes in many colours and often appears in fairytales as a symbol of love.

12 A native of Australasia and made up of a cluster of bright-red spikes of flowers, this flowerhead looks like it could be used for cleaning.

13 In Europe, this pretty trumpet-shaped flower is a sure sign that spring has arrived.

14 Prized in Asia, the petals of this aquatic flower open during the day and close at night, perhaps to stop the pollen from being damaged by morning dew.

15 Fragrant oils from this flower are used to sooth cuts and grazes, and to repel mosquitoes.

The central disc is made of up to 2,000 tiny flowers.

16 These tall, nodding, bright-yellow flowers always grow facing the Sun. One record-breaking specimen grew to a height of 9.17 m (30 ft).

17 Found in the Himalayas, this blue flower has a red European relative that is a symbol of remembrance of war.

18 The national flower of South Africa survives wildfires by growing buds from an underground stem.

TEST YOURSELF

STARTER
- Daffodil
- Sunflower
- Tulip
- Chrysanthemum
- Foxglove
- Rose

CHALLENGER
- Hibiscus
- Marigold
- Lily
- Blue poppy
- Crocus
- Lavender

GENIUS!
- Lady's slipper orchid
- Bird-of-paradise flower
- King protea
- Red-hot poker
- Bottlebrush
- Lotus

ANSWERS: 1. Lady's slipper orchid 2. Hibiscus 3. Foxglove 4. Marigold 5. Crocus 6. Red-hot poker 7. Chrysanthemum 8. Lily 9. Tulip 10. Bird-of-paradise flower 11. Rose 12. Bottlebrush 13. Daffodil 14. Lotus 15. Lavender 16. Sunflower 17. Blue poppy 18. King protea

Fruit and nuts

Fruits grow from the flowers of plants – they are the parts we can eat. They come in different colours that entice you to dive in for a bite. This is exactly what the plants want – by eating the fruits, animals help scatter the seeds inside in their waste.

1 This fruit can taste sour – but when cooked with sugar it can be used to make pies and puddings.

Fruit can be bright green or red in colour

2 When ripe, this tree-borne fruit tastes like the sweet, creamy sauce you might pour over a dessert.

Smooth-skinned yellow variety grows in warm areas such as Hawaii, USA

Sweet, creamy flesh

3 This seed-packed fruit is sour when fresh. The purple varieties can only be eaten when the skin is brown and wrinkled – unlike this orange variety, which is ripe and ready for you to tuck into!

Shiny black seeds

Woody shell

4 Traditionally grown in Central Asia, the two halves of this nut's shell break open to reveal a softer inside.

In North America, crops are flooded to protect fruit from cold and wind.

5 Crushed to make a sauce or jelly, these berries are popular at Christmas and Thanksgiving.

6 Found in Southeast Asia, the "King of the Fruits" is one of the stinkiest in the world, but has a delicious taste.

Thorny rind

7 These are not technically fruits, but an expanded part of the stem that contains tiny flowers, which are fertilized by wasps who enter inside through a hole at the bottom.

Tiny seeds embedded in reddish-pink flesh

Inside every round fruitlet is a seed.

8 After developing from white flowers, these berries are best picked when they are at their darkest – but watch out for thorns on the bush!

9 You'll find these fruits growing on a cactus in deserts and other dry places.

Sharp spine

10 Most of these small, soft, distinctively coloured fruits are grown in North America.

The fruit is pale green before it ripens and takes a darker colour.

11 This bright fruit originated in the Caribbean and is consumed for its delicious juice.

12 Expect lots of small seeds, surrounded by juicy red flesh, when you cut open the tough pink skin of this fruit.

13 Originating from Peru and related to tomatoes, these sweet fruits grow inside papery husks.

14 This small, round, smooth-shelled nut, also called a cobnut, is a favourite food of woodland squirrels.

15 This huge, juicy fruit – that grows on vines – is just what you need to quench a raging thirst!

The biggest can weigh more than 90 kg (200 lb).

Edible seeds

16 These seeds are produced inside the cones of a type of evergreen tree, but only 20 per cent of species have seeds big enough to be worth eating.

These berries come in a variety of colours, including black and white.

17 This fruit grows on a tree that has a double use – the sweet berries are delicious and its leaves are food for silkworm caterpillars.

TEST YOURSELF

STARTER
- Blackberries
- Walnuts
- Hazelnuts
- Blueberries
- Grapefruit
- Gooseberries

CHALLENGER
- Figs
- Cranberries
- Pomegranate
- Passion fruit
- Watermelon

GENIUS!
- Custard apple
- Mulberries
- Durian
- Prickly pears
- Cape gooseberries
- Pine nuts

ANSWERS: 1. Gooseberries 2. Custard apple 3. Passion fruit 4. Walnuts 5. Cranberries 6. Durian 7. Figs 8. Blackberries 9. Prickly pears 10. Blueberries 11. Grapefruit 12. Pomegranate 13. Cape gooseberries 14. Hazelnuts 15. Watermelon 16. Pine nuts 17. Mulberries

① Each bulb is divided into cloves that pack a very strong taste.

The stalks can be red, light pink, or light green.

② The pink leafstalks here are popular in sweet desserts – but the big green leaves are poisonous.

③ The crinkly leaves look as good as they taste, and are full of vitamins.

④ Packed with sticky starch, called tapioca, this tropical root vegetable is used for baking.

Fat roots grow under the soil.

Deep-red colour

Plant food

"Vegetable" is not a scientific term, it's simply the name we give to plants grown for food. A few that contain seeds are technically fruits, but because they are used in savoury dishes, they are known as vegetables. They are all versions of wild plants that farmers have learned to cultivate over thousands of years.

⑦ The shape and colour of an organ in the human body, these are usually dried, and must then be soaked and cooked before they are safe to eat.

Tube-like shape

⑤ This small-bud variety of cabbage gets its name from a city in Europe.

Made of several packed layers

⑥ This is in fact a giant berry, which can be stewed, fried, roasted, or mashed.

Deep-purple skin

⑩ First grown in the Andes, this root vegetable (meaning it grows underground) is crammed full of nutrients.

⑧ In North America and Europe, this is a favourite for celebrating Halloween and Thanksgiving.

⑨ The tasty "spears" of this vegetable are actually young shoots that have just emerged from the ground.

11 The bright-orange pigment in this vegetable helps us make vitamin A, which is essential for healthy vision.

12 This vegetable produces long tasty seed pods, picked before the seeds inside mature and grow tough.

13 This root vegetable grows best in the tropics, and has a distinctive sugary flavour.

14 The crisp, peppery roots of this vegetable are eaten raw in Europe, and are found in pickles and stews further east.

15 Growing from a vine, this sweet fruit turns a deeper orange as it ripens and is used in soups, pies, and stews.

Soft, rounded leaves

16 The name of this variety of Chinese smooth-leaved cabbage means "white vegetable" in Cantonese.

This vegetable comes in many different colours.

Used in most tinned baked beans

17 In America, these are also known as "navy beans" because they were a popular food with sailors.

18 As well as being tasty, this tropical fruit's flesh can be scooped out and the shell made into a sturdy container.

19 A popular salad vegetable, this is grown in water and has hollow stems, which make it float.

Each floret is a mini version of the whole vegetable.

20 This crunchy root vegetable grows in muddy marshes in Asia.

21 With its origins in Italy, this vegetable is a variety of cauliflower that produces edible flower buds.

TEST YOURSELF

STARTER
- Garlic
- Carrots
- Sweet potato
- Green beans
- Pumpkin
- Aubergine
- Kidney beans

CHALLENGER
- Asparagus
- Radishes
- Watercress
- Brussels sprouts
- Butternut squash
- Rhubarb
- Haricot beans

GENIUS!
- Oca
- Kale
- Pak choi
- Calabash
- Water chestnut
- Cassava root
- Romanesco broccoli

ANSWERS: 1. Garlic 2. Rhubarb 3. Kale 4. Cassava root 5. Brussels sprouts 6. Aubergine 7. Kidney beans 8. Pumpkin 9. Asparagus 10. Oca 11. Carrots 12. Green beans 13. Sweet potato 14. Radishes 15. Butternut squash 16. Pak choi 17. Haricot beans 18. Calabash 19. Watercress 20. Water chestnut 21. Romanesco broccoli

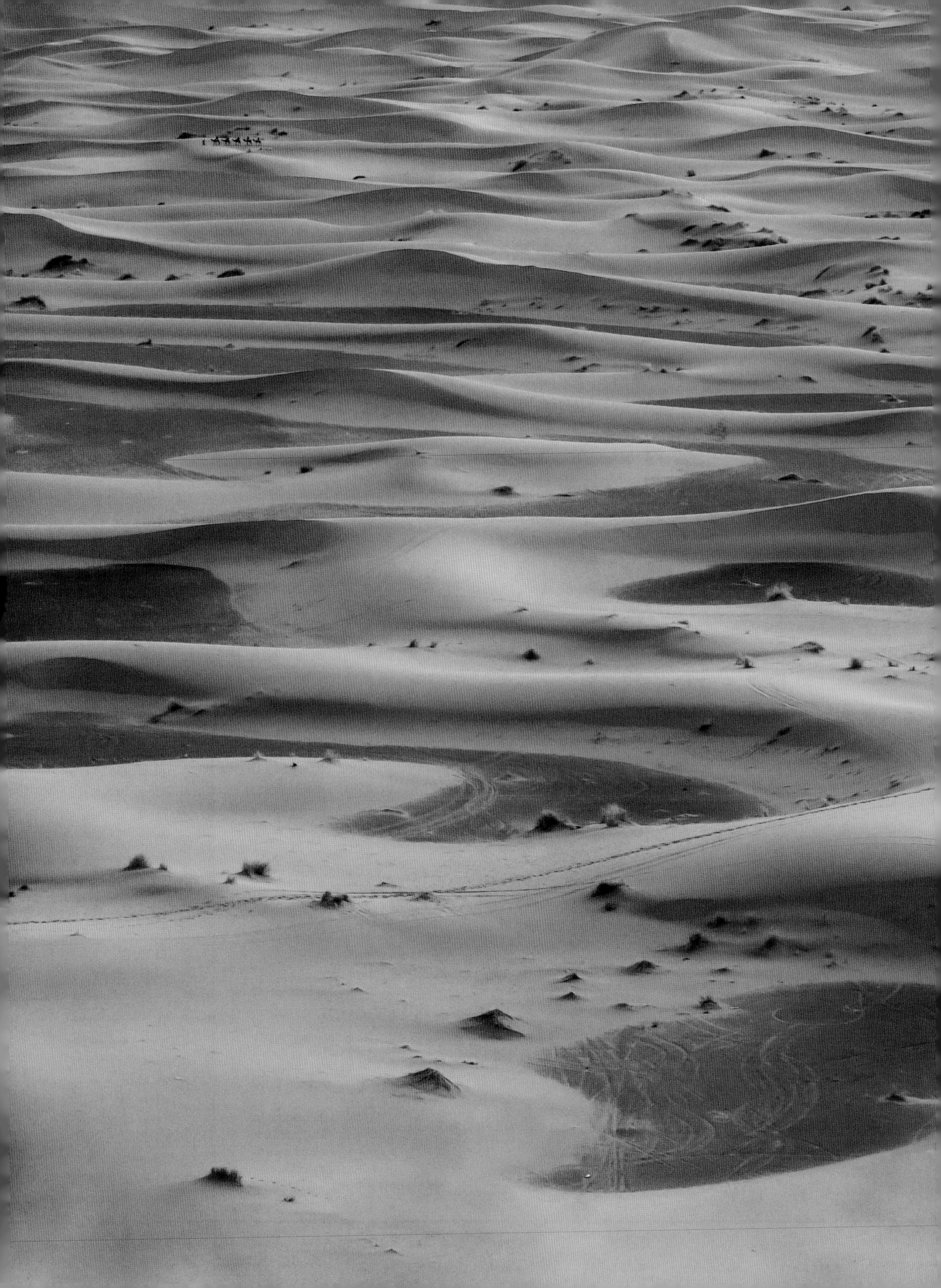

3 GEOGRAPHY GENIUS

Spot the camels
Natural wonders are found all across the globe, but there is more to some of them than meets the eye. See if you can spy the camels moving across this stretch of the Sahara desert. They are not just a mirage!

Earth

Our planet is a ball of hot rock and metal, with a cool, brittle shell and an airy atmosphere. Its surface is just the right temperature to hold oceans of liquid water – a substance vital to the survival of all living things. Many forms of life thrive on Earth, making their homes in a diverse range of habitats.

What's inside Earth?

Soon after it formed, Earth got so hot that it melted. This allowed most of its heavy iron to sink to the centre, forming a metallic core. This lies within a deep layer of hot rock called the mantle, which is covered by a thin crust.

Inner core: Earth's inner core is made of solid iron and nickel.

Oceans: Water covers two-thirds of the planet's surface.

Earth is the only known planet with life!

How the continents formed

01. Earth's crust is split into plates that keep moving, carrying the continents with them. 335 million years ago, the continents joined up.

02. Known as Pangaea, this huge supercontinent began to break up 175 million years ago.

03. As America moved away from Asia and Africa, India and Australia drifted north, creating the world we know today.

In numbers

4.6 billion
The number of years planet Earth has been in existence since it formed from a gigantic cloud of dust and gases.

6,371 km
(3,958 miles) The distance to Earth's centre.

11 km
(7 miles) The depth of the Mariana Trench in the Pacific Ocean – the deepest point on Earth.

Habitats

Deserts: A desert can be hot or cold, but is always very dry, with little life.

Grasslands: These get more rain than deserts, but not enough for forests to grow.

Tundra: Life must survive long, dark, freezing winters in this near-polar habitat.

Polar regions: Nearly all life in the icy polar regions lives in the seas and oceans.

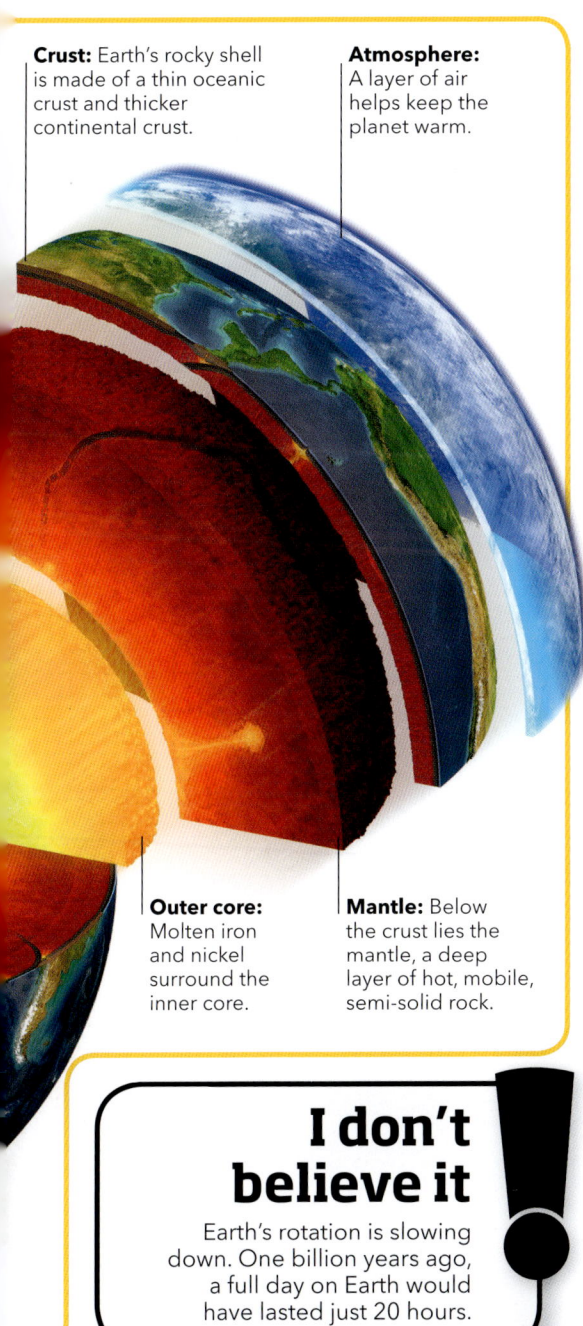

Crust: Earth's rocky shell is made of a thin oceanic crust and thicker continental crust.

Atmosphere: A layer of air helps keep the planet warm.

Outer core: Molten iron and nickel surround the inner core.

Mantle: Below the crust lies the mantle, a deep layer of hot, mobile, semi-solid rock.

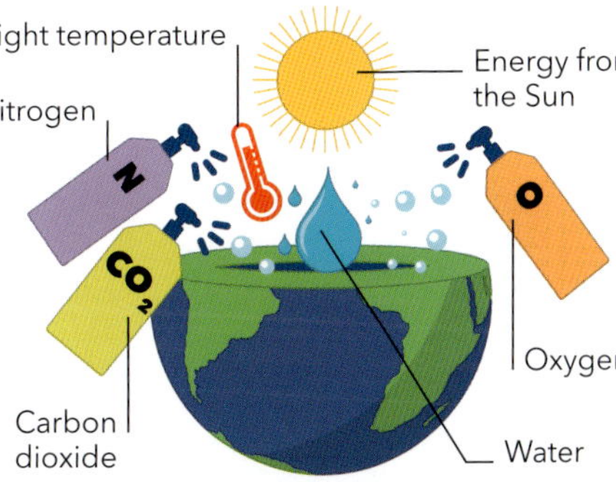

Just right!

Earth has just the right temperature to ensure that water doesn't freeze or boil away into space. The air also has the perfect mixture of gases needed to support life.

Right temperature · Nitrogen · Energy from the Sun · Carbon dioxide · Oxygen · Water

Endless water cycle

Much of Earth's life depends on the water cycle - the way moisture circulates between the oceans, air, and land. Many plants and animals rely on the rainfall it creates.

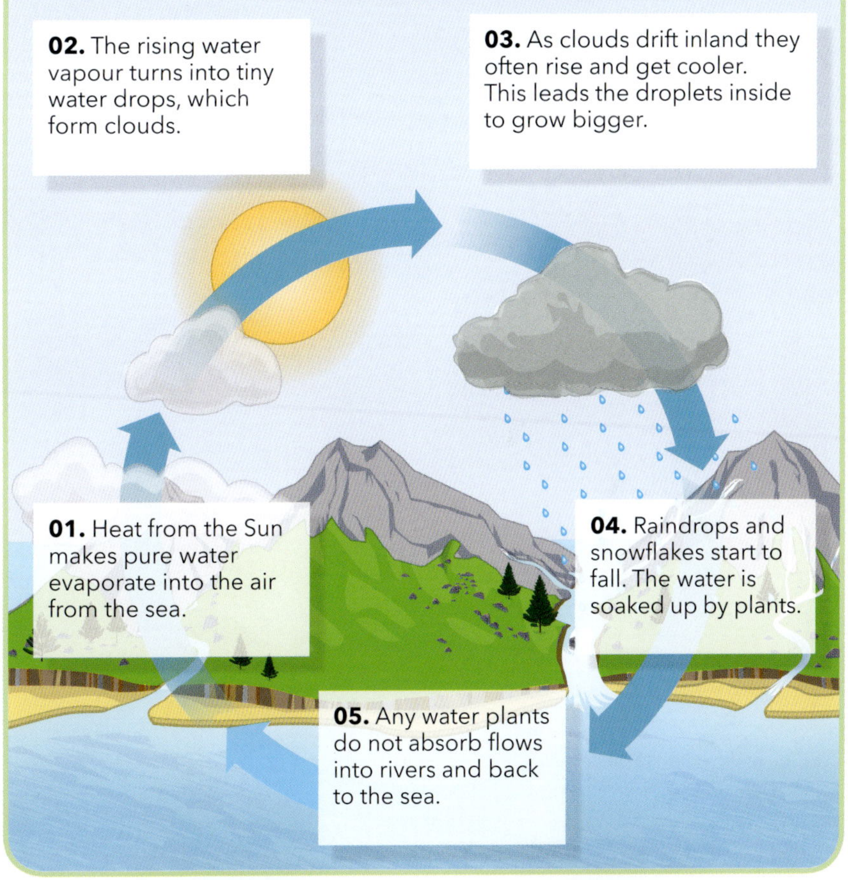

01. Heat from the Sun makes pure water evaporate into the air from the sea.

02. The rising water vapour turns into tiny water drops, which form clouds.

03. As clouds drift inland they often rise and get cooler. This leads the droplets inside to grow bigger.

04. Raindrops and snowflakes start to fall. The water is soaked up by plants.

05. Any water plants do not absorb flows into rivers and back to the sea.

I don't believe it!

Earth's rotation is slowing down. One billion years ago, a full day on Earth would have lasted just 20 hours.

Mountains: The air is cold at high altitudes, so this habitat is similar to tundra.

Oceans: These include a wide variety of habitats, from icy polar seas to coral reefs.

Rivers and wetlands: These rich habitats support lots of plants and animals.

Forests: A dense forest can be home to a huge variety of life in all its forms.

GEOGRAPHY GENIUS

High seas

More than two-thirds of Earth's surface is covered by seawater. Most of this water lies in deep oceans, but there are also other smaller, shallower seas around the coasts of the continents. Sometimes parts of a sea can be almost entirely surrounded by land – these are known as gulfs.

① The swampy shores of this water body, lined with lagoons and beaches, are often battered by destructive hurricanes.

② This cold sea is dotted with icebergs that drift south from Greenland.

③ Dividing America from Europe and Africa, the second-largest ocean covers about 106,460,000 sq km (41,100,000 sq miles).

④ Cut off from the ocean by a chain of around 7,000 islands, such as Saint Lucia (below), this tropical sea is home to coral reefs.

⑤ By far the biggest ocean in the world, at around 161,760,000 sq km (62½ million sq miles), this water body covers almost half the globe and has an average depth of more than 4,000 m (13,000 ft) – which is more than four times the height of the tallest building in the world, Dubai's Burj Khalifa.

⑥ Named after a British expedition ship that sailed here, this Antarctic sea has floating ice on which penguins live and cold, rocky islands where they nest.

TEST YOURSELF

STARTER	CHALLENGER	GENIUS!
Atlantic Ocean	North Sea	Sea of Okhotsk
Pacific Ocean	Red Sea	Persian Gulf
Indian Ocean	Yellow Sea	Labrador Sea
Gulf of Mexico	Caspian Sea	Scotia Sea
Mediterranean Sea	Black Sea	Coral Sea
Arabian Sea	Adriatic Sea	Laptev Sea
Caribbean Sea	South China Sea	Java Sea

7 Chalk cliffs line parts of this shallow coastal sea in Northern Europe.

8 This scenic European sea lies between the coasts of Italy and Croatia.

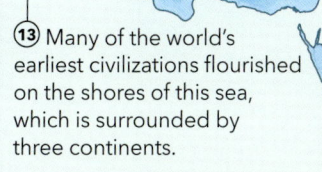

9 Despite its dark, sinister name, this almost completely land-locked sea near Turkey is a beautiful, tranquil stretch of water.

10 Frozen for half the year, this Russian sea lies on the edge of the Arctic Ocean.

11 Though it is called a sea, this is actually the biggest salt lake on Earth, at around 371,000 sq km (143,000 sq miles).

12 Floating ice in winter is a danger to ships crossing this large, cold sea.

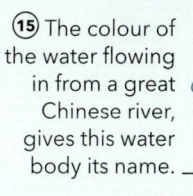

13 Many of the world's earliest civilizations flourished on the shores of this sea, which is surrounded by three continents.

14 A vital trade route for centuries, this sea also supports a huge fishing industry.

15 The colour of the water flowing in from a great Chinese river, gives this water body its name.

16 Rocky islands dot the waters of Halong Bay (below) at the southern edge of this sea in the Far East.

17 The shallow coastal waters of this narrow sea between Africa and Asia support coral reefs. Floating algae can sometimes tint the water pale red.

18 Best known for its oil reserves, this water body is named after the nation that is known as Iran today.

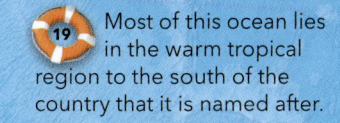

19 Most of this ocean lies in the warm tropical region to the south of the country that it is named after.

20 Islands made of hard granite are a feature of this shallow Indonesian sea.

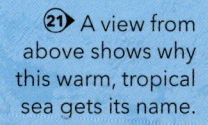

21 A view from above shows why this warm, tropical sea gets its name.

ANSWERS: 1. Gulf of Mexico 2. Labrador Sea 3. Atlantic Ocean 4. Caribbean Sea 5. Pacific Ocean 6. Scotia Sea 7. North Sea 8. Adriatic Sea 9. Black Sea 10. Laptev Sea 11. Caspian Sea 12. Sea of Okhotsk 13. Mediterranean Sea 14. Arabian Sea 15. Yellow Sea 16. South China Sea 17. Red Sea 18. Persian Gulf 19. Indian Ocean 20. Java Sea 21. Coral Sea

GEOGRAPHY GENIUS

World waterways

When rain falls on the land, it trickles downhill in streams, which flow into rivers, and eventually ends up in the deep blue sea. Some of these winding rivers are quite short, but others cover huge distances. Can you name these mighty rivers?

8 The capital city of France is divided in two by this river, which has been painted by many artists.

7 One of Europe's biggest rivers flows from the Swiss Alps to Holland.

2 Famous for the steamboats which paddle along this huge river.

1 Its name means "white water river" and it flows through one of the coldest regions of North America.

5 Cutting through huge areas of tropical rainforests, this is the world's biggest river, in terms of volume of water.

4 This tropical river winds around some of South America's oldest mountains and flows through Venezuela and Colombia.

3 Beginning at the famous Rocky Mountains, this river has carved one of the deepest rocky canyons on Earth and the "Horseshoe Bend" (left).

9 This river cuts through Africa's largest tropical rainforest, and is the second-longest river in Africa at over 4,670 km (2,900 miles) long.

6 Big ocean-going ships can use this wide river to reach cities in Argentina and Paraguay.

15 The waters of this southern African river tumble over the spectacular Victoria Falls.

ANSWERS: 1. Yukon 2. Mississippi 3. Colorado 4. Orinoco 5. Amazon 6. Paraná 7. Rhine 8. Seine 9. Congo 10. Danube 11. Volga 12. Indus 13. Nile 14. Euphrates 15. Zambezi 16. Lena 17. Shinano 18. Yangtze 19. Ganges 20. Mekong 21. Murray

10 This European river flows through ten countries on its way to the sea. Here it is shown going through Budapest, Hungary.

16 One-third of the population of China lives near this 4,350-km- (2,700-mile-) long river.

18 For more than half the year this Siberian river is covered by thick ice.

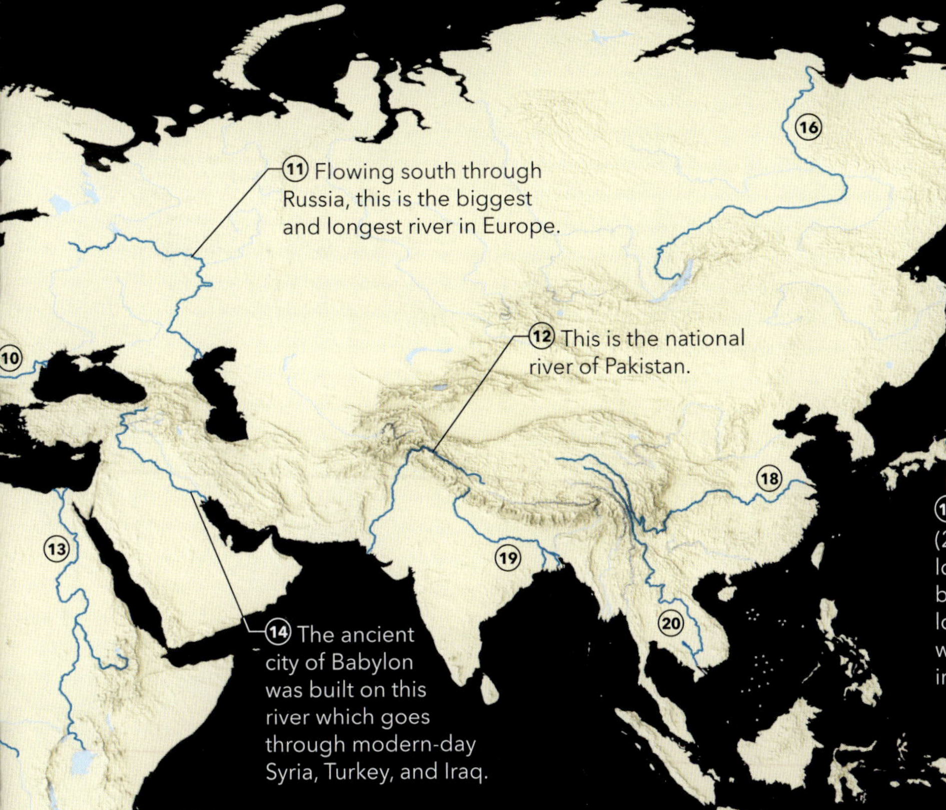

11 Flowing south through Russia, this is the biggest and longest river in Europe.

12 This is the national river of Pakistan.

19 Sacred to the Hindu religion, this river flows from the Himalayas to the Bay of Bengal.

17 At 367 km (228 miles) long, this is both the longest and widest river in Japan.

20 This river passes through five southeast Asian nations, including Vietnam (below).

14 The ancient city of Babylon was built on this river which goes through modern-day Syria, Turkey, and Iraq.

13 Two rivers – one white and one blue – meet in the Sahara desert to make one of the world's longest rivers, reaching a length of 6,695 km (4,160 miles).

21 This river forms the northern border of the Australian state of Victoria and flows from the Snowy Mountains.

TEST YOURSELF

STARTER
Seine
Colorado
Amazon
Nile
Ganges
Murray
Mississippi

CHALLENGER
Danube
Rhine
Zambezi
Congo
Indus
Mekong
Shinano

GENIUS!
Lena
Volga
Yukon
Orinoco
Paraná
Euphrates
Yangtze

112 GEOGRAPHY GENIUS

① Formerly known as Mount McKinley, this is the highest mountain peak in North America, at 6,190 m (20,308 ft).

② This giant active volcano rises from the floor of the Pacific Ocean to form a volcanic island.

④ The Aztec name for this peak means "smoking mountain" and it is the most active volcano in Mexico.

③ The jagged ridges of this spectacular mountain are also home to bears and even mountain lions.

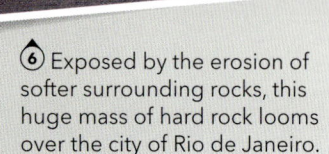

⑥ Exposed by the erosion of softer surrounding rocks, this huge mass of hard rock looms over the city of Rio de Janeiro.

⑤ The highest point of the Andes – the world's longest mountain range – this peak is also the highest outside Asia, at 6,962 m (22,841 ft).

⑧ Few mountains have a more recognizable profile than this one, which forms the backdrop to Cape Town at the southern tip of Africa.

⑦ Only discovered as recently as 1958, this wall of rock is the highest point in Antarctica.

TEST YOURSELF

STARTER	CHALLENGER	GENIUS!
Mount Everest	K2	Mount Ararat
Mount Fuji	Denali	Mount Kosciuszko
Mount Kilimanjaro	Mount Elbrus	Mount Cook
Table Mountain	Mount Whitney	Vinson Massif
Mont Blanc	Sugarloaf Mountain	Aconcagua
Mount Olympus	Mount Kinabalu	Mount Wilhelm
Mauna Loa	Popocatépetl	Lianhua Feng

Peak puzzle

Earth's crust is made of vast, slowly moving plates of rock. In some places these crunch into each other, pushing the land up into dramatic mountain ranges, such as the Himalayas. In other places, volcanoes form where plates meet. Active at first, they may then lie dormant (sleeping) for many years then erupt suddenly.

11 The highest peak in Europe, with the largest of its two cones reaching 5,642 m (18,510 ft), this dormant volcano lies in southern Russia.

Named for the colour of its icy summit, this is the highest mountain in the Alps.

This rugged mountain was the home of the gods of ancient Greek mythology.

According to tradition, this snow-capped volcano is where Noah's Ark came to rest in the great flood.

Although the highest in the world, at 8,848 m (29,029 ft), this mountain in the Himalayas has been climbed by thousands of people.

17 The highest peak in Japan, this dormant volcano has inspired Japanese artists and poets for centuries.

Standing at 8,611 m (28,251 ft), this mountain still has the temporary name a surveyor gave it in the 1850s.

Exposed by erosion, this huge mass of granite is the highest point in Malaysia, at 4,095 m (13,435 ft).

This is the tallest mountain in Papua New Guinea, named in 1888 by a German climber who visited it.

13 Despite lying close to the equator, this dormant African volcano is so high that its summit is covered in snow and ice.

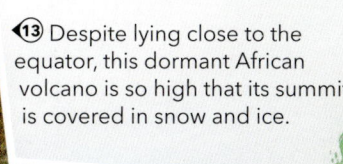

21 This triple-peaked mountain in New Zealand is named after a famous 18th-century British explorer.

Despite its Polish name, given by an explorer from Poland, this is the highest peak of the Snowy Mountains, which lie in eastern Australia.

16 At 1,864 m (6,115 ft), this is the highest point of the Huangshan, the spectacular rocky range in China. It is sometimes called "Lotus Peak" because it resembles a lotus flower.

ANSWERS: 1. Denali 2. Mauna Loa 3. Mount Whitney 4. Popocatepetl 5. Aconcagua 6. Sugarloaf Mountain 7. Vinson Massif 8. Table Mountain 9. Mont Blanc 10. Mount Olympus 11. Mount Elbrus 12. Mount Ararat 13. Kilimanjaro 14. K2 15. Lianhua Feng 16. Mount Everest 17. Mount Fuji 18. Mount Kinabalu 19. Mount Wilhelm 20. Mount Kosciuszko 21. Mount Cook

Wonders of the world

Spectacular natural features created from rock, ice, and water are found all over the world. Many are the result of centuries of rock erosion, while others mark places where molten rock or superheated water boil up from deep in Earth's crust. How many do you recognize?

1) In winter, beneath the icy surface of this Canadian lake, methane gas rises from decaying vegetation on the lake bed, to give an amazing frozen bubble effect.

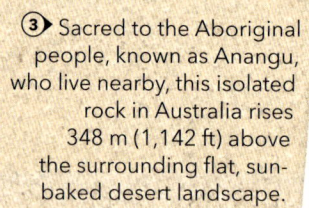

2) Located in Belize, and formed by the collapse of a cave beneath a Caribbean coral reef, this is one of the world's most famous scuba diving sites.

3) Sacred to the Aboriginal people, known as Anangu, who live nearby, this isolated rock in Australia rises 348 m (1,142 ft) above the surrounding flat, sun-baked desert landscape.

4) This vast expanse of white crystals in Bolivia is the largest salt flat on Earth, formed by the evaporation of an ancient salt lake.

5) Yellow sulfur dotted with pools of green sulfuric acid make this landscape in Ethiopia look like an alien planet!

6) This huge slab of ancient, hard sandstone in Venezuela forms a tepui – a flat-topped mountain with sheer cliff edges.

7) Over thousands of years these layers of rock in Argentina have been carved by wind and rain into a dazzling zigzag of colour.

8. Pamukkale Springs 9. Strokkur geyser 10. Giant's Causeway 11. Hoodoos, Cappadocia 12. Erta Ale 13. Perito Moreno Glacier 14. Zhangye Danxia 15. Monument Valley

8 Hot water, rich in dissolved minerals, has built up these terraces of white rock in Turkey, which shimmer with blue water.

9 Fuelled by hot rock deep below ground, this Icelandic hot spring regularly erupts into the air, reaching heights of up to 40 m (131 ft).

10 These rocks may look like stepping-stones, but are a natural pattern of geometric shapes formed by a mass of hot molten rock, which shrank as it cooled, splitting into columns.

11 These spires of soft volcanic ash in Turkey are capped with harder rock that protects them from the rain.

12 This Ethiopian volcano contains a lake of searing hot molten lava. The cooling surface of the lava is crusted with black basalt rock.

13 This Argentinian river of ice flows off the Andes mountains into a lake, where the ice breaks off to form a sheer cliff 74 m (243 ft) high and 5 km (3 miles) long.

14 These multicoloured rock layers exposed in this desert region of China took millions of years to form.

15 Used as a backdrop to countless films about the American West, this desert landscape in the USA consists of giant sandstone buttes rising above the valley floor.

TEST YOURSELF

STARTER	CHALLENGER	GENIUS!
Uluru	Giant's Causeway	Zhangye Danxia
Perito Moreno Glacier	Salar de Uyuni	Pamukkale Springs
Great Blue Hole	Lake Abraham	Erta Ale
Monument Valley	Serranía de Hornocal	Danakil Depression
Mount Roraima	Hoodoos, Cappadocia	Strokkur geyser

ANSWERS: 1. Lake Abraham 2. Great Blue Hole 3. Uluru 4. Salar de Uyuni 5. Danakil Depression 6. Mount Roraima 7. Serranía de Hornocal

GEOGRAPHY GENIUS

① With 11 different time zones, this is the world's biggest country. It stretches across two continents and shares borders with 14 other nations.

Approximately 75 per cent of this country – the eastern region – lies in Asia. The rest is in Europe.

One third of the country is covered in rainforest.

② Surrounded by the Indian and Pacific oceans, most of the world's largest island is desert, with its big cities along the coast.

③ The largest country in South America has a tropical climate. The Amazon river, which carries more water than any other on Earth, passes through it.

To the north, the country borders the Caspian Sea.

There are no rivers in this country – 95 per cent of it is desert!

④ Once known as Persia, this is the second-largest country in the Middle East.

⑤ Most of the Arabian Peninsula is taken up by this desert nation, which supplies almost a quarter of the world's oil.

⑥ The Sahara Desert occupies most of Africa's largest country, which borders the Mediterranean Sea in the north.

⑦ This narrow nation in South America is the world's longest country with more than 6,000 km (3,700 miles) of Pacific Ocean coastline.

⑧ Landlocked by five other East African nations, this is the oldest independent country on the continent.

⑨ Found off the east coast of Africa, this island is best known for its unique wildlife, including lemurs.

TEST YOURSELF

STARTER
- Australia
- Chile
- Canada
- Japan
- New Zealand
- United Kingdom
- Italy
- Russia

CHALLENGER
- Brazil
- Madagascar
- Mexico
- South Africa
- Spain
- Norway
- Greece
- Egypt

GENIUS!
- Saudi Arabia
- Algeria
- Ethiopia
- Indonesia
- Vietnam
- Cuba
- Bangladesh
- Panama
- Iran

Countries of the world

Grab your globe and dust down that atlas! There are a total of 195 countries in the world today, and here are some of them, but shown only as their outlines on a map. Use these border shapes and the clues to identify each nation and prove your geographical genius.

- Islands in the Arctic Ocean, where polar bears and Arctic foxes live, also make up this nation.

10 The second-largest country in the world has vast conifer forests and more lakes than anywhere else on Earth.

11 The largest country in Central America has more Spanish speakers than any other nation and is known for its ancient ruins of the Aztec and Mayan civilizations.

- The western border with Libya cuts through the Sahara Desert.

12 Made up of more than 13,000 islands, this country in Southeast Asia has a tropical climate and exotic wildlife, including orangutans and Komodo dragons.

13 On the southernmost tip of Africa, the richest country on the continent has gold and diamond mines.

14 This northeast African nation borders the Mediterranean Sea to the north and the Red Sea to the east.

15 About 3,000 islands form this Asian country, characterized by modern cities and active volcanoes.

- There are more sheep than people on these volcanic islands.

- Borders Russia, Finland, and Sweden to the east

16 To the north, the Pyrenees mountains divide this country from France.

17 Two main islands in the Pacific Ocean make up this nation of earthquakes, volcanoes, and geysers.

18 One of the four Scandinavian countries, this nation has a long coastline lined with deep sea inlets called fjords.

19 With the South China Sea to the east, this country has land borders with China, Laos, and Cambodia.

20 This European country looks like a boot kicking an island into the Mediterranean Sea.

- The crocodile-like shape of this island gives it the nickname "El Cocodrilo".

- This country lies to the east of India, on the Bay of Bengal.

21 Made up of the largest island in Europe, this nation includes a northern region of the island to the west.

22 Sugar cane is grown on the largest island in the Caribbean, which has a range of habitats – from deserts to jungles.

23 Called the Cradle of Western Civilization, this European country has more than 2,000 islands off the mainland.

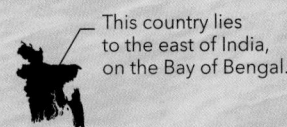

24 This low-lying tropical land experiences a monsoon season. It boasts lush vegetation and a population of tigers.

25 A canal across this country links the Atlantic and Pacific oceans.

ANSWERS: 1. Russia 2. Australia 3. Brazil 4. Iran 5. Saudi Arabia 6. Algeria 7. Chile 8. Ethiopia 9. Madagascar 10. Canada 11. Mexico 12. Indonesia 13. South Africa 14. Egypt 15. Japan 16. Spain 17. New Zealand 18. Norway 19. Vietnam 20. Italy 21. United Kingdom 22. Cuba 23. Greece 24. Bangladesh 25. Panama

Cities

More than half of today's global population lives in a city. The first large urban areas were built thousands of years ago as the power bases of great empires. Modern cities still serve the same purpose, providing homes and a base for government and businesses.

In numbers

38 million
The population of Tokyo and its surrounding towns, which have merged to form the world's largest, most populous urban area.

150 m
(492 ft) The minimum height for a building to be called a skyscraper.

74 km/h
(46 mph) The speed of the world's fastest lift, travelling between the 121 storeys of the Shanghai Tower in China's largest city.

How to build a city

01. Pick the right location. Choose somewhere with plenty of space, a water supply, and good transport links.

02. Cities need homes. Plan houses and apartments in different sizes and styles to accommodate a growing population.

03. Your city must provide a base for businesses. Where office space is scarce, you will have to build upwards.

04. To keep traffic moving, lay out a fixed system of well-surfaced roads and make use of space below ground with underground trains.

05. Don't build a concrete jungle. Make room for green spaces and outdoor activities.

I don't believe it

In the caves of Cappadocia in Turkey, 36 underground cities have been excavated, dating back hundreds of years.

Depths of the city

Beneath the bustle of a city, a subterranean system of pipes, tunnels, and cables supplies clean water, removes waste, and provides services and transport.

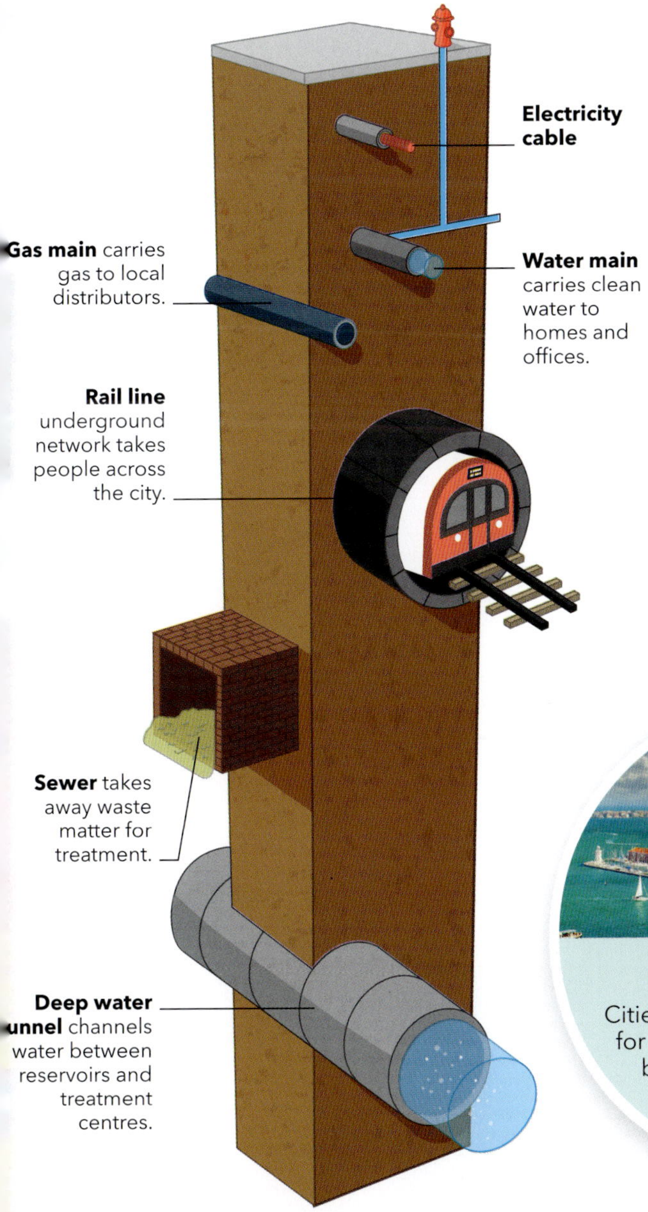

Electricity cable

Gas main carries gas to local distributors.

Water main carries clean water to homes and offices.

Rail line underground network takes people across the city.

Sewer takes away waste matter for treatment.

Deep water tunnel channels water between reservoirs and treatment centres.

Extreme living

- The world's highest city is La Rinconada in the Peruvian Andes, at 5,100 m (16,700 ft) above sea level.
- The world's lowest city is Jericho in the Middle East, at 260 m (853 ft) below sea level.
- Monrovia, in Liberia, is the world's wettest city, averaging 4,622 mm (182 in) of rain a year.
- Aswan, in Egypt, is the driest city, with only 1 mm ($1/33$ in) of rain a year.

Cities on water

Cities often develop close to water for trade and transport. Venice is built on 118 islands in Italy's Venetian Lagoon.

Above the clouds

Towering 828 m (2,716 ½ ft) high, the Burj Khalifa in Dubai is the world's tallest building. Constructed from 10,000 km (6,200 miles) of steel, it has 163 floors of homes, offices, and hotels.

City plans

Grid: New York, nicknamed the "Big Apple", is laid out in a rectangular grid of streets.

Radial: Some avenues of the French capital Paris extend from the centre like the Sun's rays.

Canal: Built during the 17th century, Amsterdam, the Dutch capital, has a neat network of canals.

Star/Pentagon: The world's biggest city, Tokyo, sprawls out in a star shape from the central hub.

② Explosive dynamite was used to carve the four giant heads of these noteworthy American presidents into the rock.

④ This Italian bell tower started to lean to one side in the soft ground during its construction, but has miraculously survived for more than 600 years!

① This unique multi-spired Spanish cathedral has been under construction for more than 130 years – and is still not finished.

③ This gleaming shrine was built on a site that is sacred to both the Islamic and Jewish religions in Israel.

Cool constructions

Since the dawn of civilization, humans have built some astonishing structures. Some are dazzlingly beautiful, others stupendously big, and some built many centuries ago are miraculously still standing! Many of these constructions may look familiar, but can you name them all?

⑤ Stretching for more than 21,000 km (13,048 miles) across Asia, this is the longest human-made structure on the planet.

⑥ In the United Arab Emirates (UAE), the tallest building in the world rises to a height of 828 m (2,716½ ft), and has over 200 storeys.

⑦ A spectacular example of modern architecture, the roof of this arts venue resembles the sails of a ship.

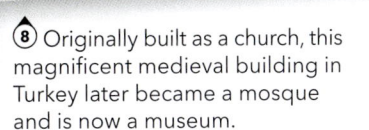

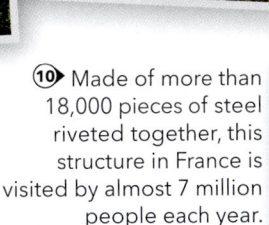

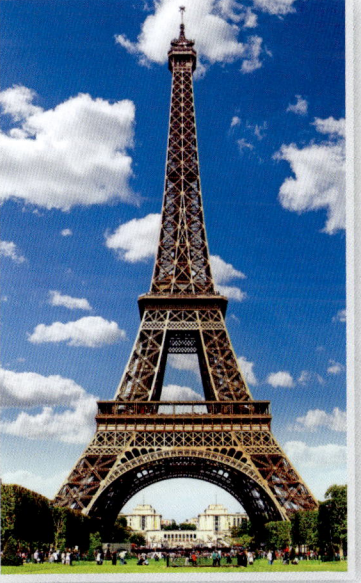

TEST YOURSELF

STARTER
- Eiffel Tower, Paris
- Taj Mahal, Agra
- The Great Wall
- Tower of Pisa
- Great Sphinx of Giza

CHALLENGER
- Sydney Opera House
- Parthenon, Athens
- St Basil's Cathedral, Moscow
- Leshan Giant Buddha
- Christ the Redeemer, Rio de Janeiro

GENIUS!
- Mount Rushmore, South Dakota
- Dome of the Rock, Jerusalem
- Burj Khalifa, Dubai
- Hagia Sophia, Istanbul
- Sagrada Família, Barcelona

8 Originally built as a church, this magnificent medieval building in Turkey later became a mosque and is now a museum.

9 This 30-m- (98-ft-) tall statue of a religious figure stands on the summit of a mountain, overlooking a city in Brazil.

10 Made of more than 18,000 pieces of steel riveted together, this structure in France is visited by almost 7 million people each year.

11 Carved out of a sandstone cliff in China more than 1,200 years ago, this colossal seated figure is an amazing 71 m (233 ft) high.

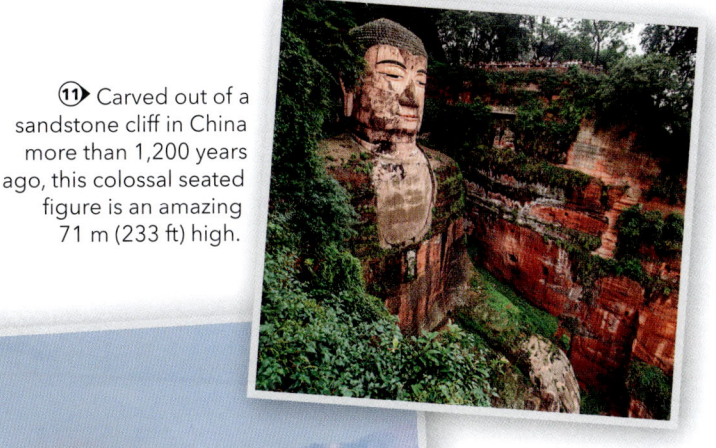

12 Despite being 2,450 years old, this temple to the ancient Greek goddess Athena still dominates the capital city of Greece.

13 Originally cut from solid rock, this giant ancient Egyptian sculpture has the body of a lion and a human head.

14 Made of white marble, this beautiful building was built by a Mughal emperor as a memorial to his wife.

15 Found in Red Square in the capital city of Russia, this 16th-century structure was originally white, red, and gold, with the dazzling colour scheme seen today appearing only in the 17th century.

ANSWERS: 1. Sagrada Família, Barcelona 2. Mount Rushmore, South Dakota 3. Dome of the Rock, Jerusalem 4. Burj Khalifa, Dubai 5. The Great Wall 6. Tower of Pisa 7. Sydney Opera House 8. Hagia Sophia, Istanbul 9. Christ the Redeemer, Rio de Janeiro 10. Eiffel Tower, Paris 11. Leshan Giant Buddha 12. Parthenon, Athens 13. Great Sphinx of Giza 14. Taj Mahal, Agra 15. St Basil's Cathedral, Moscow

GEOGRAPHY GENIUS

City skylines

From skyscrapers to sacred sites, stunning structures both old and new dominate the skylines of many urban hubs around the world. Can you correctly identify the cities from their silhouettes?

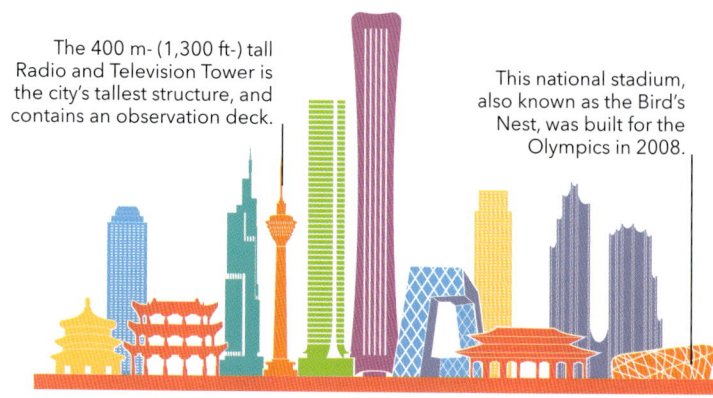

The 400 m- (1,300 ft-) tall Radio and Television Tower is the city's tallest structure, and contains an observation deck.

This national stadium, also known as the Bird's Nest, was built for the Olympics in 2008.

① This densely populated capital city is a mixture of modern skyscrapers and historical sites, such as the Forbidden City – the palace of the ruling emperor for nearly 600 years.

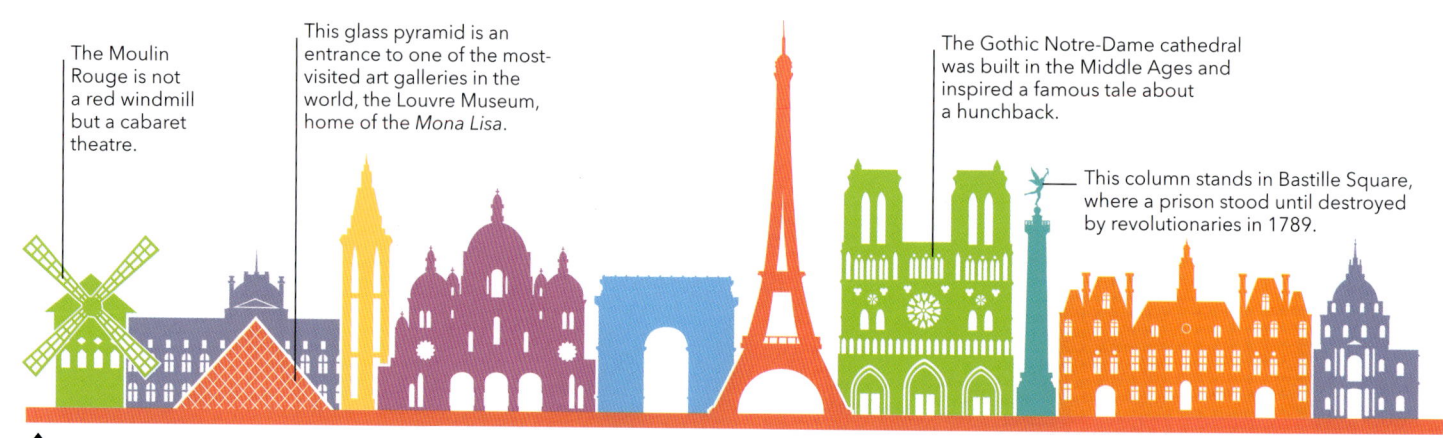

The Moulin Rouge is not a red windmill but a cabaret theatre.

This glass pyramid is an entrance to one of the most-visited art galleries in the world, the Louvre Museum, home of the *Mona Lisa*.

The Gothic Notre-Dame cathedral was built in the Middle Ages and inspired a famous tale about a hunchback.

This column stands in Bastille Square, where a prison stood until destroyed by revolutionaries in 1789.

② Surrounded by majestic churches and cathedrals, the Eiffel Tower is the dominant landmark in this historic capital, sometimes known as the "City of Love".

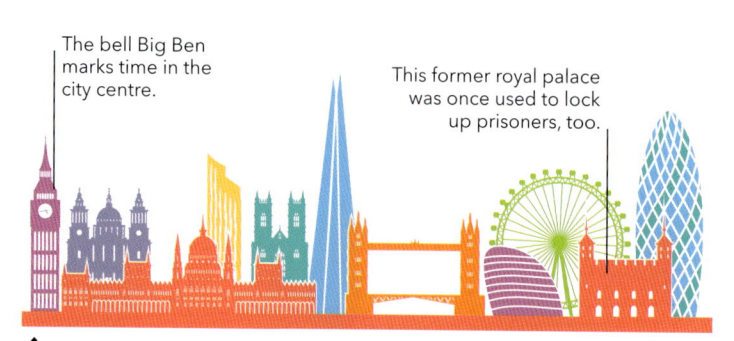

The bell Big Ben marks time in the city centre.

This former royal palace was once used to lock up prisoners, too.

The Reichstag is home to the nation's parliament.

The Brandenburg Gate was built as a symbol of peace.

③ Sitting on the banks of the River Thames, one of the world's oldest cities is home to a large parliament building, where the nation's politicians meet.

④ This European capital was divided by a wall, between east and west, from 1961 until 1989 when it was torn down to unite the city and the country.

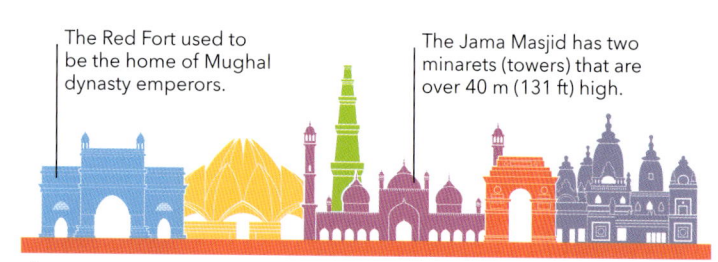

The Red Fort used to be the home of Mughal dynasty emperors.

The Jama Masjid has two minarets (towers) that are over 40 m (131 ft) high.

The central church roof of St. Basil's Cathedral is 61 m (200 ft) high.

⑤ This Asian capital city has many preserved historical buildings, including religious shrines, temples, tombs, and gardens.

⑥ At 74,322 sq m (800,000 sq ft) Red Square is huge, and lies at the heart of this city, acting as both a political and cultural centre.

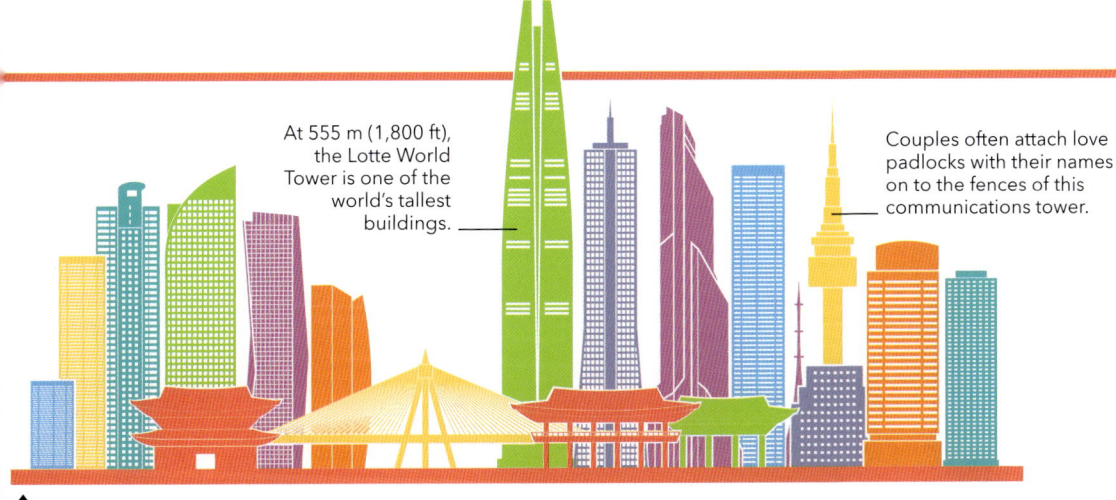

123

TEST YOURSELF

STARTER
New York, USA
Paris, France
Rome, Italy
London, UK

CHALLENGER
Dubai, UAE
Berlin, Germany
Beijing, China
Moscow, Russia

GENIUS!
Tokyo, Japan
Seoul, South Korea
Delhi, India
Kuala Lumpur, Malaysia

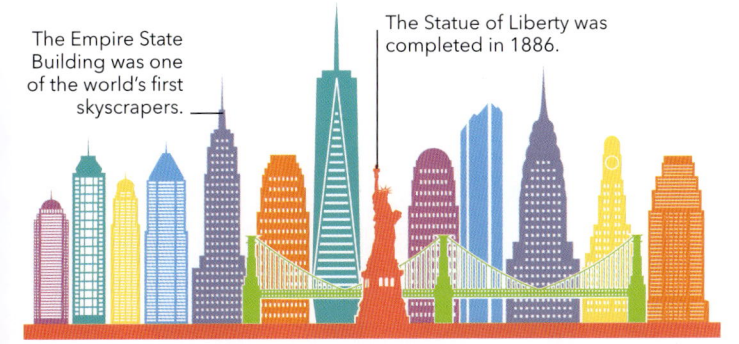

At 555 m (1,800 ft), the Lotte World Tower is one of the world's tallest buildings.

Couples often attach love padlocks with their names on to the fences of this communications tower.

⑦ An eye-catching skyline of high-rise buildings sits against the backdrop of the Namsan mountain in this capital, which also includes historic sites such as palaces.

Standing 88 storeys high, the Petronas Towers are the world's tallest twin structures.

Built at a site where two rivers join, the Jamek mosque is the city's oldest mosque.

⑧ Traditional Asian architecture mixes with modern skyscrapers in this vibrant young capital, which was only given city status in 1972.

The Empire State Building was one of the world's first skyscrapers.

The Statue of Liberty was completed in 1886.

A high-end hotel with its own helipad, the Burj Al Arab stands on its own artificial island.

At 828 m (2,716½ ft) tall, Burj Khalifa has been the world's tallest building since 2008.

⑨ The office buildings constructed in the 19th and 20th centuries turned this coastal city into a high-rise hub, with nicknames ranging from the "Big Apple" to "The City that Never Sleeps".

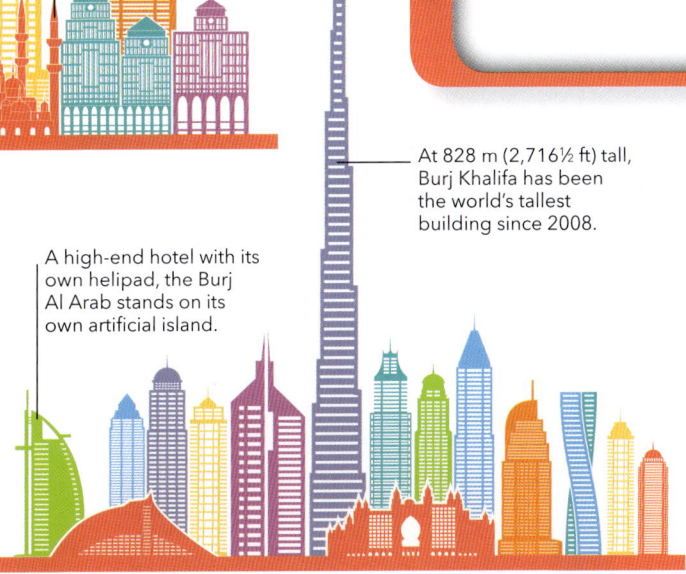

⑩ Construction on a rapid scale has produced this modern high-rise city, known for its luxury hotels and shopping centres.

The world's largest amphitheatre once held chariot races and gladiatorial combats.

This tower, similar to one in a European capital, was opened in 1958.

⑪ Once the heart of a large empire, this ancient city boasts many ruins and relics, as well as churches full of classical art.

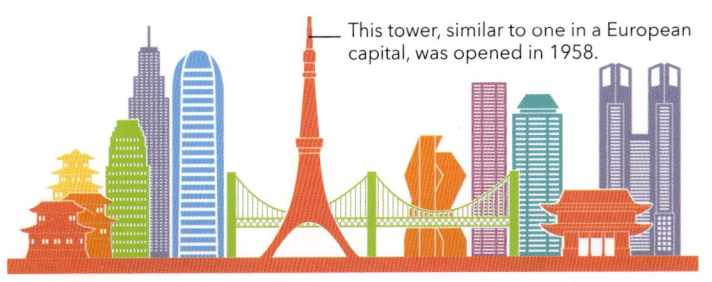

⑫ Earthquakes prove a problem in this large city, so the skyline spreads outwards rather than upwards.

ANSWERS: 1. Beijing, China 2. Paris, France 3. London, UK 4. Berlin, Germany 5. Delhi, India 6. Moscow, Russia 7. Seoul, South Korea 8. Kuala Lumpur, Malaysia 9. New York, USA 10. Dubai, UAE 11. Rome, Italy 12. Tokyo, Japan

Capital cities

Pack your bags because you're off on a round-the-world trip! Whether it is the centre of government, or a hub of trade and culture, each one of these capital cities has its own unique history and identity.

② Standing an impressive 2,240 m (7,350 ft) above sea level, this city and its major monuments were built around the ruins of an ancient Aztec capital.

① Canada's government building – Parliament Hill – is located in one of the coldest capitals in the world, where temperatures can reach −16°C (−3°F) on an average in winter.

③ Cuba's colourful capital is home to classic cars, bright buildings, and the sounds of traditional salsa music.

④ Costa Rica's capital is a cultural hub filled with museums and theatres.

⑤ Peru's coastal capital was founded by the Spanish explorer Francisco Pizarro in 1535 and today is one of the largest cities in South America.

⑥ Famed for its modernist architecture, this young city was only established in 1960.

⑦ Argentina's capital boasts the widest street in the world – 9 de Julio Avenue.

TEST YOURSELF

STARTER	CHALLENGER	GENIUS!
Cairo	Ottawa	Abu Dhabi
Tokyo	Canberra	Kinshasa
Brasília	Nairobi	Ankara
Moscow	Dhaka	San José
Berlin	Lima	Kuala Lumpur
Madrid	Buenos Aires	Bucharest
Bangkok	Stockholm	Abuja
Mexico City	Havana	Kabul
		Antananarivo

⑧ With around 1.5 million inhabitants, Sweden's most populated city consists of 14 islands joined by 57 bridges.

⑳ Originally called Edo, the Japanese capital is known for its advanced technology and fast transport.

Divided in two by a famous wall until 1989, Germany's capital city has played an important part in European history.

The heart of modern-day Russia holds lots of beautiful palaces and cathedrals, many found inside its central fortress known as the Kremlin.

The stunning architecture of this Romanian capital once earned it the nickname "Little Paris".

Nestled amongst the snowy Hindu Kush mountains, Afghanistan's capital used to be a key trading centre on the Silk Road.

Europe's highest capital city, at 694 m (2,277 ft) above sea level, boasts a sunny Spanish climate and famous football teams.

Bangladesh's capital since 1971, this is one of the most densely populated cities in the world.

⑱ Floating markets and grand temples are all hallmarks of Thailand's capital.

A massive granite monolith, called Aso Rock, dominates the skyline of this influential Nigerian city.

A mix of Asian and European cultures and architectural styles meet in this historic Turkish city.

Animals in Kenya's oldest established national park roam alongside this bustling urban city.

The capital of the Democratic Republic of Congo grew from a small trading town, which was established in 1881.

A range of diverse habitats filled with unique wildlife surround the hilltop capital of Madagascar.

This small inland city was chosen to be Australia's capital in 1911, beating two larger rivals.

⑮ Lying just off the coast on an island, this city in the United Arab Emirates is best recognized by the stunning domes of its grand mosque.

⑭ Full of fascinating historical wonders, including the pyramids, Egypt's capital city lies on the River Nile.

⑲ The iconic Petronas Towers are just one of the impressive skyscrapers found in this busy Malaysian city.

ANSWERS: 1. Ottawa 2. Mexico City 3. Havana 4. San José 5. Lima 6. Brasilia 7. Buenos Aires 8. Stockholm 9. Berlin 10. Moscow 11. Bucharest 12. Madrid 13. Ankara 14. Cairo 15. Abu Dhabi 16. Kabul 17. Dhaka 18. Bangkok 19. Kuala Lumpur 20. Tokyo 21. Abuja 22. Kinshasa 23. Nairobi 24. Antananarivo 25. Canberra

GEOGRAPHY GENIUS

Eye in the sky

Satellites and spacecraft that circle Earth and other planets have cameras onboard that take detailed photographs of their surface. Some show natural features such as rivers, while others show great cities and other structures created by humans.

③ Built nearly 600 years ago, this complex of almost 1,000 buildings surrounds a Chinese palace.

A 6-m- (20-ft-) deep moat surrounds the complex.

② At 24 km (15 miles) high, the largest volcano in the Solar System is one of the most spectacular features of the Red Planet.

① Carved by the Colorado River over millions of years, this gorge in North America is more than 1.8 km (1 mile) deep and 29 km (18 miles) wide in certain places – making it one of the biggest in the world.

One of the three cliffs is 57 m (188 ft) tall.

⑥ More than 2.8 million litres (740,000 gallons) of water tumbles over these huge cliffs in North America every second.

④ Shaped like a boot, this European country glows at night with millions of lights from buildings and streets.

⑤ The world's highest mountain range has snowy peaks divided by valleys carved by streams that flow into great rivers.

ANSWERS: 1. The Grand Canyon 2. Olympus Mons, Mars 3. Forbidden City 4. Italy 5. Himalayas 6. Niagara Falls 7. Nile Delta 8. San Andreas Fault 9. Great Barrier Reef 10. New York 11. Ganges Delta 12. Pyramids of Giza

7 Fertile land marks the mouth of the longest river in the world, before it joins the Mediterranean Sea.

A well-known statue of a woman holding a flaming torch stands on this smaller island.

8 Running through California, USA, this 1,300-km- (800-mile-) long fracture divides Earth's two biggest tectonic plates.

9 This famous island, part of a big US city, has a large green park, surrounded by skyscrapers.

10 One of the largest rivers in Asia flows into the Bay of Bengal, splitting into many channels lined with mangrove swamps.

12 Located off the coast of Australia and made by millions of sea creatures, this is the only structure on Earth made by living things that is visible from space.

11 More than 4,500 years old, these huge structures in the desert are the tombs of Egyptian pharaohs.

TEST YOURSELF

STARTER	CHALLENGER	GENIUS!
Italy Nile Delta Pyramids of Giza San Andreas Fault	Himalayas The Grand Canyon Niagara Falls Great Barrier Reef	Olympus Mons, Mars Ganges Delta Forbidden City Manhattan Island, New York

GEOGRAPHY GENIUS

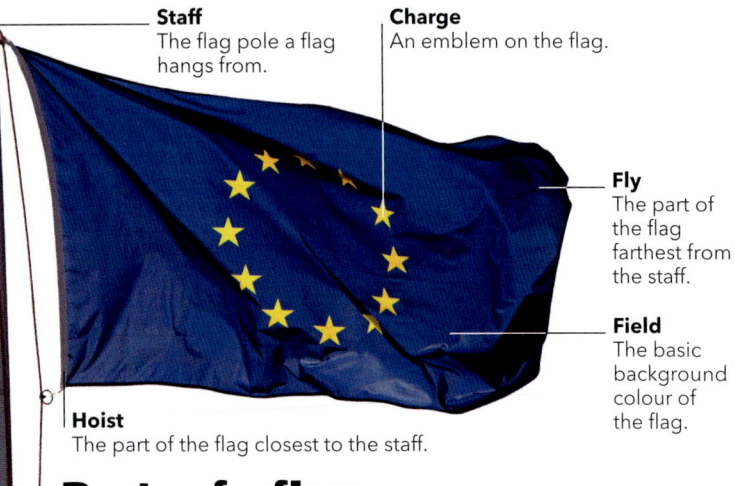

Staff The flag pole a flag hangs from.

Charge An emblem on the flag.

Fly The part of the flag farthest from the staff.

Field The basic background colour of the flag.

Hoist The part of the flag closest to the staff.

Parts of a flag

Flags come in a great variety of colours, patterns, and designs, but they all share the same features and parts.

Flags

Flags developed out of the coat of arms that armies carried into battle. Some countries have used the same flag design for centuries while others have changed their look. Afghanistan, for instance, has had more than 20 different flags in the past 150 years!

How to plant a flag on the Moon

The first flag to fly on the Moon was a US flag bought for just $5.50. It was fitted inside an aluminium tube, and was flown to the Moon on board the Apollo 11 spacecraft in 1969.

01. There's no wind on the Moon to fly a flag. Get engineers to fit a wire into a hem sewn into the top of the flag so it will stick out straight.

I don't believe it

The 27 stars on Brazil's flag show the pattern in the night sky above the city of Rio de Janeiro on 15 November 1889 – Brazil's independence day.

In numbers

4,261 m (13,979 ft) The distance below sea level that the Mir-1 submersible dived to plant a Russian flag at the bottom of the Arctic Ocean in 2007.

2,058 sq m (22,152 sq ft) The area of a Mexican flag made in 2011. The biggest flag ever flown from a flag pole, its area was bigger than 7 tennis courts.

12 The most colours found on a national flag, those of San Marino and Ecuador.

Star state

Each of the stars on the US flag represents one of the 50 US states. Over time, as states joined the union of American states, the flag has had more than 25 changes.

Where else are flags used?

Regional: A giant holding a club features on the flag of the Finnish region of Lapland.

State: All 50 states in the USA, including Arizona (above), have their own flag.

Nepal's flag is the only national flag that has more than four sides.

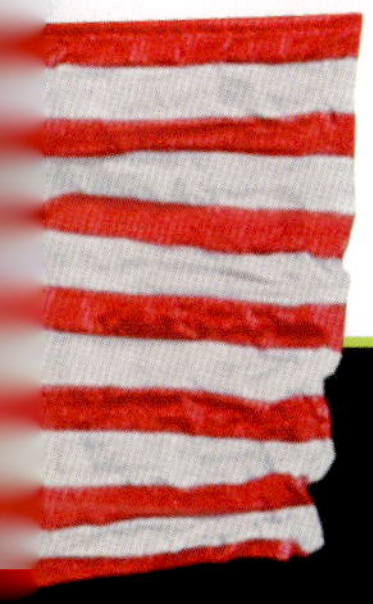

Flag study

Vexillology is the name given to the study of flags. It comes from the latin word *vexillum*, meaning "flag". Vexillologists even have their own flag (above).

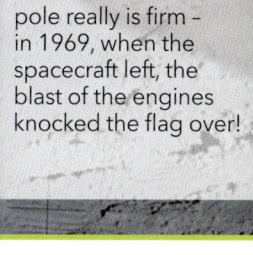

Flag laws

- In many countries it's against the law to damage or destroy the national flag. In France, for example, the punishment is up to six months in prison, while in Israel the punishment can be up to three years in prison.

- In Denmark it is against the law to destroy the flags of other countries but not Denmark's own national flag.

- According to Finnish law, when a national flag of Finland is washed, it can only be dried indoors.

- Some countries have rules about what time of the day their flag can be flown. In Iceland, for instance, the flag must never be raised before seven o'clock in the morning.

02. Find a good new spot. Six Apollo missions have planted flags on the Moon, and they are all still there today.

03. Try to plant the flag pole into the lunar surface – this is not easy, the ground is very hard.

04. Check the pole really is firm – in 1969, when the spacecraft left, the blast of the engines knocked the flag over!

FLAG FACTS

- Jamaica is the only country with a national flag that does not feature the colours red, white, or blue.

- The latest design of the US flag was adopted in 1960 and was created by 17-year-old Robert G Heft as a school assignment. He only gained a B- grade in class!

- At the 1936 Olympics, Haiti and Liechtenstein discovered their national flags were the same. Liechtenstein later added a crown to their flag.

- All official national flags in India are made in one factory in Bengeri village, in the state of Karnataka.

Sports: A chequered flag is waved to signal the end of many motor races.

Organizations: The United Nations flag features olive leaves, representing peace.

Pirates: Skulls and swords were designed to strike fear into other ships' crews.

GEOGRAPHY GENIUS

① A sun with 32 rays adorns the flag of South America's second-biggest country.

② Traditional carpet weaving patterns are part of this former Soviet republic's flag.

③ This mountainous European nation is one of the few to fly a square flag.

④ This flag flies in a country that's home to more than 1,400 million people.

⑤ This nation manufactures the highest number of cars in all of Europe.

⑥ Spears and a shield are said to protect this African nation's people.

⑦ This island kingdom's flag was formed by combining three flags into one.

Raise the flag

Every nation of the world flies their own flag design. Each has been chosen to reflect the country's history, colours, and identity. They represent the pride of the people, uniting everyone under one big banner.

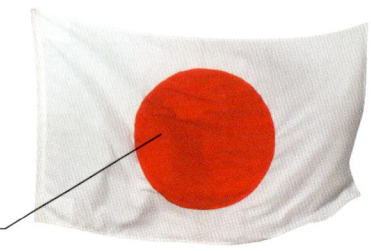

⑧ The country known for its cherry blossom season and very fast trains features a crimson sun on its flag.

Red symbolizes "brightness"

⑨ A bird of paradise stars on this South Pacific island flag, designed by a 15-year-old schoolgirl in 1971.

⑩ A thunder dragon dominates the flag of this rugged, mountainous Asian kingdom.

⑪ This flag was first flown in 1960, when this African country became independent.

⑫ The eagle sitting on a cactus is based on historic symbols of the Aztec empire.

⑬ This country is famed for its African wildlife and its Maasai peoples whose shield is found on the flag.

⑭ The colours of the ancient Inca civilization are depicted on this Andean nation's flag.

131

15 Depicting the many colours of the "rainbow nation", this flag first flew in 1994, the year in which Nelson Mandela became its president.

16 Formed by freed slaves, this African state based its design on the US flag.

17 All the official flags of this nation are made of khadi – a cloth popularized by Mahatma Gandhi.

18 The flag of the world's biggest country and hosts of the 2018 FIFA World Cup.

19 This country, which the Amazon river flows through, has the words "Order and Progress" on its flag.

21 The circular symbol at the centre of this Asian nation's flag means balance in the universe.

22 The world's best-known long-distance cycling race has been hosted by this nation since 1903.

20 Blue represents the Mediterranean Sea on the flag of this land of ancient gods, where the first Olympic Games took place.

23 A maple leaf reflects the large forests found in this North American nation.

24 The *shahādah* (a Muslim statement of faith) is written in Arabic on this oil-producing nation's flag.

25 This country is famously shaped like a boot, when looked at from space.

26 Southern hemisphere stars dot the flag of a country famous for its kangaroos.

27 A crossroads between Europe and Asia, this country's flag features an Islamic star and crescent moon symbols.

TEST YOURSELF

STARTER
- United Kingdom
- Japan
- Switzerland
- Canada
- South Africa
- China
- Brazil
- France
- Greece

CHALLENGER
- Australia
- Argentina
- Russian Federation
- Nigeria
- Turkey
- Mexico
- India
- Germany
- Italy

GENIUS!
- Liberia
- Kenya
- Bhutan
- Turkmenistan
- South Korea
- Papua New Guinea
- Saudi Arabia
- Swaziland
- Peru

ANSWERS: 1. Argentina 2. Turkmenistan 3. Switzerland 4. China 5. Germany 6. Swaziland 7. United Kingdom 8. Japan 9. Papua New Guinea 10. Bhutan 11. Nigeria 12. Mexico 13. Kenya 14. Peru 15. South Africa 16. Liberia 17. India 18. Russian Federation 19. Brazil 20. Greece 21. South Korea 22. France 23. Canada 24. Saudi Arabia 25. Italy 26. Australia 27. Turkey

Weather

All the weather we experience occurs in the troposphere, the lowest level of Earth's atmosphere. Temperature, air pressure, wind speed, humidity, and the Sun all affect our weather. Around the world the weather varies along with the changing landscape, from cold, snowcapped mountains, to humid, tropical rainforests.

Some tornadoes can be around 4 km (2½ miles) wide!

Heavy Snow

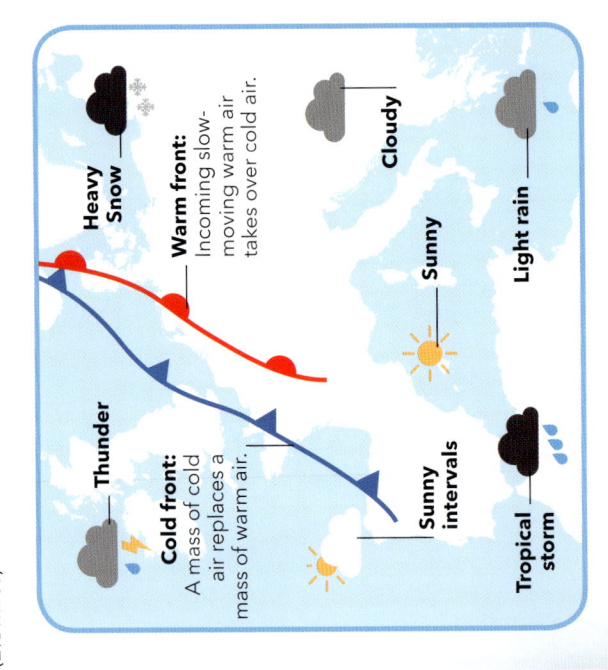

Warm front: Incoming slow-moving warm air takes over cold air.

Cloudy

Light rain

Sunny

Thunder

Cold front: A mass of cold air replaces a mass of warm air.

Sunny intervals

Tropical storm

What's the forecast?

Meteorologists (weather scientists) study weather systems and use symbols on regional maps to indicate the coming weather. This is very important when extreme weather is forecast, such as tornadoes, when staying at home is advised. Today satellites in space linked to powerful computers can track severe weather.

Tornadoes are typically less than about 600 m (1,969 ft) in height.

Lake Maracaibo has 1.2 million lightning strikes a year.

Everlasting storm

A unique series of storm clouds develops over Lake Maracaibo, Venezuela, almost every night, generating dramatic thunderstorms.

Extreme weather

❄ The Meghalaya state in India receives the most precipitation in the world per year with an average of 11,872 mm (467²⁄₅ in).

❄ 1,182 cm (465 in) of snow fell on Japan's Mount Ibuki in 1927 – a record amount.

❄ Over 45,000 thunderstorms rumble daily on Earth.

❄ Ice storms occur when rain or water spray freeze onto very cold objects, turning buildings into ice statues – like this lighthouse on Lake Michigan, USA.

I don't believe it

Frogs and fish have actually dropped from the skies – having been swept up into clouds by powerful winds, they then fall like rain!

How a tornado forms

01. Moist, warm air rising from the land cools as it rises, creating a huge, dark storm cloud.

02. Strong winds high in the air set the cloud spinning. These huge rotating clouds are called supercells.

03. Surrounding air is pulled in, and the air in the cloud starts to spin faster. A funnel then forms, reaching the ground.

04. The fast, strong, swirling tornado destroys anything in its path, leaving a trail of devastation behind.

In numbers

325 km/h (200 mph) The top speed of the winds inside a tornado.

100 The number of lightning bolts that strike somewhere on Earth every second.

1.825 m (6 ft) The amount of rain that fell on the Indian Ocean island of Réunion in 24 hours in 1966.

1 The number of lightning flashes needed to create enough electricity to light a town for a year.

Strange weather

Moonbow: When moonlight shines through water droplets, the reflection can make a faint moonbow in the sky.

Firewhirl: If raging fires on the ground meet powerful winds, flames can shoot up into the air in a dangerous display of firewhirls.

Dust storm: Strong winds blowing over dusty landscapes can produce huge banks of sand and dust.

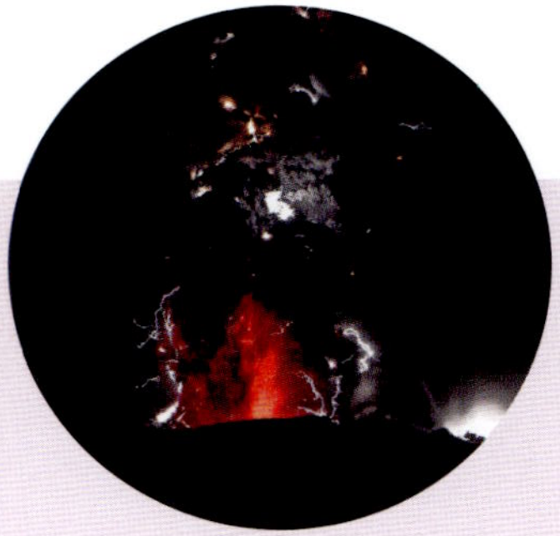

Volcanic lightning: This occurs when an erupting volcano generates an electric storm.

Giant hailstones: Hailstones form from ice crystals blown around in thunderclouds – some are bigger than golf balls.

TEST YOURSELF

STARTER
- Cirrus
- Cumulonimbus
- Stratus
- Cumulus

CHALLENGER
- Cirrocumulus
- Stratocumulus
- Nimbostratus
- Cirrostratus

GENIUS!
- Lenticular
- Mammatus
- Altocumulus
- Altostratus

Cloudspotting

Those fluffy clouds in the sky may look like floating cotton wool, but they are actually made of tiny water drops, or even ice crystals suspended in the air. If the water droplets or ice crystals in the cloud get too big, they fall as rain or snow. Knowing your clouds may help you predict if this might happen, so you can grab that umbrella!

① These very high-flying clouds form wispy trails of ice crystals.

② Blue sky can be seen through the small fluffy cushions of this high cloud.

③ Thin sheets of this high-altitude cloud can turn the sky white.

④ This fluffy mid-altitude cloud can form beautiful patterns in the sky.

These clouds are made of both water and ice.

⑤ Sheets of this grey cloud at mid-altitude can cause steady light rain.

Another name given to this type is "The King of Clouds".

⑦ A fluffy, low-level cloud type, which can form almost continuous sheets especially over the sea.

⑥ These odd-looking clouds form shapes that look like glass lenses.

⑧ This low-level cloud forms a grey sheet that can hide the Sun.

⑩ Resembling heaps of cotton wool, this cloud type often forms in fine weather.

⑨ This massive column of cloud causes thunderstorms and hail.

⑪ Rounded lobes of this cloud hang below the main cloud mass.

⑫ Dark grey sheets of this low-level cloud cause continuous heavy rain.

ANSWERS: 1. Cirrus 2. Cirrocumulus 3. Cirrostratus 4. Altocumulus 5. Altostratus 6. Lenticular 7. Stratocumulus 8. Stratus 9. Cumulonimbus 10. Cumulus 11. Mammatus 12. Nimbostratus

Rocks and minerals

Rock types

Syenite

Igneous rocks are formed when magma (molten rock) either solidifies underground or when it reaches Earth's surface.

Gneiss

Metamorphic rocks are formed from existing rocks that change under extreme temperatures and pressures underground.

Sandstone

Sedimentary rock is usually made by tiny pieces of rock, worn away by wind and rain, joining together.

Earth's crust is a layer of rocky minerals up to 50 km (31 miles) thick. Heat from inside our planet keeps the crust moving, constantly creating and destroying the rocks and minerals over millions of years.

Hot stuff!
Igneous rock that forms at Earth's surface takes hours to cool, but underground this can take thousands of years!

What is the rock cycle?

The effects of erosion, pressure, and heat recycle rocks from one form to another – a never-ending process called the rock cycle.

01. Wind and rain wear away rock, breaking it down into tiny particles, known as sediment.

The effect of wind and rain on rock is called weathering.

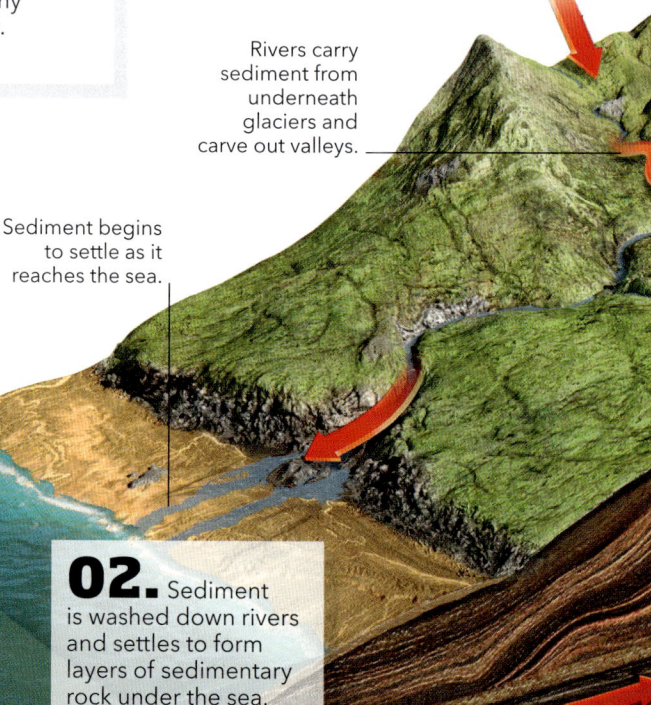

Rivers carry sediment from underneath glaciers and carve out valleys.

As the weight of the sediment layers builds, it squashes the particles down and they stick together, a process called cementation.

Sediment begins to settle as it reaches the sea.

02. Sediment is washed down rivers and settles to form layers of sedimentary rock under the sea.

In numbers

£2.3 million
(US $3 million) The price of a single carat (0.2 g/ 1⁄14 oz) of jadeite, a rare kind of jade and the most expensive mineral today.

75 per cent
The amount of Earth's land surface covered by sedimentary rock. Below this layer lies mainly igneous and metamorphic rock.

66 tonnes
Weight of the largest meteorite to strike Earth. These stony or metallic rocks enter Earth's atmosphere from space!

What's the difference?

Minerals: A mineral is made up of one chemical combination – this quartz is a mix of silicon and oxygen – and is identified by the shape of its crystals.

Hexagonal crystals

Feldspar comes in a variety of different colours.

Rocks: A rock is a mixture of different minerals. This granite contains feldspar (pink), quartz (grey), and mica (black).

Everyday minerals

Chalk
Chalcite, the mineral in chalk, crumbles and sticks to surfaces. It is good for writing on blackboards.

Talc
This mineral crumbles into powder that soaks up moisture, helping to keep skin dry.

Toothpaste
Minerals can be useful in toothpaste because their rough textures help to clean or polish teeth.

I don't believe it
Zircon, the oldest-known mineral crystal, formed 4.4 billion years ago, just after the formation of planet Earth.

What a strike!
It is no coincidence that this looks like compacted sand. It is called fulgurite and is formed when a lightning bolt strikes sand and turns it into a glassy rock.

Glaciers grind the rocks into sediment.

04. Heat deep underground melts rock to form magma, which erupts as lava from volcanoes. Both turn to igneous rock as they cool.

03. Squeezing and heating underground, caused by activity inside Earth, change sedimentary and igneous rocks into metamorphic rocks.

Fascinating facts

- Pumice is a rock that floats because it's full of holes made by bubbles of gas when the hot volcanic rock erupted.

- Coal is a rock that formed millions of years ago from the remains of prehistoric swamp forests that fossilized in the ground.

- Glassy obsidian forms when lava cools very quickly. Its edges are so sharp they are used in surgical scalpels.

- In 2000, a cave in Mexico was discovered to be full of gypsum crystals up to 11 m (36 ft) long!

Rock stars

138 GEOGRAPHY GENIUS

Do you have what it takes to separate the rocks from the minerals? Some are not as hard as they look! They are all found in the ground beneath our feet, but some have the colour or sparkle to really catch your eye. And a few are as precious as gemstones.

1 The blood-red colour in this mineral ore is caused by the presence of rusty iron.

Pea-sized mineral grain

2 This mineral contains a mixture of ingredients, but its main importance is as a source of aluminium.

3 The metallic shine and yellowish colour of this mineral gave it the nickname "fool's gold".

4 Although it looks like silver, this precious metal is actually more valuable than either silver or gold.

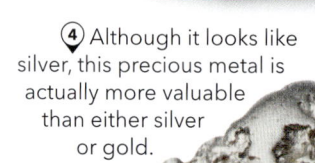

5 This rock can crumble into dust, but is good for writing on the wall.

6 Here is a mineral that you shouldn't play around with – it's deadly poisonous.

7 This rock is made up of tiny marine shells and can sometimes contain bigger fossils as well.

8 This tough rock – used in building – forms most of the solid foundation beneath Earth's continents.

A mix of minerals gives this rock a grainy look.

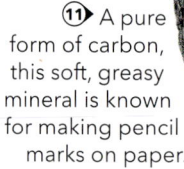

9 Crystals of this flower-pink mineral can be cut and polished into valuable gemstones.

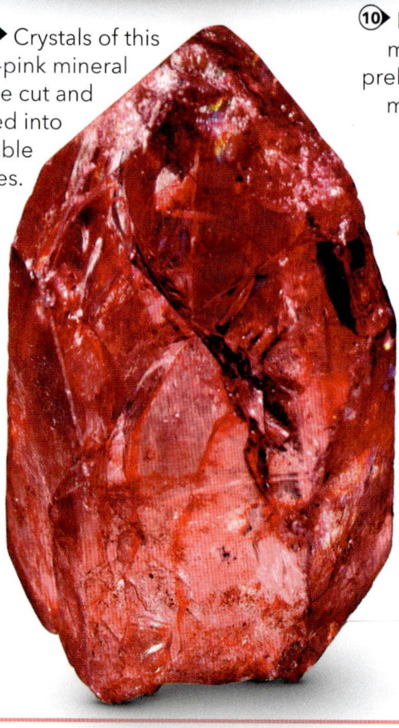

10 In the Stone Age, this mineral was used by prehistoric people to make axe blades.

11 A pure form of carbon, this soft, greasy mineral is known for making pencil marks on paper.

ANSWERS: 1. Haematite 2. Bauxite 3. Pyrite 4. Platinum 5. Chalk 6. Arsenic 7. Limestone 8. Granite 9. Rose quartz 10. Flint 11. Graphite 12. Agate 13. Cinnabar 14. Marble 15. Gold 16. Halite 17. Obsidian 18. Meteorite 19. Sulfur 20. Malachite 21. Sandstone

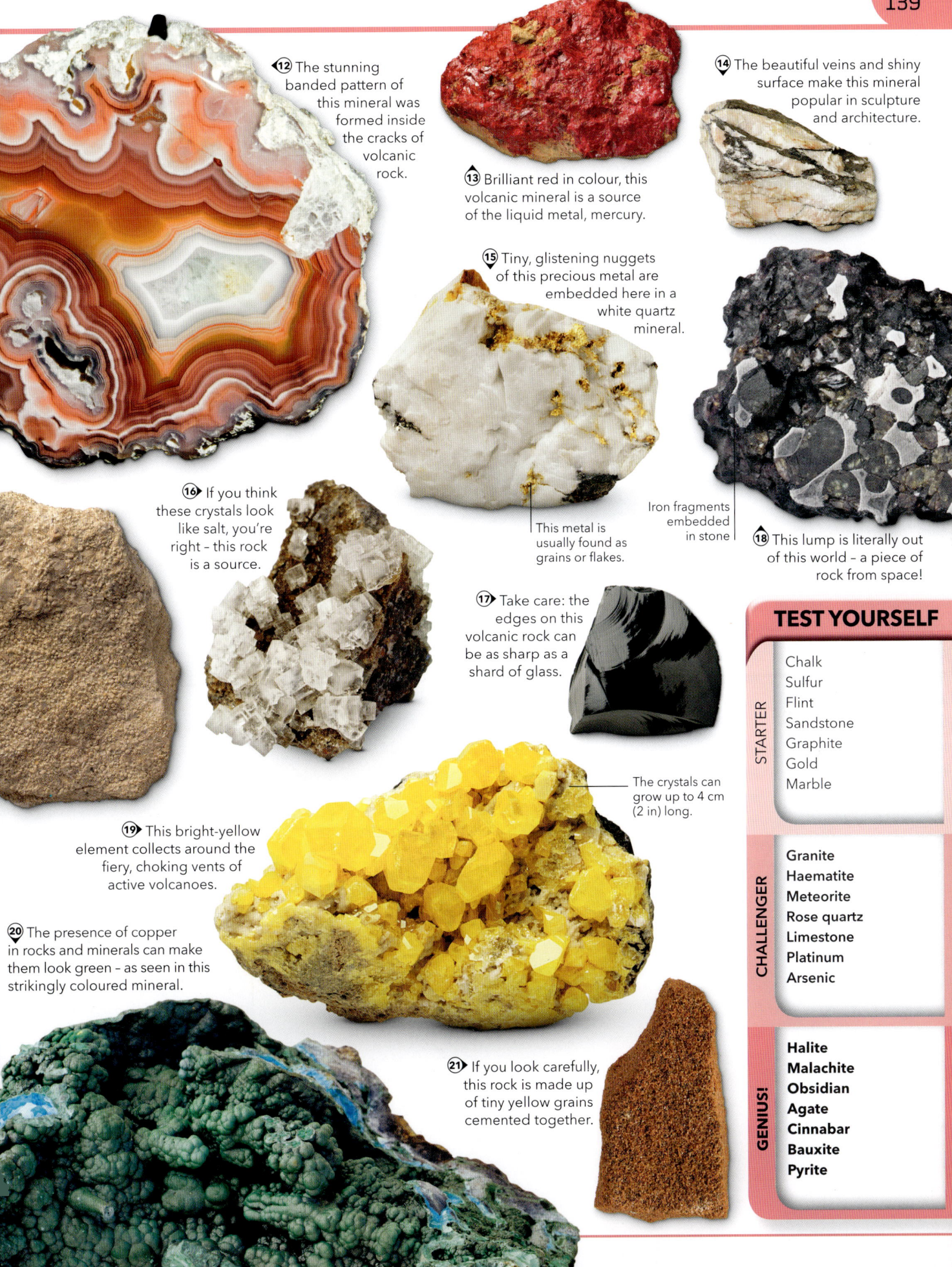

12 The stunning banded pattern of this mineral was formed inside the cracks of volcanic rock.

13 Brilliant red in colour, this volcanic mineral is a source of the liquid metal, mercury.

14 The beautiful veins and shiny surface make this mineral popular in sculpture and architecture.

15 Tiny, glistening nuggets of this precious metal are embedded here in a white quartz mineral.

This metal is usually found as grains or flakes.

Iron fragments embedded in stone

18 This lump is literally out of this world – a piece of rock from space!

16 If you think these crystals look like salt, you're right – this rock is a source.

17 Take care: the edges on this volcanic rock can be as sharp as a shard of glass.

The crystals can grow up to 4 cm (2 in) long.

19 This bright-yellow element collects around the fiery, choking vents of active volcanoes.

20 The presence of copper in rocks and minerals can make them look green – as seen in this strikingly coloured mineral.

21 If you look carefully, this rock is made up of tiny yellow grains cemented together.

TEST YOURSELF

STARTER
Chalk
Sulfur
Flint
Sandstone
Graphite
Gold
Marble

CHALLENGER
Granite
Haematite
Meteorite
Rose quartz
Limestone
Platinum
Arsenic

GENIUS!
Halite
Malachite
Obsidian
Agate
Cinnabar
Bauxite
Pyrite

Precious gemstones

Some minerals form crystals that can be cut and polished into stunning gems, making them popular in jewellery. Many are highly valuable and a few even cost millions – do you have an eye for quality?

1 ▶ The most popular type of this gem is deep purple in colour. The ancient Greeks believed it was created by the god of wine, Bacchus.

2 ▶ No other gemstone has the striking black and white banding pattern of this one.

3 ▶ This semiprecious gemstone is often found in granite. For centuries, Native Americans have given it as funeral gifts.

This heart-shaped gem is surrounded by 29 smaller gems.

4 ▶ The name of this variety of the mineral beryl reminds you that it has the colour of the sea.

5 ▶ The name of this stone comes from the Latin for "seed" – possibly inspired by pomegranate seeds, which are similar in shape and colour.

6 ▶ Grinding down this stone produces a deep blue pigment that was used by many artists. It was also used in ancient jewellery.

7 ▶ The iron in this gemstone gives it an olive-green colour – the more iron, the deeper the shade of green.

Cut and polished beads

8 ▶ Made of pure crystallized carbon, this gem is one of the hardest materials and is sometimes used in cutting tools.

9 ▶ Formed from tree resin that hardened millions of years ago, this gem sometimes contains fossilized animals.

ANSWERS: 1. Amethyst 2. Onyx 3. Tourmaline 4. Aquamarine 5. Garnet 6. Lapis lazuli 7. Peridot 8. Diamond 9. Amber 10. Sapphire 11. Emerald 12. Topaz 13. Jasper 14. Ruby 15. Moonstone 16. Jet 17. Malachite 18. Turquoise 19. Tiger's eye 20. Pearl 21. Opal

10 This gemstone can come in yellow, purple, or green, but is best known for its blue form.

11 The green colour of this well-known gemstone, shown here decorating a Turkish dagger, comes from metals: chromium and vanadium.

12 Impurities in the crystal make this gemstone come in different colours, including red, yellow, or green.

13 When polished, this gemstone can be carved into ornamental shapes, such as vases and bowls.

14 A blood-red gemstone of this kind, called "Sunrise", sold for more than US $30 million in 2015.

15 The white sheen that gives this gemstone its name comes from the way it scatters light.

16 Gemstones don't get much blacker than this. Like coal, it is formed from prehistoric dead wood.

17 This gemstone can have a green-marbled effect, and was once used to make green paint.

18 Lacking the sparkle of other gemstones, this one makes up for it with its distinctive blue shade and veined pattern.

19 Different minerals give this polished gem a deep red-brown colour – like the fiery gaze of a big cat.

20 When an oyster is irritated by a speck of grit, it turns the grit into this smooth, glistening gemstone.

21 This stunning multicoloured gem is mostly mined in Australia, where it is the national gemstone.

TEST YOURSELF

STARTER	CHALLENGER	GENIUS!
Amber	Amethyst	Malachite
Sapphire	Topaz	Tourmaline
Diamond	Lapis lazuli	Peridot
Turquoise	Opal	Jasper
Pearl	Onyx	Moonstone
Ruby	Garnet	Aquamarine
Emerald	Jet	Tiger's eye

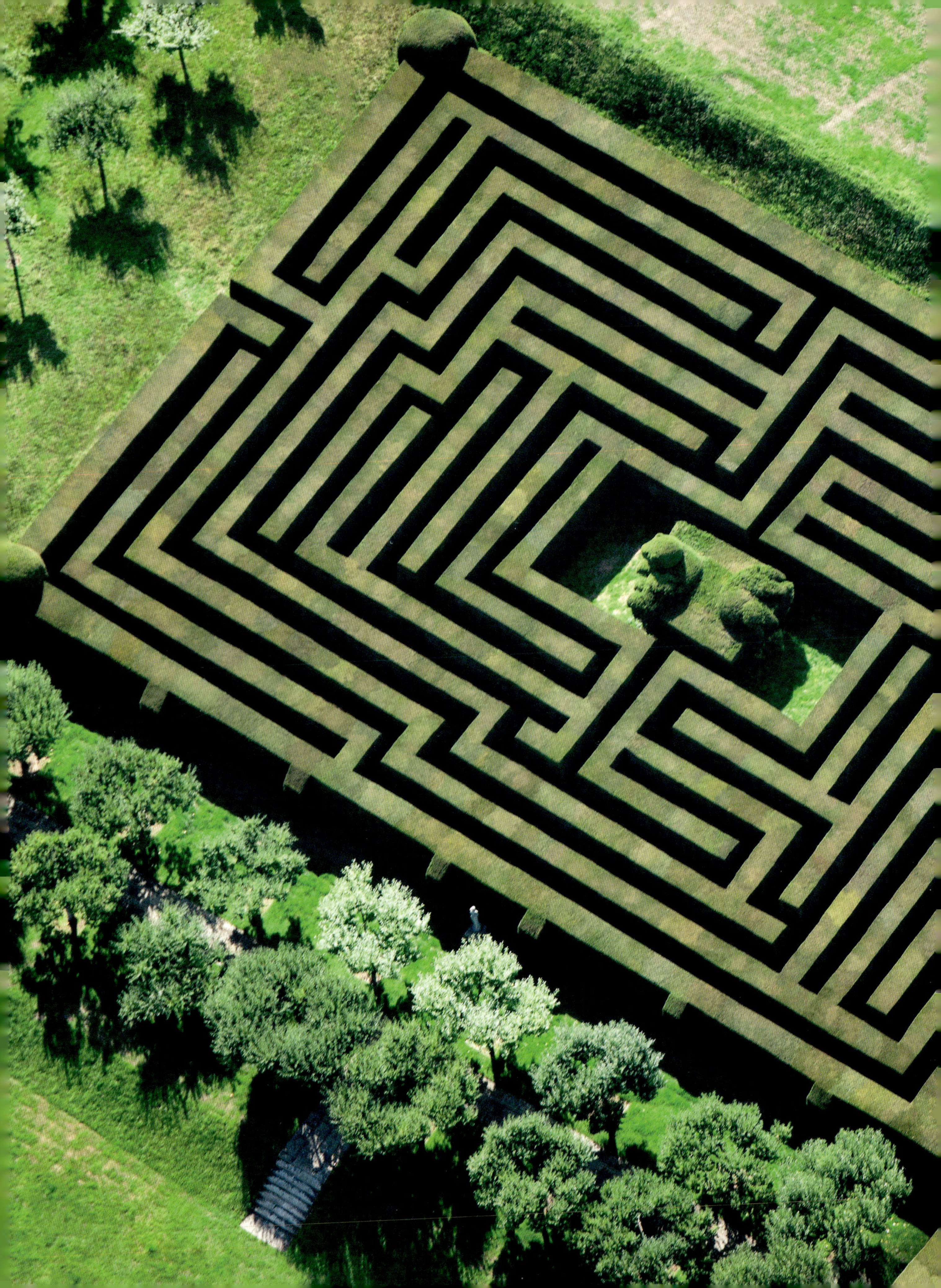

4 HISTORY BUFF

Master the maze
History doesn't always follow a clear path, as leaders often change and civilizations rise and fall. But humans in every era have always sought to entertain themselves. Why not pick up a pastime of the past and see if you can plot a course through this maze?

Timeline

Sumerian
The earliest cities were built by the Sumerians, who lived in what is now Southern Iraq.
5000–2350 BCE

Indus Valley
Many sites of well-planned cities have been excavated in the Indus Valley of Northwest India and Pakistan.
3300–1300 BCE

Egypt
The Egyptians created the longest-lasting ancient civilization, which spanned more than 3,000 years.
3300–30 BCE

Norte Chico
The oldest-known civilization of the Americas was established at Norte Chico in Peru.
3100–1800 BCE

Greece
The civilizations of ancient Greece gave the world ideas such as democracy, as well as the Olympic Games.
1600–146 BCE

Ancient civilizations

When a population comes together and establishes a distinctive way of life, with its own rulers (in the ancient world, usually kings), religion, and culture, a new civilization is born. Many civilizations of the distant past are still known to us today, often through the fascinating buildings they left behind.

How to build a pyramid

01. Recruit an army of thousands of labourers – building an ancient Egyptian royal tomb is a monumental task.

02. Send labourers to quarries to cut stone blocks by hand and then drag them on sleds to the site.

Outer covering of polished limestone

Calendars

To keep track of time, the first civilizations invented calendars, which recorded the years and named the days and months. Calendars set dates for important festivals.

In the Chinese calendar, each year is named after one of 12 animal signs – the dragon for example.

This carved stone is a Roman calendar, with months named after gods, rulers, and numbers.

The centaur is Sagittarius, the archer, one of the signs of the zodiac.

In numbers

400,000 km
(250,000 miles) Total length of the roads built by the Romans throughout their empire.

40,000 km
(25,000 miles) Total length of the roads built by the Incas of Peru.

21,196 km
(13,170 miles) Length of the Great Wall of China, built more than 2,000 years ago to keep invaders out.

Ancient theatre
Theatre was a big part of the ancient classical world. The all-male casts wore masks to play both men and women.

Theatre comes from "theatron", Greek for "viewing"

Rome
The ancient Romans built an empire that included all the lands around the Mediterranean.

753 BCE–476 CE

China
United by the First Emperor, China remained under imperial rule for more than 2,000 years.

221 BCE–1912 CE

Maya
The Maya built cities, with pyramid temples and palaces, in the jungles of Central America.

250–1697 CE

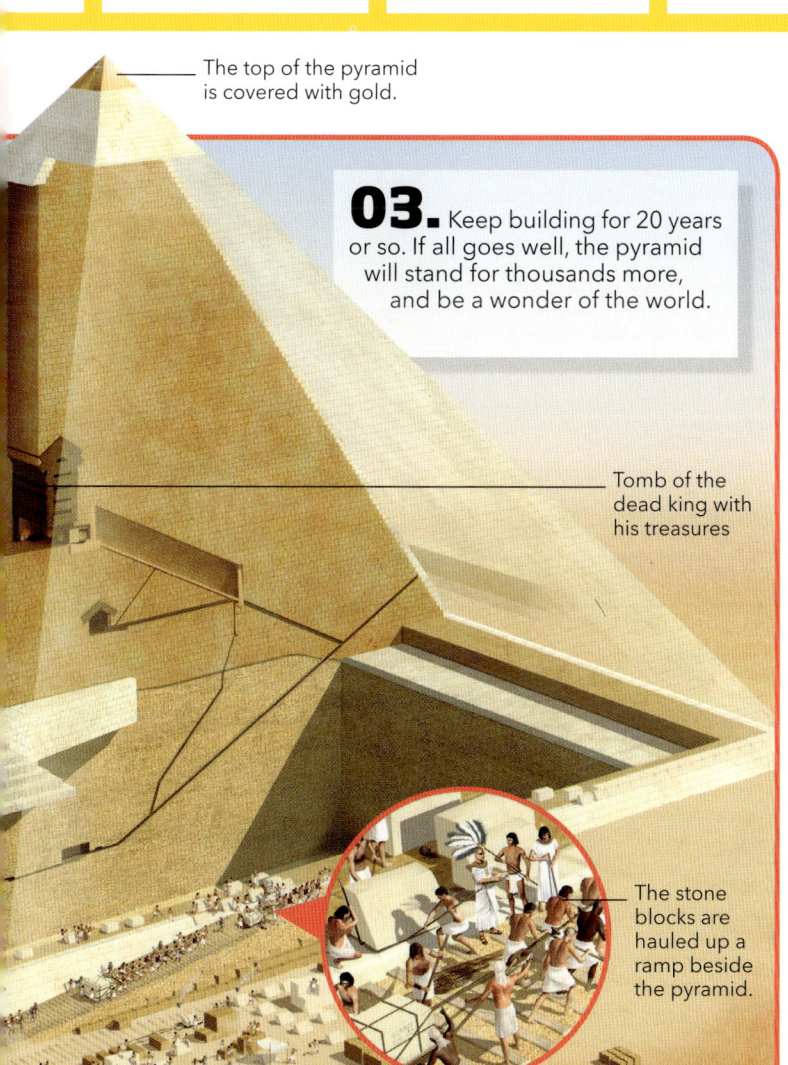

The top of the pyramid is covered with gold.

03. Keep building for 20 years or so. If all goes well, the pyramid will stand for thousands more, and be a wonder of the world.

Tomb of the dead king with his treasures

The stone blocks are hauled up a ramp beside the pyramid.

Top tombs

- A curse was said to bring death to anyone who entered the tomb of the Egyptian king Tutankhamun.
- The First Emperor of China's tomb is guarded by an army of 7,000 life-size terracotta (pottery) warriors.
- In the Sumerian royal burial tombs of Ur, archaeologists found the remains of many human sacrifices.
- The Mayans thought jade was more precious than gold. The Mayan king Pacal of Palenque was buried wearing a jade mask.

I don't believe it
The Incas of Peru had no writing, but they kept records with lengths of knotted string of different colours.

Mayan: The Mayans built temples shaped like steep pyramids, with steps leading to a room on top.

Greek: Stone columns were typical of Greek temples. A statue of a god stood inside.

Egyptian: To enter an Egyptian temple, you had to pass through gateways called pylons.

Hindu: The outside walls of Hindu temples were richly decorated with carvings.

Roman: The Romans copied Greek temples, but built them with brick and concrete instead of stone.

HISTORY BUFF

① Built by the Greeks in what is now Turkey, this ancient city's impressive library and amphitheatre still stand today.

② Known for its "Avenue of the Dead", this complex of pyramids in Mexico was the largest city in the Americas in 500 CE.

③ Once the heart of a great pre-Incan empire in Peru, this meticulously planned capital boasts unique walls and carvings.

Decorative earth walls

Lost cities

Over the centuries, civilizations have risen and fallen from power, their abandoned cities forgotten, buried by desert sands or overgrown by forests. Can you identify these ancient sites from around the world, rediscovered by explorers and archaeologists?

④ When the Incas abandoned this sacred site high in the Andes mountains in 1572, it remained hidden from the outside world until 1911.

About 200 buildings make up the site.

⑤ A soapstone bird statue found in the ruins of this medieval city features on the flag of a modern African country.

⑥ Stone chariots, elephant stables, and temples are just some of the remains at this grand 14th-century capital of a former Hindu empire.

⑦ This temple city in Cambodia, built in the 12th century, is one of the largest religious monuments in the world.

⑧ When the volcano Vesuvius erupted in Italy in 79 CE, it completely buried this Roman town in thick ash.

ANSWERS: 1. Ephesus 2. Teotihuacan 3. Chan Chan 4. Machu Picchu 5. Great Zimbabwe 6. Hampi 7. Angkor Wat 8. Pompeii 9. Thebes 10. Roman Forum 11. Chichen Itza 12. Gaochang 13. Bagan 14. Persepolis 15. Petra

9 This ancient Egyptian city, by the River Nile, held a great temple to the ram-headed god, Amun.

10 At this site, in the middle of the capital of Italy, the toga-clad citizens of a mighty empire once walked and went to public meetings.

11 A 24-m- (79-ft-) tall step pyramid is just one of the archaeological wonders of this ancient Mayan city in Mexico.

12 An ancient oasis city in the Taklamakan Desert in China was once an important trading post on the Silk Road.

13 It is thought more than 10,000 Buddhist temples once stood in this sacred city in Myanmar.

14 In Iran, towering columns mark the site of a great Persian king's audience hall.

15 Also known as the "Rose-Red City", this site in Jordan is named after the colour of its buildings carved out of sandstone cliffs.

TEST YOURSELF

STARTER	CHALLENGER	GENIUS!
Petra	Persepolis	Ephesus
Pompeii	Angkor Wat	Chan Chan
Machu Picchu	Hampi	Great Zimbabwe
Chichen Itza	Teotihuacan	Gaochang
Roman Forum	Thebes	Bagan

HISTORY BUFF

Guess the gods

The ancient Romans worshipped many gods. They built temples where they sacrificed animals to honour them. Each one ruled over a different area of life – from marriage and love, to war and fire. Can you recognize the gods in this gallery?

① This god ruled over the dead in the kingdom of the underworld, guarded by the three-headed dog Cerberus.

② This goddess was taken by the king of the dead to be his queen.

③ Known for his trident – a fishing spear with three prongs – this god ruled the sea.

④ The messenger of the gods was a speedy traveller, aided by his winged helmet.

⑤ A two-faced god of beginnings, this one gave his name to the first month of the year.

⑥ The goddess of wisdom, crafts, and war is usually shown wearing a helmet and armed with a spear.

⑦ The word "volcano" comes from the name of this god of fire and metalworkers.

Usually shown holding a blacksmith's hammer, this god forged armour for heroes and gods.

⑧ The sixth month of the year is named after the queen of the gods and the goddess of marriage, who is shown here wearing her royal headband called a diadem.

⑨ Armed with thunderbolts, the king of the gods ruled over the sky.

⑩ A drinking cup and a bunch of grapes help identify the god of agriculture, wine, and fertility.

⑪ The brightest planet in the night sky is named after this goddess of love and beauty.

This goddess is often shown holding a mirror in her hand.

⑫ Armed with arrows, this is the goddess of the hunt.

⑬ Shown as a young man without a beard, the god of light, healing, and music carries a lyre.

⑭ The god of desire fired arrows to make people fall in love.

⑮ Ready for battle and wearing a warrior's helmet, this fiery god of war gave his name to the Red Planet in our Solar System.

TEST YOURSELF

STARTER
- Diana
- Juno
- Jupiter
- Mars
- Venus

CHALLENGER
- Apollo
- Cupid
- Janus
- Mercury
- Neptune

GENIUS!
- Bacchus
- Minerva
- Pluto
- Proserpina
- Vulcan

ANSWERS: 1. Pluto 2. Proserpina 3. Neptune 4. Mercury 5. Janus 6. Minerva 7. Vulcan 8. Juno 9. Jupiter 10. Bacchus 11. Venus 12. Diana 13. Apollo 14. Cupid 15. Mars

Mythical creatures

Myths and legends are timeless tales, exploring the mysteries of nature and the big questions of life. These stories feature gods, heroes, demons, and monsters, who often have magical powers.

1 This ancient Greek monster is a lion with a goat's head on its back, and a snake for a tail.

This monster could breathe fire.

2 In Greek myths, this creature, part lion and part eagle, guarded golden treasures and was known for its strength.

The horn is said to contain healing powers.

4 This dragon with a cockerel's head could kill people with a glance.

3 In the Middle Ages, Europeans told stories of horses with horns, living in remote forests.

The dragon also has the feet of a cockerel.

5 Myths of humans with the ability to turn into wolves have been told across Europe.

6 Across Europe and Asia, there are stories of women with the tails of fish.

7 The Greek sea god's chariot was pulled by this creature – half horse and half fish.

The body is covered with thick hair.

8 This tall, hairy ape-like beast is said to live in the Himalayan mountains of Asia.

9 A beast, with the body of a man and the head of a bull, was hidden in a labyrinth by King Minos of Crete.

10 This player of tricks, who can appear as a spider or a man, appears in African and Caribbean stories.

11 A bird which never dies, this creature has the ability to be reborn out of fire.

ANSWERS: 1. Chimera 2. Griffin 3. Unicorn 4. Cockatrice 5. Werewolf 6. Mermaid 7. Hippocampus 8. Yeti 9. Minotaur 10. Anansi 11. Phoenix 12. Thunderbird 13. Chinese dragon 14. Manticore 15. Centaur 16. Cyclops 17. Kappa 18. Faun

12 A giant bird which creates storms and flashes of lightning appears in the myths of North American peoples.

13 In East Asia, this creature with a snake-like body and four legs is thought to bring good luck.

Eagle claws are on the feet.

14 This Persian creature has a lion's body, a human face, and a tail that shoots deadly spines.

15 This ancient Greek mythical creature has the upper body of a man on a horse's body and legs.

16 Greek myths feature this scary one-eyed giant, said to feed on human flesh.

The dish-like depression on the head is this creature's source of power.

17 Japan's ponds and rivers are still thought to be home to this web-footed creature with a turtle's shell.

18 Ancient Roman myths often tell of wild men with the legs and horns of goats.

TEST YOURSELF

STARTER
Chinese dragon
Mermaid
Phoenix
Unicorn
Werewolf
Yeti

CHALLENGER
Centaur
Cyclops
Faun
Griffin
Minotaur
Thunderbird

GENIUS!
Anansi
Chimera
Cockatrice
Hippocampus
Kappa
Manticore

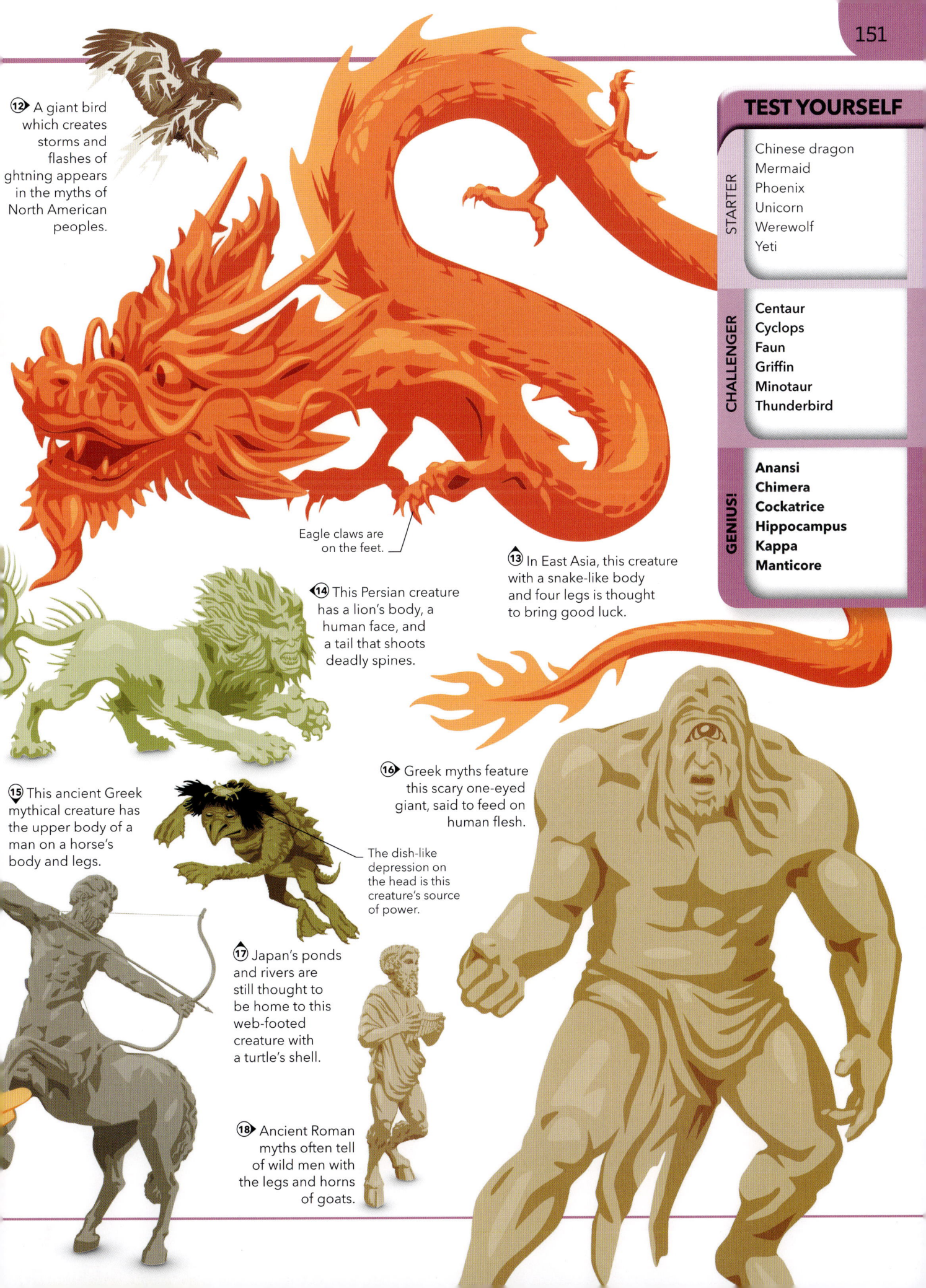

HISTORY BUFF

Castles

The many amazing castles around the world were not just the homes of kings and queens. They were also important defence posts against enemies. Some of the earliest castles date back to the 11th century and their styles have changed a lot over time.

Battlements
The jagged tops of the castle walls allowed defenders to shoot arrows as well as hide from enemy fire during battle.

Types of castle

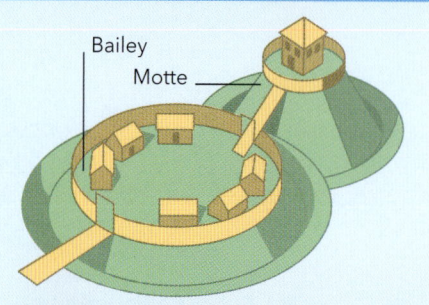

Motte and Bailey: This type of castle, built during the 11th and 12th centuries, had a courtyard (bailey) protected by a wall and a tall, steep mound (motte).

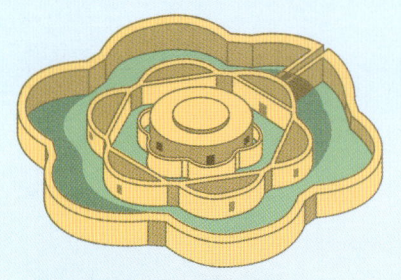

Concentric: From the 12th century onwards, castles were built with two or more stone walls to give greater protection from enemy attacks.

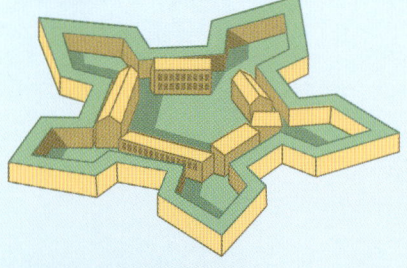

Star-shaped: First built in the mid-15th century, the complex structure of these castles let the defenders fire cannons from different angles.

Drawbridge
The only entrance was a wooden bridge, which could be raised to keep enemies out.

Castle defences

To capture this castle, attackers would have to cross a moat and then break through two walls. All the while, defenders would be shooting arrows at them from the battlements and towers above.

Moat
A large water-filled ditch surrounded the castle, keeping attackers at bay.

How to attack a castle

01. Move your army forwards, towards the castle. Protect your forces by using wooden siege towers as shields.

02. Use cannons to shoot heavy balls at the castle walls, so they can smash through the defences.

Corner towers
Round towers at the corners allowed defenders to look out in all directions.

Castle careers

🃏 **Jesters** (below) were performers who entertained guests at castle feasts. Often wearing brightly coloured clothes, they told jokes and played tricks, and were even allowed to poke fun at the lords and ladies.

🃏 **A gong farmer** was a person who emptied the cesspit beneath the castle toilet. This smelly job could only be done at night, when everyone else was asleep - nice!

🃏 **The lady-in-waiting** was a high-ranking attendant, acting as a companion to a queen or noblewoman. She helped her mistress dress, and sat with her, usually doing embroidery, reading, or playing music.

When nature calls!
A castle toilet was a small room with a hole opening onto the outside, from which waste fell into the cesspit below.

I don't believe it
In the 13th century, a polar bear lived in the Tower of London. It used to swim in the River Thames hunting for fish!

03. The defenders will fire arrows at your army, but don't turn back - fire your own at them and keep moving forward.

Some castle walls were 6 m (20 ft) thick!

What's what?

Castles were strongholds, built both for defence and as a residence. They came in all shapes and sizes - this is Himeji castle in Japan.

Forts were built for defensive and military purposes, not for permanent residence. Mehrangarh is one of India's largest forts.

Palaces, such as England's Buckingham Palace, were designed for luxury and comfort - not to withstand military attacks.

Hold the fort

Across the world, rulers and nobles have built forts, castles, and palaces. While castles and forts usually have thick stone walls to defend them from attack, palaces were built to display the wealth and power of those who lived in them.

② Built by King Louis XIV, this vast palace outside Paris, France, was the home of the royal family until the French Revolution. Richly decorated, it is famous for its Hall of Mirrors.

③ This fort and palace in Granada, Spain, was built by the Muslim sultans who ruled the country 700 years ago. Its gardens and courtyards are full of orange trees and fountains.

① Although this fairytale castle in Germany looks medieval, it was built in the 19th century in the style of knights' castles of old.

The tallest tower is 65 m (213 ft) high.

Painting shows St George slaying a dragon.

④ Chinese emperors once relaxed in this palace in Beijing, known for its wonderful gardens, lakes, pavilions, temples, and pagodas.

⑤ Medieval knights from Europe built this castle as a stronghold in Syria, during the Crusades.

6 On the coast of Egypt sits this fort, which once defended the city of Alexandria from attack.

7 This English castle is the largest in the world that is still lived in as a home – by the British royal family!

8 In the 15th century, this palace of domes and towers in Istanbul was the residence of the Ottoman sultans of Turkey.

9 Also known as Dracula's castle, this stronghold stands in a Romanian forest.

10 This grand palace in St Petersburg, Russia, has 1,057 rooms and was once the home of the Russian royal family.

11 With its distinctive sandstone walls, this fort in Delhi, India, was lived in by the country's Mughal emperors.

12 Kings began living in this palace in Thailand in 1782. Today, it is only used for state occasions.

TEST YOURSELF

STARTER
Alhambra
Palace of Versailles
Windsor Castle
Neuschwanstein Castle

CHALLENGER
Bran Castle
Summer Palace
Red Fort
Grand Palace of Bangkok

GENIUS!
Citadel of Qaitbay
Krak de Chevaliers
Topkapi Palace
Winter Palace

ANSWERS: 1. Neuschwanstein Castle 2. Palace of Versailles 3. Alhambra 4. Summer Palace 5. Krak de Chevaliers 6. Citadel of Qaitbay 7. Windsor Castle 8. Topkapi Palace 9. Bran Castle 10. Winter Palace 11. Red Fort 12. Grand Palace of Bangkok

⑤ South Africa's Zulu warriors carried these long cowhide shields for protection in close combat.

⑥ The spikes on this type of heavy metal club could pierce through armour.

⑨ A medieval knight needed two hands to wield this long, slashing sword.

⑩ This ancient Greek wooden weapon had an iron spearhead at one end and a bronze spike at the other, to stand it up in the ground.

⑦ European medieval knights swung this weapon in the air at their enemies.

④ Japanese warriors, called samurai, used these weapons – the sharpest steel swords ever made.

③ The Aztecs of Mexico had swords with razor-sharp blades made from obsidian, a volcanic rock.

⑧ Pirates and naval marines fought on the decks of ships with these short, curving swords.

② The word "gladiator" comes from the name of this sword, which was carried by Roman foot soldiers.

Leaf-shaped spearhead

① This bow, made of springy yew wood, was as tall as the European archer who fired it.

Battle ready!

Warfare has been a part of history for thousands of years, and weapons have come in a wide range of forms. They have been wielded by warriors in many types of combat – from battles and sieges, to wars and duels – and were used to both defend and attack.

⑫ In western Asia, horsemen used this light, curved sword to slash at their enemies.

⑪ The flame-like shape of this medieval sword's long blade inspired its French name.

⑬ Ancient Greek foot soldiers – called hoplites – were named after the shield each carried.

⑮ European cavalry soldiers in the 18th and 19th centuries often fought with long, curving swords such as this one.

⑯ In the 14th and 15th centuries European foot soldiers used this weapon like a spear, an axe, or a hook.

Usually 1.5–1.8 m (5–8 ft) long

⑭ This throwing knife, with a beak-shaped blade, is a traditional weapon from Central Africa.

⑰ A long-handled axe was a favourite weapon of fierce medieval raiders from Scandinavia.

⑱ Carried by Indian soldiers into battle, this 19th-century shield had handles at the back and was gripped in the left hand to fend off blows.

㉑ These shields were used by Roman legionaries and could be put together to form a shield wall.

This formation is called the tortoise.

⑲ New Zealand's Maori warriors fought hand-to-hand with beautifully carved clubs, made from wood or whale bone.

Trigger

⑳ This East Asian weapon has a bronze trigger, which is pulled to release an arrow.

TEST YOURSELF

STARTER
- Cutlass
- Longbow
- Viking battleaxe
- Sabre
- Flail
- Longsword
- Scutum

CHALLENGER
- Qin crossbow
- Mace
- Dhal
- Dory
- Gladius
- Hoplon
- Bird-headed throwing knife

GENIUS!
- Macuahuitl
- Isihlangu
- Halberd
- Wahaika
- Scimitar
- Katana
- Flamberge

ANSWERS: 1. Longbow 2. Gladius 3. Macuahuitl 4. Katana 5. Isihlangu 6. Longsword 10. Dory 11. Flamberge 12. Scimitar 13. Hoplon 14. Bird-headed throwing knife 15. Sabre 16. Halberd 17. Viking battleaxe 18. Dhal 19. Wahaika 20. Qin crossbow 21. Scutum

HISTORY BUFF

Fighting fashion

For thousands of years, warriors have waged wars across the world. The helmets soldiers wore, both for protection and for show, can tell you a lot about them. While a tall helmet crest made a warrior look bigger and more threatening, a richly decorated one showed its wearer's high rank.

1 Warriors in the Middle East wore this helmet in the 16th century. It is decorated with inscriptions from the Qur'an, the Islamic religious text.

2 Named after a sea creature with a distinctive tail, this helmet was worn in 17th-century Europe.

Elongated neck guard

3 In the 7th century CE, a king was buried in a ship with this helmet. It was discovered in 1939 in England.

4 The eagle on this leather helmet, worn between 1842 and 1918, is the emblem of a German state.

5 Foot soldiers of an ancient empire wore helmets such as this one, which was designed to protect the head without blocking vision or hearing.

6 Expensive materials, such as gold, silver, and eagle feathers, on this East Asian helmet, indicate that it belonged to a high-ranking official.

7 Named after a city-state in ancient Greece, this bronze helmet covered the entire head, except the eyes and the mouth.

The crest was probably made of dyed red horsehair or feathers.

8 This helmet was worn by the famous Scandinavian sea-raiding people. It was made by welding iron plates together.

Face guard to protect nose and eyes

Cockerel's head for decoration

9 Made mainly of chain mail, this helmet was worn by a warrior of an Indian Muslim empire.

10 Highly decorated helmets, such as this one, were mostly worn for parades in 16th-century Germany.

Triangular chain mail covered the face

Pierced holes for breathing

11 From the 1220s to 1350, European knights protected their heads with big bucket-shaped helmets.

12 Made of leather, with a tall feather plume, this helmet was worn by soldiers on horses during the Napoleonic wars in the early 19th century.

Decoration representing stag antlers

13 Spanish soldiers who conquered the Aztec and Inca empires of South America wore helmets like this one.

14 This elaborately decorated helmet was worn for display by Japanese warriors.

TEST YOURSELF

STARTER
- Viking helmet
- Roman Legionary helmet
- Samurai helmet
- Lobster-tail pot helmet

CHALLENGER
- Turkish helmet
- Anglo-Saxon helmet
- Chinese helmet
- Great helm
- Corinthian helmet

GENIUS!
- Mughal helmet
- British cavalry helmet
- Morion
- Armet
- Prussian helmet

ANSWERS: 1. Turkish helmet 2. Lobster-tail pot helmet 3. Anglo-Saxon helmet 4. Prussian helmet 5. Roman Legionary helmet 6. Chinese helmet 7. Corinthian helmet 8. Viking helmet 9. Mughal helmet 10. Armet 11. Great helm 12. British cavalry helmet 13. Morion 14. Samurai helmet

HISTORY BUFF

In numbers

49
The number of countries ruled by a dictatorship.

44
The number of countries with a monarchy.

41
The number of countries where the president is head of both state and government.

7
Countries where the monarch is head of both state and government.

Leaders

Throughout history, countries have been governed in different ways. Once, most states were ruled by monarchs (kings or queens who had total power). In many countries today, power has passed to the people, who have a say (by voting) in how they are governed. Many people have had to fight for this right, through political campaigns. Monarchs have also been overthrown, through revolutions.

How to be a queen

01. To qualify, you must be the closest living relative of the last monarch.

02. Discuss arrangements for your coronation. It must be held somewhere grand, such as an abbey or cathedral.

03. Be dignified and calm during the ceremony. The most solemn moment is when holy oil is dabbed on your forehead.

Gold rod, called a sceptre

Elizabeth I of England wore golden robes for her coronation.

Ancient Greeks held elections over 2,500 years ago.

Votes for women

Around the world, women had to fight for the right to vote - known as suffrage. The first country to give women the vote was New Zealand in 1893. One of the fiercest struggles was in Britain, where "suffragettes" led by Emmeline Pankhurst (left in 1914) were often arrested when they protested. British women got the vote in 1918.

Forms of government

☑ **Democracy**
The word democracy means "rule by people". In modern democracies, citizens vote to elect representatives, officials who make decisions on their behalf. Representatives include British members of Parliament and US senators.

☑ **Dictatorship**
A dictatorship is rule by a single leader who has seized power, backed by military force. Dictators ban all political opposition. They strictly control the press so that the people never read any criticism of them.

Who's in charge?

Monarch: Although some countries still have kings and queens, their modern role is often ceremonial, as head of state.

President: Countries without a monarchy often have a president as their head of state. Some presidents have real power, others a ceremonial role.

Prime minister: In countries with a ceremonial monarch or president, the head of the government is a prime minister.

Revolutions!

American Revolution 1775-1783: This war ended rule in the US by the British monarchy.

French Revolution 1789-1799: The ordinary citizens overthrew the king and founded a republic.

Russian Revolution 1917: The last tsar was toppled and Russia became a communist state.

Cuban Revolution 1956-1959: Revolutionaries took power from an unpopular dictator.

I don't believe it!

Shot in a duel, American president Andrew Jackson (1829-1837) lived for another 40 years with the bullet still in his chest.

Sticky ends!

- Around 35 Roman emperors were murdered by their fellow Romans.
- In 1460, King James II of Scotland stood too near a cannon and was killed when it exploded.
- In 1918, Nicholas II, last tsar of Russia, with his wife and five children, was executed by revolutionaries.
- In 1793, in France, King Louis XVI and Queen Marie-Antoinette had their heads chopped off by a guillotine.

04. Sit on a throne wearing a jewelled crown and holding royal regalia, such as an orb and sceptre. You are now a queen. Swear an oath to uphold the law.

English kings and queens are presented with a jewelled sphere called an orb, representing the globe.

Voting matters

In a democratic election, voters mark a cross next to their chosen candidate, and the winner is the one with the most votes!

HISTORY BUFF

Famous faces

While many famous world leaders in history were warriors who conquered great empires, others led political movements or triggered revolutions. Some used force, others used peaceful methods, but all of them made a big impact on the world.

1 This king of Macedon conquered Persian lands and created an empire stretching over three continents, all before dying at the age of 32 in 322 BCE.

2 After making himself ruler of ancient Rome, this famous general was assassinated by senators on the Ides of March in 44 BCE.

3 Ancient Egypt's last pharaoh was a famous queen who killed herself – possibly by allowing a snake to bite her – after being defeated in a war against Rome.

4 After uniting the Mongol tribes, this 13th-century warrior used his mighty army to create an empire that stretched across Asia.

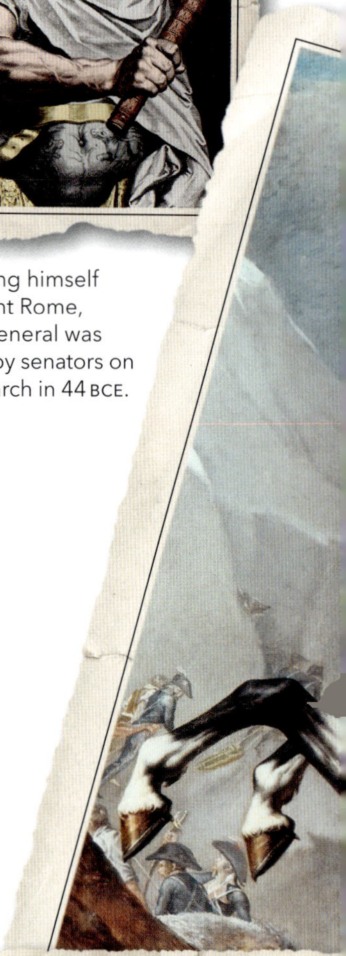

5 After leading the American army to victory over Great Britain, this war hero became the first president of the United States in 1789.

6 This 18th-century empress of Russia encouraged science and education, and made her empire a strong European power.

⑦ After this general made himself emperor of France in 1804, he went on to conquer many European empires, before being defeated in the Battle of Waterloo in 1815.

⑧ Called the "Father of the Nation", this activist used peaceful methods to lead India's fight for freedom from British rule in the 20th century.

⑨ After 27 years in prison, this civil rights leader became South Africa's first black president in 1994.

This famous portrait shows the general crossing the Alps to conquer Austria.

⑩ This revolutionary leader founded the People's Republic of China in 1949, which he ruled for 27 years.

⑪ This Argentinian leader of the 1950s Cuban Revolution is now a famous symbol of rebellion.

⑫ A pastor and civil rights leader, this man led a non-violent campaign for equal rights for African-Americans in the 1950s and 1960s.

This famous war horse was called Marengo.

TEST YOURSELF

STARTER
Catherine the Great
Mahatma Gandhi
Nelson Mandela
Cleopatra

CHALLENGER
Martin Luther King Jr
Napoleon Bonaparte
Julius Caesar
Alexander the Great

GENIUS!
Genghis Khan
Mao Zedong
George Washington
Che Guevara

ANSWERS: 1. Alexander the Great 2. Julius Caesar 3. Cleopatra 4. Genghis Khan 5. George Washington 6. Catherine the Great 7. Napoleon Bonaparte 8. Mahatma Gandhi 9. Nelson Mandela 10. Mao Zedong 11. Che Guevara 12. Martin Luther King Jr

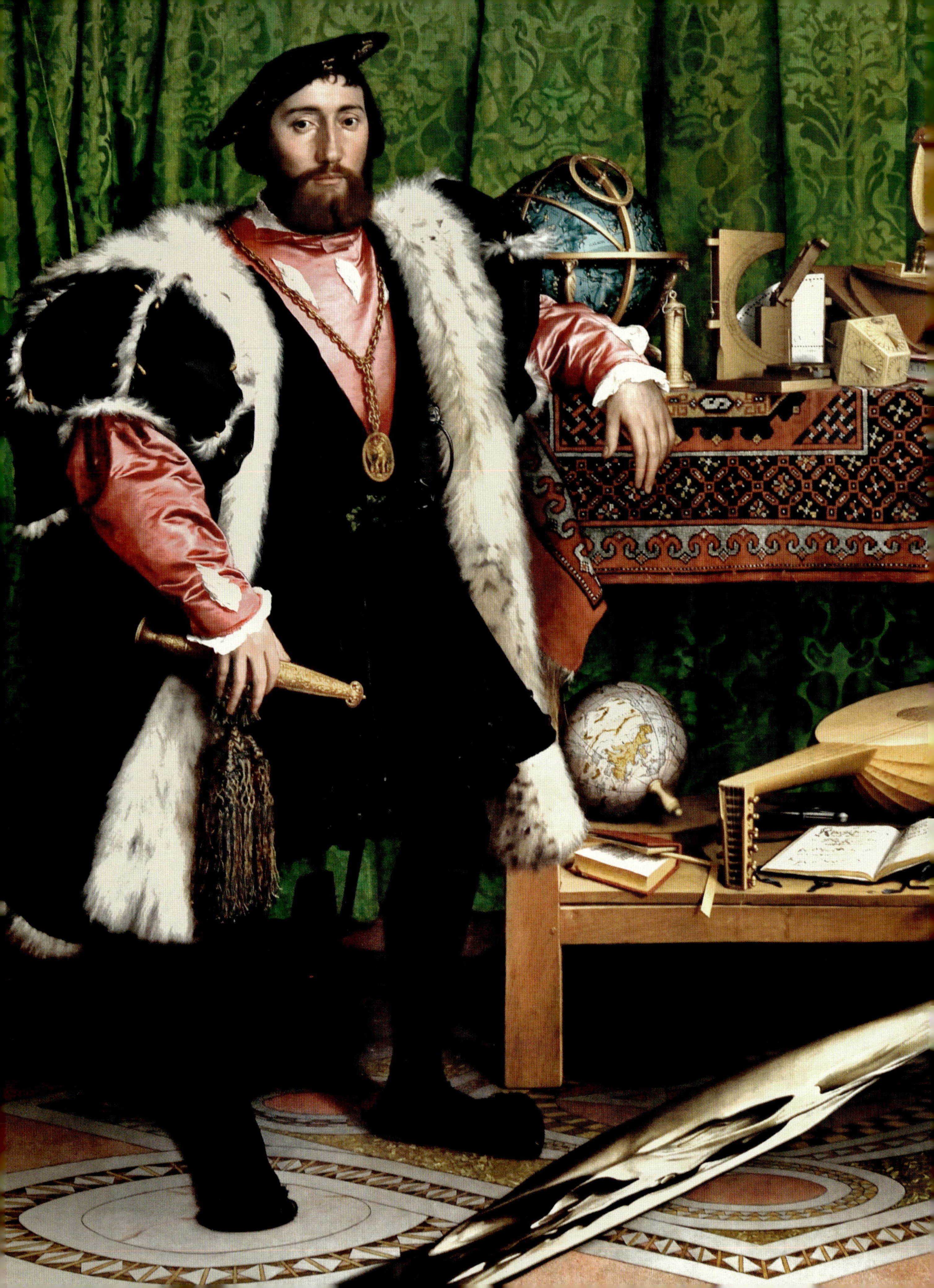

5 CULTURE VULTURE

Picture puzzle
Making a masterpiece is a great art, but some artists have even packed puzzles into their paintings as well. Can you see the skull hidden in this picture by Renaissance artist Hans Holbein the Younger?

CULTURE VULTURE

Art

Traditionally art was drawing, painting, and sculpture. Today, anything goes and the artist's imagination is the only limit. What some may regard as weird, others see as wonderful – take a look and see which styles of art inspire you.

In numbers

32,000
The age in years of the earliest cave paintings found in Chauvet, France, showing animals being hunted.

4
The number of years it took Italian artist Michelangelo (1475–1564) to paint the ceiling and upper walls of the Sistine Chapel in Rome.

Types of paintings

Portrait
Individual people are the subject of portraits. The style can be realistic or abstract.

Still life
Everyday objects, such as fruit or even shoes, are captured in still-life paintings.

Landscape
Scenes of the countryside have been depicted in paintings for many centuries.

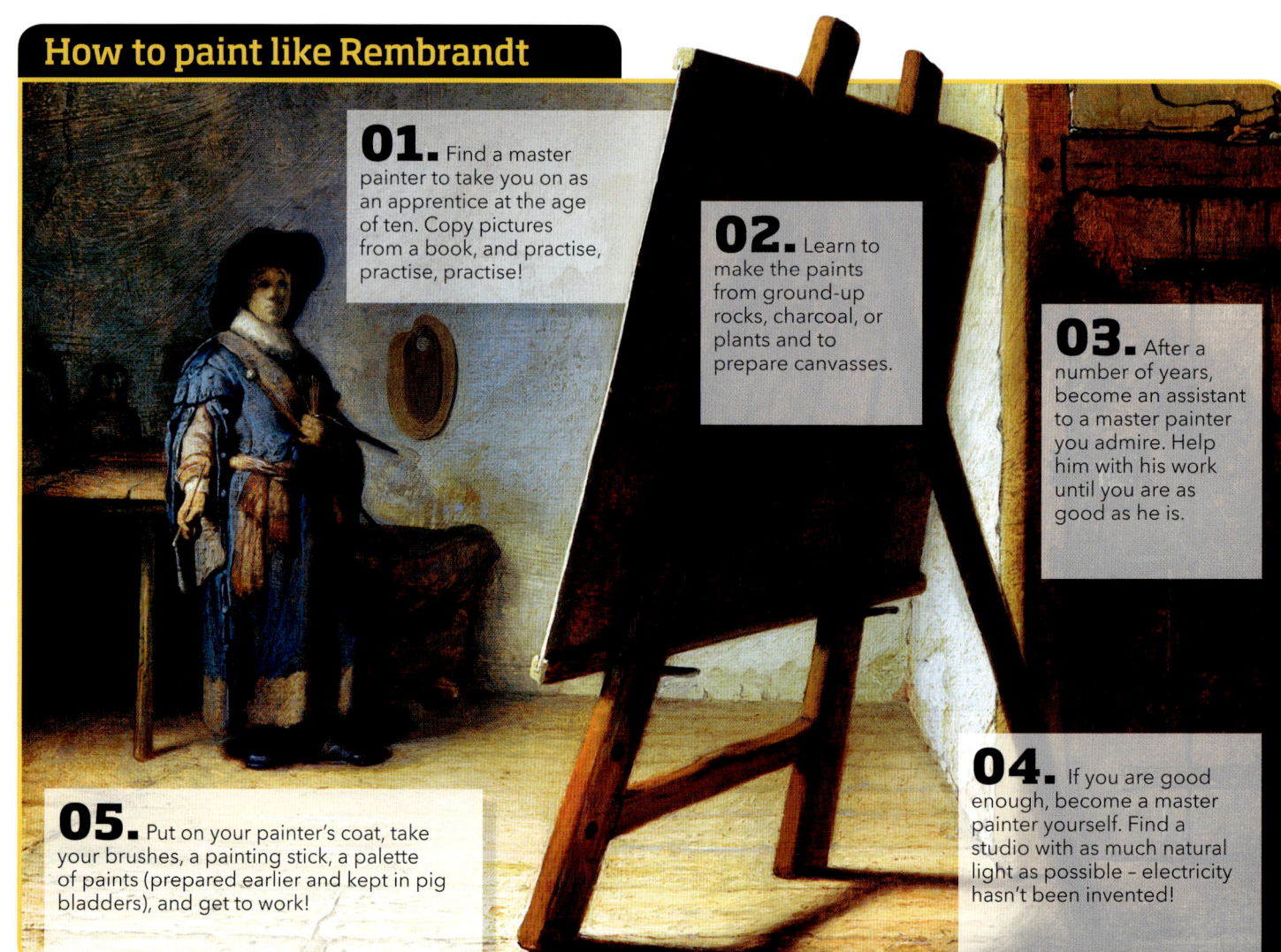

How to paint like Rembrandt

01. Find a master painter to take you on as an apprentice at the age of ten. Copy pictures from a book, and practise, practise, practise!

02. Learn to make the paints from ground-up rocks, charcoal, or plants and to prepare canvasses.

03. After a number of years, become an assistant to a master painter you admire. Help him with his work until you are as good as he is.

04. If you are good enough, become a master painter yourself. Find a studio with as much natural light as possible – electricity hasn't been invented!

05. Put on your painter's coat, take your brushes, a painting stick, a palette of paints (prepared earlier and kept in pig bladders), and get to work!

Art styles

Mosaic: Tiny pieces of hard material, such as glass, stone, or pottery, are used to make pictures.

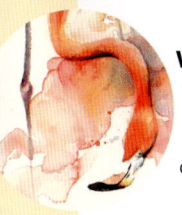

Watercolour: Paints that dissolve in water are applied in layers to give a delicate, light effect.

Oil paints: Pigment mixed with oil result in a slow-drying paint that gives rich colours and textures.

Pastels: A small stick of pure pigment combined with a gum or resin produces a dry, chalky colour.

Steel giant
The Angel of the North, in England, is a sculpture by British artist Antony Gormley. It is 20 m (65 ft) tall with a wingspan of 54 m (177 ft).

Creating colour
Pigments are used to make an artist's palette of colours. They can be either natural (from rock, soil, or plants) or human-made (from chemicals). In the past, unusual ingredients were used to create different colours.

Red is still made from crushed cochineal beetles.

Yellow came from the urine of cows fed on mango leaves in Bengal, southern Asia.

White came from the ash of burned animal bones.

Green was once made from a deadly poison called arsenic.

Purple was produced using the mucus of sea snails.

Supersized sculpture

- The Colossus of Constantine was made in 312–315 CE to honour the Roman emperor. It was 12 m (40 ft) tall, but only fragments remain, including the head (right).

- The Spring Temple Buddha, China, was completed in 2008, and stands a mighty 128 m (420 ft) tall.

- The Statue of Unity, India, became the tallest statue in the world in 2018. It reaches 182 m (597 ft)!

I don't believe it!
Salvator Mundi by Leonardo da Vinci (1452–1519) is the world's most expensive painting. It sold for $450 million (£346 million) in 2017.

Gallery of the greats

Every age has its great artists, the "masters" with unique skills who create new styles, use clever techniques, and inspire others. Here is a gallery of famous paintings by some of the great masters – do you know what they are called?

2) The world's most famous painting is by the Italian artist Leonardo da Vinci. It shows a woman with a mysterious smile – what is she called?

3) In a style known as Cubism, the Spanish artist Pablo Picasso used jagged lines to convey the feeling of sadness.

1) This painting by the Dutch artist Rembrandt is huge – more than 3.5 m (11¼ ft) tall and 4.5 m (14½ ft) wide. It was unusual because it portrayed the civil guards in action, rather than a traditional formal scene – there is even a dog!

4) Japanese artist Katsushika Hokusai's woodblock print is so dramatic, you almost feel seasick! Can you spot Mount Fuji in the background?

5) The self-taught French artist Henri Rousseau painted wild animals in jungle scenes based on visits to the Botanical Gardens in Paris, France.

⑥ In 1470, the Italian artist Paolo Uccello was inspired to paint the mythical story of a hero rescuing a princess from a terrifying monster.

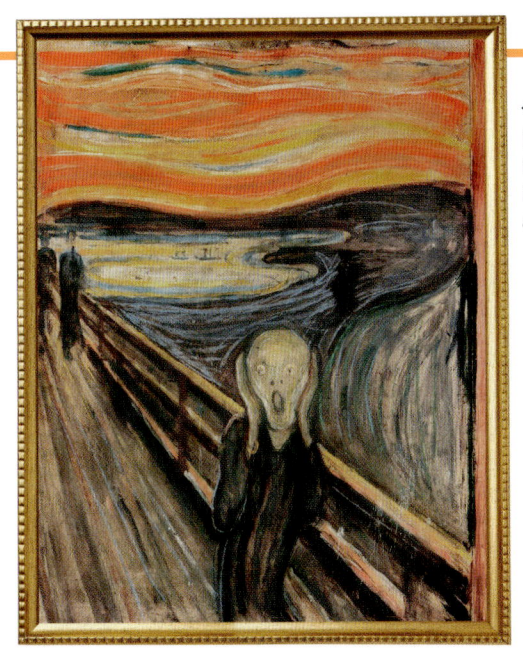

⑦ This painting by the Norwegian artist Edvard Munch may not be realistic in style, but is powerful and haunting.

TEST YOURSELF

STARTER
Tiger in a Tropical Storm
St George and the Dragon
Mona Lisa
The Great Wave off Kanagawa

CHALLENGER
The Starry Night
Green Mountains and White Clouds
Water Lilies
The Scream

GENIUS!
Girl with a Pearl Earring
Weeping Woman
The Star
The Night Watch

⑧ The swirling sky by Dutch artist Vincent van Gogh has a distinctive style, created using thick oil paint with fat brushes, or squeezed straight from the tube.

⑨ Fascinated by the world of ballet, French artist Edgar Degas made hundreds of paintings of dancers in class and on stage.

⑩ This 350-year-old work is painted on silk. Chinese artist, calligrapher, and poet Wu Li's landscape captures the grandness of nature.

⑪ French Impressionist Claude Monet loved these flowers in his garden so much he painted them about 250 times.

⑫ This painting by Dutch artist Johannes Vermeer glows with light, bringing out the detail of his subject.

ANSWERS: 1. The Night Watch 2. Mona Lisa 3. Weeping Woman 4. The Great Wave off Kanagawa 5. Tiger in a Tropical Storm 6. St George and the Dragon 7. The Scream 8. The Starry Night 9. The Star 10. Green Mountains and White Clouds 11. Water Lilies 12. Girl with a Pearl Earring

① This triangular instrument has 47 strings – the shorter the string the higher the note.

② This large percussion instrument makes a deep boom when struck with a soft-headed stick.

③ First developed in the 1500s, this instrument is played by drawing a wooden bow, strung with horsehair, across strings.

Chin rest

④ This brass instrument has three valves, which are pressed down to produce different notes and pitches (whether a sound is high or low).

⑤ This popular woodwind instrument is played by blowing air through a mouthpiece at the top.

⑦ Usually made of metal, this woodwind instrument is held horizontally and played by blowing air over a hole at one end.

⑥ Wooden bars are laid out like a keyboard and struck with a mallet. The hollow tubes below pick up the vibrations and amplify the sound.

⑧ By moving a tube (called a slide), to make the instrument longer or shorter, a player produces different notes and pitches.

Slide

⑨ Also known as a kettle drum, this instrument is played by striking the membrane (skin) with wool-topped sticks.

Pedal can loosen or tighten the skin, producing different pitches

TEST YOURSELF

STARTER	CHALLENGER	GENIUS!
Violin	Cello	Oboe
Flute	Tuba	Bassoon
Saxophone	Trombone	Bass drum
Trumpet	Clarinet	Snare drum
Cymbals	Xylophone	Timpani
Harp		Vibraphone

Playing the classics

In a classical orchestra, there are many kinds of instrument, played in different ways. These instruments are usually grouped in four sections – percussion, brass, woodwind, and string.

Valves are pressed to change notes

Mouthpiece

10 Invented in 1840, this brass woodwind instrument became a popular feature in jazz and swing bands.

Mouthpiece is made of two pieces of wood strapped together

11 This woodwind instrument is about 65 cm (25½ in) long.

12 Usually played sitting down, this large, heavy brass instrument has a bellowing sound.

13 This woodwind instrument is made of a long tube, folded back on itself.

14 Striking these metal plates together makes a crashing sound.

Metal bars

15 A set of wires on the underside of this instrument creates a buzzing sound.

16 A player rests this instrument on the floor on its metal spike, and sits to draw the bow across the strings.

17 The tuned metal bars on top of the instrument are lightly struck to produce a mellow sound.

Hollow tubes produce a trembling quality.

ANSWERS: 1. Harp 2. Bass drum 3. Violin 4. Trumpet 5. Clarinet 6. Xylophone 7. Flute 8. Trombone 9. Timpani 10. Saxophone 11. Oboe 12. Tuba 13. Bassoon 14. Cymbals 15. Snare drum 16. Cello 17. Vibraphone

Making music

Folk music is a form of traditional music created, and passed on, by ordinary people rather than professional composers. Around the world, folk musicians play many different, unusual, and wonderful instruments, some very old in origin. Can you identify these instruments?

1 This West African hand drum has a carved wooden base and a goatskin head.

2 Russian folk music often features this three-stringed instrument with a triangular body.

3 This instrument has a round body covered with a skin, which vibrates when the strings are plucked.

4 The goat-legged Greek god of shepherds gave his name to these pipes.

5 Pipers make music by blowing air into the bag with a blowpipe and squeezing it out through a set of pipes.
- Blowpipe

6 In India and other parts of South Asia, musicians beat both ends of this drum.
- Barrel-like shape

7 This instrument is nicknamed a squeezebox because bellows are pulled and squeezed to make air vibrate the metal strips inside.
- Keys alter the sound.
- Bellows

8 This cheap tin whistle, popular in Ireland and Scotland, is named after a British coin.

9 Popular in Korea, this bamboo flute makes a buzzing sound when played.

10 Australian aborigines make this pipe from a eucalyptus branch hollowed out by termites.

ANSWERS: 1. Djembe 2. Balalaika 3. Banjo 4. Panpipes 5. Bagpipes 6. Dhol 7. Accordion 8. Penny whistle 9. Daegeum 10. Didgeridoo 11. Steelpan 12. Harmonica 13. Ocarina 14. Ukulele 15. Erhu 16. Maracas 17. Tanpura 18. Hurdy-gurdy

173

Different-shaped dents make different notes.

11 Though this Caribbean instrument looks like a drum, it can also be used to play melodies.

Mouthpiece

12 Invented in Europe in the early 19th century, this instrument is played by blowing and sucking air.

The pegs are turned to tune the strings.

13 For thousands of years, people have played instruments like this, blowing through the mouthpiece and covering the holes to create different sounds.

A horse-hair bow is drawn over the strings.

15 This Chinese two-stringed instrument has a sound box at the bottom, which is covered with python skin.

Carved decoration

14 The name of this small stringed instrument, from Hawaii, means "jumping flea".

Sound box

16 These Latin American rattles are often made from dried gourds or wood, filled with beans or pebbles.

Three strings are made from steel, and the fourth one is made from brass.

17 Indian folk and classical musicians pluck the strings of this long-necked instrument.

Panel protects wheel

18 This European instrument is played by turning a handle, which makes a wheel rub against strings, creating music!

Handle

This instrument can sometimes be up to 3 m (10 ft) long.

TEST YOURSELF

STARTER
- Accordion
- Bagpipes
- Didgeridoo
- Harmonica
- Penny whistle
- Maracas

CHALLENGER
- **Balalaika**
- **Ukulele**
- **Hurdy-gurdy**
- **Panpipes**
- **Steelpan**
- **Banjo**

GENIUS!
- **Daegeum**
- **Dhol**
- **Djembe**
- **Erhu**
- **Ocarina**
- **Tanpura**

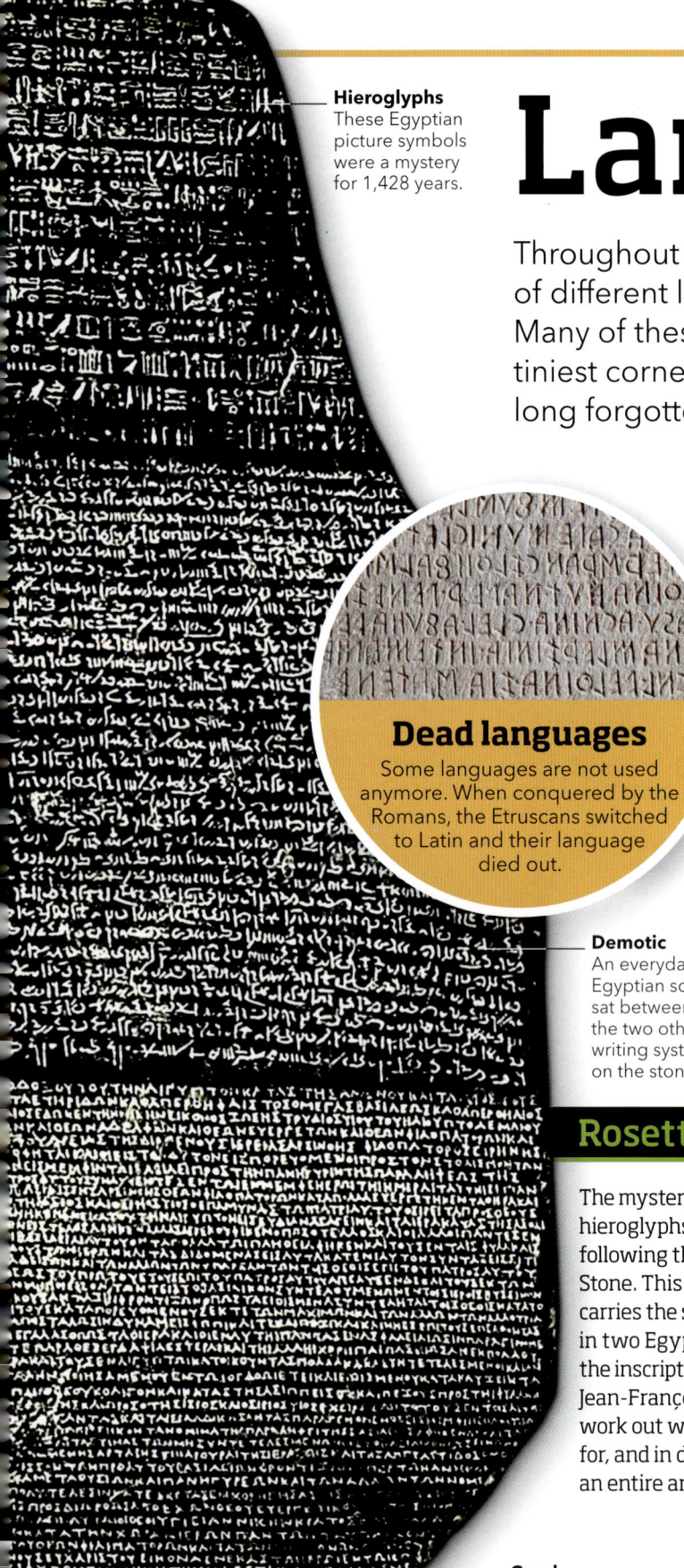

Hieroglyphs
These Egyptian picture symbols were a mystery for 1,428 years.

Languages

Throughout history, humans have used a vast variety of different languages to communicate with each other. Many of these live on today, even if only spoken in the tiniest corners of the world. However, others have been long forgotten and are now a mystery to us.

Words and pictures

Hieroglyphs, perhaps the world's first writing system was invented around 3,300 BCE in Egypt. The Egyptians used small beautiful picture signs to represent sounds, words, and ideas.

Symbols
A loaf of bread is used as the sign for the "t" sound.

Dead languages
Some languages are not used anymore. When conquered by the Romans, the Etruscans switched to Latin and their language died out.

Demotic
An everyday Egyptian script sat between the two other writing systems on the stone.

Rosetta stone

The mystery of how to read Egyptian hieroglyphs was revealed in 1822, following the discovery of the Rosetta Stone. This 112 cm ($3^{7}/_{10}$ ft) tall tablet carries the same text in Greek as well as in two Egyptian scripts. By comparing the inscriptions, a French scholar called Jean-François Champollion was able to work out what the hieroglyphs stood for, and in doing so gave us access to an entire ancient civilisation.

Greek
The lowest level of the slab contained Greek, a language already known to historians.

In numbers

2,473
The number of languages classed at risk of dying out by UNESCO. This is around 43 per cent of all the languages in existence.

16
The number of official languages of Zimbabwe – the most of any country.

12
The number of letters in the Rotokas alphabet. Spoken only on the island of Bougainville, Papua New Guinea, it has the smallest alphabet ever!

Sign language

Mostly used by people with a hearing impairment, sign languages use hand shapes and body movements to communicate, rather than words. There are many different forms – below is the sign for "friend" used in three different countries.

The hands twist as the fingers hook first one side, then the other.

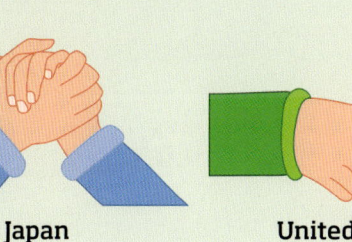

Japan | United Kingdom | USA

I don't believe it

It is thought that more than 200 of today's languages are spoken by fewer than 10 people.

Face with cold sweat
This emoticon can be used to mean stress or hard work.

Say it in pictures

People are again using pictures in communication, to get across their emotions. Emoticons are typed on a keyboard, for example :) is a smiling face, whilst emojis (above) are actual images that can be inserted into a message.

Mandarin
Around 909 million people speak the world's most popular first language.

4,445 million people speak other first languages.

World languages

Although there are 7,097 languages spoken today, most of the world uses only a small number of them. Mandarin is the most popular first language, but if you count how many people speak additional languages (called second languages), then English would be the most widely spoken.

Chinese	Spanish	English	Arabic	Hindi	Bengali	Portuguese	Russian	Japanese	Punjabi
12%	6%	5%	4.1%	3.4%	3.2%	2.9%	2%	1.7%	1.2%

Fictional languages

Some languages were invented just for characters in films and books.

Klingon: In the *Star Trek* films, the alien Klingons have their own language. They greet with "nuqneH!" meaning "what do you want?"

Na'vi: Na'vi is another invented language, spoken by the aliens in the 2009 film *Avatar*. It contains more than 2,200 words.

Lapine: The rabbits in Richard Adams' novel *Watership Down* speak English mixed with a rabbit language, called Lapine.

Quenya: British author J.R.R. Tolkien created many languages for the elves in *The Lord of the Rings*. Only Quenya is used in the films.

CULTURE VULTURE

Greetings!

There are more than 7,000 ways of greeting someone – that's the number of languages spoken around the world today. Some languages are spoken by millions, while many people speak more than one language.

aloha — a-lo-ha

ciao — chow

hola — oh-lah

olá — oh-lah

مرحبا — mar-ha-ban

hello — heh-low

bonjour — bohn-zhoor

नमस्ते — nuh-muh-stay

สวัสดี — sa-was-dee

merhaba — mer-ha-ba

① The world's second most spoken language is used by more than 400 million people in 21 countries.

② People on the Pacific Ocean islands use this greeting, which means "love and kindness".

③ In a Southern European country, friends use this word to say hello and goodbye.

④ This language was first used by people living on a European island and now it is one of the most widely spoken languages in the world.

⑤ This western European language is also spoken in parts of South America, Africa, and East Asia.

⑥ The religious text of Islam, the Qur'an, is written in this language. This greeting means "welcome".

⑦ This western European language is spoken by people in five continents. People say "good day" when they meet.

⑧ People in Southeast Asia often fold their hands and bow when using this greeting. It means "I bow to you".

⑨ This greeting is in a Southeast Asian language, used in the country that sits between Myanmar and Cambodia.

⑩ This greeting is used in a nation bordered by eight countries, including Greece and Iran.

This language is written from right to left.

This language is written in the Devanagari script.

The African grey parrot can mimic human speech and can be taught to greet people.

ANSWERS: 1. Spanish 2. Hawaiian 3. Italian 4. English 5. Portuguese 6. Arabic 7. French 8. Hindi 9. Thai 10. Turkish 11. Greek 12. Polish 13. Russian 14. Mandarin 15. German 16. Korean 17. Japanese 18. Latin 19. Swedish

Χαίρετε
kee-air-ai-tay

11 Meaning "be glad", this language used in a Mediterranean country, has a long history – at least 3,400 years.

cześć!
chesh-ch

12 This eastern European greeting, meaning "honour", was originally used to show respect.

Goodbye

здравствуйте
zdras-tvu-tyeh

13 This language is spoken in the biggest country in the world, stretching from Eastern Europe across Asia.

This writing system has 50,000 different characters.

您好
nee-how

14 A billion East Asians use this word to greet each other in the world's most spoken language.

여보세요
ann-yeong

16 The inhabitants of an East Asian peninsula, divided into two countries, greet each other in this language.

15 The greeting is used by people living in a large European country, which lies between France and Poland.

hallo
ha-low

salve
sal-way

18 The language of ancient Rome may not be spoken today, but is still used for scientific terms.

こんにちは
kon-ni-chi-wa

17 An East Asian island-nation uses this greeting. It means "today", and is short for "How are you today?"

One of three different scripts used to write this language

hallå
ha-low-ah

19 This is one of the languages of Scandinavia, and is related to English, Dutch, and German.

TEST YOURSELF

STARTER	CHALLENGER	GENIUS!
Hawaiian	Russian	Thai
Italian	German	Turkish
Arabic	Hindi	Swedish
Portuguese	Japanese	Greek
French	Polish	Latin
English	Spanish	Korean
	Mandarin	

Sports

Games and sports have been played since ancient times to settle disputes, encourage fitness, and crown champions. Today, competitions are held all around the world, turning individual players into celebrated heroes and uniting nations as their teams compete for the top trophies on a global stage.

A flaming torch is carried into the Olympic stadium. It lights the Olympic flame, which will burn until the closing ceremony.

Ancient games

The Olympic Games started in ancient Greece in 776 BCE. The competition is still held today, every four years. The first winners received a crown of olive leaves, but gold medals have been awarded since 1904.

Top of their game

Jamaican sprinter Usain Bolt is the world's fastest man, holding records for the 100 metres and 200 metres.

American tennis ace, Serena Williams, is the world's most successful current player, with 23 Grand Slam singles titles to her name.

South Korea's Yuna Kim was the first figure skater to win Olympic, World, Four Continents, and Grand Prix Final gold.

American swimmer Michael Phelps, with 28 medals, is the most successful Olympian of all time.

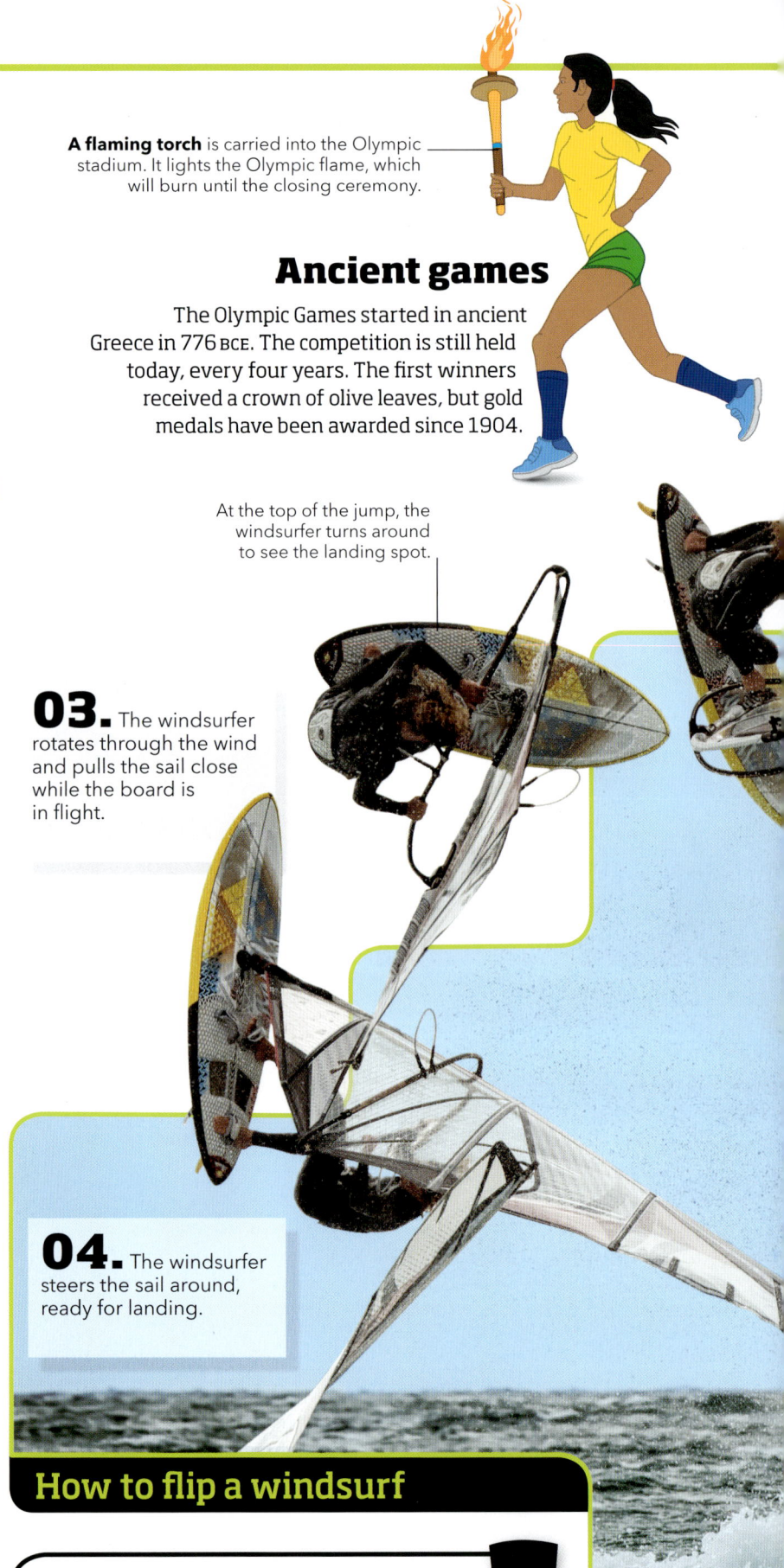

At the top of the jump, the windsurfer turns around to see the landing spot.

03. The windsurfer rotates through the wind and pulls the sail close while the board is in flight.

04. The windsurfer steers the sail around, ready for landing.

How to flip a windsurf

I don't believe it

Golf is the only sport that has been played on the Moon. In 1971, Alan Shepard hit a golf ball from the surface of the Moon into space.

The new sport

Gamers compete in online tournaments of sports video games – called eSports. These competitions are so popular, crowds of spectators now gather to watch the show on screen in high-definition, very similar to watching a live sporting event.

In numbers

300 km/h
(185 mph) is the speed of the moving ball in a game of pelota – the fastest moving ball game.

170 km/h
(105 mph) The speed at which ice hockey pucks travel. The pucks are frozen before the game so they can travel faster and smoother.

92
The number of hat-tricks (three goals) Brazilian striker Pelé scored during his football career.

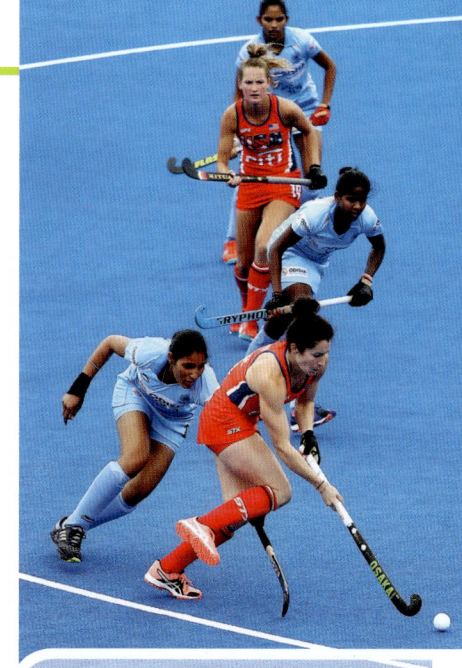

01. Professional windsurfers start this gravity-defying move by riding a wave to its highest point.

02. The wind catches the sail and lifts the board clean out of the water and high into the air.

Top windsurfers reach speeds of 96 km/h (60 mph).

Oldest sport

Wrestling is the world's oldest sport. Here, two ancient Greek wrestlers compete, in a carving dating from around 510 BCE.

Fast facts

- Despite being played since the 19th century, women's field hockey only became an Olympic sport in 1980 at the Moscow Games.

- In 1939, the longest cricket match took place between England and South Africa. It lasted 43 hours over 12 days – and ended in a tie!

- The average player in the National Basketball Association (NBA) stands 2 m (6 ft 7 in) tall – which helps with shooting hoops!

Top sports

The beautiful game, football, tops the list of the most-watched sports in the world. Four of the top five are team sports, in which spectators follow a chosen team or their national side.

Sport	Viewers
Volleyball	0.9 billion
Tennis	1 billion
Field Hockey	2 billion
Cricket	2.5 billion
Football (Soccer)	4 billion

180 | CULTURE VULTURE

On the ball

For more than 3,500 years, people all over the world have been throwing, kicking, bashing, and rolling balls for fun – can you identify these ones? Look out for two shuttlecocks too, for sports that have fun with feathers!

1 Played on a four-walled court, two to four players take turns to hit this small, rubber ball using a racket.

When holding the ball, a player can only move one foot before having to pass.

This ball can travel at speeds of more than 160 km/h (100 mph).

2 Players aim to shoot this ball through a netted hoop to score a goal.

3 Players take turns to hit this ball over a net on a table court, using small wooden bats.

4 A player kicks this into the air and then has to keep on kicking to prevent it from touching the ground.

The cork base is normally covered in thin leather.

5 Feathers help this cork fly over a net at high speed – the fastest recorded at a competitive match being 332 km/h (206 mph).

Usually made of 16 feathers, the best coming from a goose's left wing

6 Players use a hooked stick to dribble this ball across a pitch – and to try to hit it into the other team's net!

7 An oval-shaped ball used to score tries, drop-goals, or penalties.

8 Roll this ball to knock down as many pins as possible.

9 Players use different clubs to hit this ball into a hole in as few shots as possible.

10 A team of 11 players tries to kick or head this ball into an opponent's net.

The earliest balls were made of a pig's bladder.

11 Players use rackets to hit this small, bouncy ball across a rectangular-shaped court over a 1.07 m- (3½ ft-) high net.

12 Watch 18 players, playing on an oval pitch, try to kick this ball through the opponent's goal posts.

13 A team of five tries to shoot or dunk this ball into the opposing team's basket.

A player can only "handball" or kick this oval ball, they can't throw it!

14 A player will hit this leather ball and try to score runs. The ball is very hard, with insides made of cork, rubber, and tightly wound string.

15 Pitchers throw this ball at a batter and try to get them out, while the batter tries to hit it as far as they can.

Traditionally, this leather-covered ball is red with white seams.

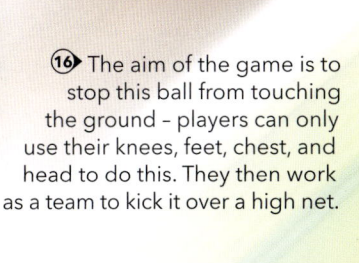

16 The aim of the game is to stop this ball from touching the ground – players can only use their knees, feet, chest, and head to do this. They then work as a team to kick it over a high net.

17 A team of 11 players scores points by combining to manoeuvre this ball into an opponent's end zone.

18 A player uses a wooden cue (which looks like a long pole) to knock coloured balls like this one into pockets on a table.

TEST YOURSELF

STARTER
- American football
- Baseball
- Basketball
- Cricket ball
- Football
- Tennis ball

CHALLENGER
- Netball
- Golf ball
- Pool ball
- Rugby ball
- Squash ball
- Table tennis ball

GENIUS!
- Australian rules football
- Hockey ball
- Jianzi shuttlecock
- Sepak takraw ball
- Bowling ball
- Shuttlecock

ANSWERS: 1. Squash ball 2. Netball 3. Table tennis ball 4. Jianzi shuttlecock 5. Shuttlecock 6. Hockey ball 7. Rugby ball 8. Bowling ball 9. Golf ball 10. Football 11. Tennis ball 12. Australian Rules football 13. Basketball 14. Cricket ball 15. Baseball 16. Sepak takraw ball 17. American football 18. Pool ball

Game on!

Modern sports stars, team players, and amateur enthusiasts stay ahead of the game by using the latest equipment. Bats, sticks, rackets, and mallets are now stronger and lighter than ever before, ensuring hot shots blast the balls further and faster. Let the games begin!

1 This curved stick is used to get the ball in the net, in an outdoor team sport.

2 Two competing players use this long stick to pot coloured balls into pockets on a cloth-covered table.

3 Shuttlecocks are smashed over a high net using this lightweight stringed racket.

Usually around 147 cm (57⅜ in) long.

Can also be made of aluminium, but the wooden versions are used by professional players.

4 Players strive to smash the ball out of the ballpark to hit a home run in this popular team game.

5 This long-handled netted stick is used to throw, carry, and catch balls in a team sport that was first played by Native Americans.

The net can be made of leather, nylon, or linen.

6 This piece of kit racks up fours and sixes in a British bat-and-ball game.

Made from the wood of willow trees, this equipment cannot measure more than 96 cm (38 in) long.

Frames used to be wooden, but now are mostly made of carbon.

7 This racket is used to hit a rubber ball in a four-walled indoor court.

8 Both teams are skating on thin ice as they use this stick to smash the puck into the opponent's net.

ANSWERS: 1. Hockey stick 2. Snooker cue 3. Badminton racket 4. Baseball bat 5. Lacrosse stick 6. Cricket bat 7. Squash racket 8. Ice hockey stick Golf club 10. Polo stick 11. Rounders bat 12. Croquet mallet 13. Basque pelota bat 14. Table tennis racket 15. Tennis racket

183

11 Since King Henry VIII's reign, this English sport has involved players striking balls long distances with a wooden bat and sprinting past four bases to win points.

12 This hammer-like equipment is used for a traditional lawn game in which players navigate balls through a series of hoops.

This kit can also be used to hit the opponent's balls off the course.

10 Teams on horseback compete to drive wooden balls into rival goals using this mallet.

9 Performances are best below par (number of hits) in this game where tee shots, pitches, and putts lead to birdies and bogeys.

In just one round, a player could use up to 14 different versions of this equipment.

13 This unusual curved paddle evolved in parts of France and Spain for use in the world's fastest ball game.

Paddle made of plaited willow twigs.

14 Players do battle across a table using these rackets to hit small balls to and fro over a low net.

15 Aces serve and strike yellow balls across courts using large carbon-fibre rackets.

TEST YOURSELF

STARTER
- Golf club
- Hockey stick
- Cricket bat
- Baseball bat
- Tennis racket

CHALLENGER
- Snooker cue
- Table tennis racket
- Lacrosse stick
- Badminton racket
- Squash racket

GENIUS!
- Croquet mallet
- Rounders bat
- Ice hockey stick
- Polo stick
- Basque pelota bat

184 CULTURE VULTURE

Sports store

It's safety first in modern sports where injuries can end careers. The correct apparel and the right equipment are essential to challenge at a competitive level or tackle tough terrain on land, snow, or water. Here is your chance to hit a home run by naming the items in this superstore of sports stuff.

① Competitors try to throw this object the greatest distance in a track and field event.

Comes in various weights and materials

② Since ancient Greece, athletes have attempted to leap over high bars by using this long apparatus to push off the ground.

Earlier made of wood, the apparatus is now usually made of fibreglass.

③ Players compete to propel this heavy ball as far as possible, from shoulder height.

The ball is usually made of iron or brass.

④ Hard headgear is needed to prevent injuries from pucks and sticks in a fast-paced team game on ice.

⑤ This oversized leather mitt is used to catch and throw the ball safely in a popular American sport.

Webbing between the thumb and forefinger helps to trap the ball.

⑥ Whether off-road or on-track, athletes ride safely with this must-have protective headgear.

⑦ Snow and ice can be treacherous, so these spiked metal frames give a good grip on slippery surfaces.

Sturdy metal frames are attached to walking boots.

Front spikes help during vertical climbs.

⑧ Athletes throw this long spear-shaped apparatus over long distances to determine the winner.

⑨ This pair of paddles makes a splash in water to propel a boat forwards at speed.

ANSWERS: 1. Discus 2. Pole vault 3. Shot put 4. Ice hockey helmet 5. Baseball glove 6. Cycling helmet 7. Crampons 8. Javelin 9. Rowing oars 10. Basketball boots 11. Ski poles 12. Snowboard 13. Curling stone 14. Football boots 15. Hammer 16. Boxing gloves 17. American football helmet 18. Fencing foil

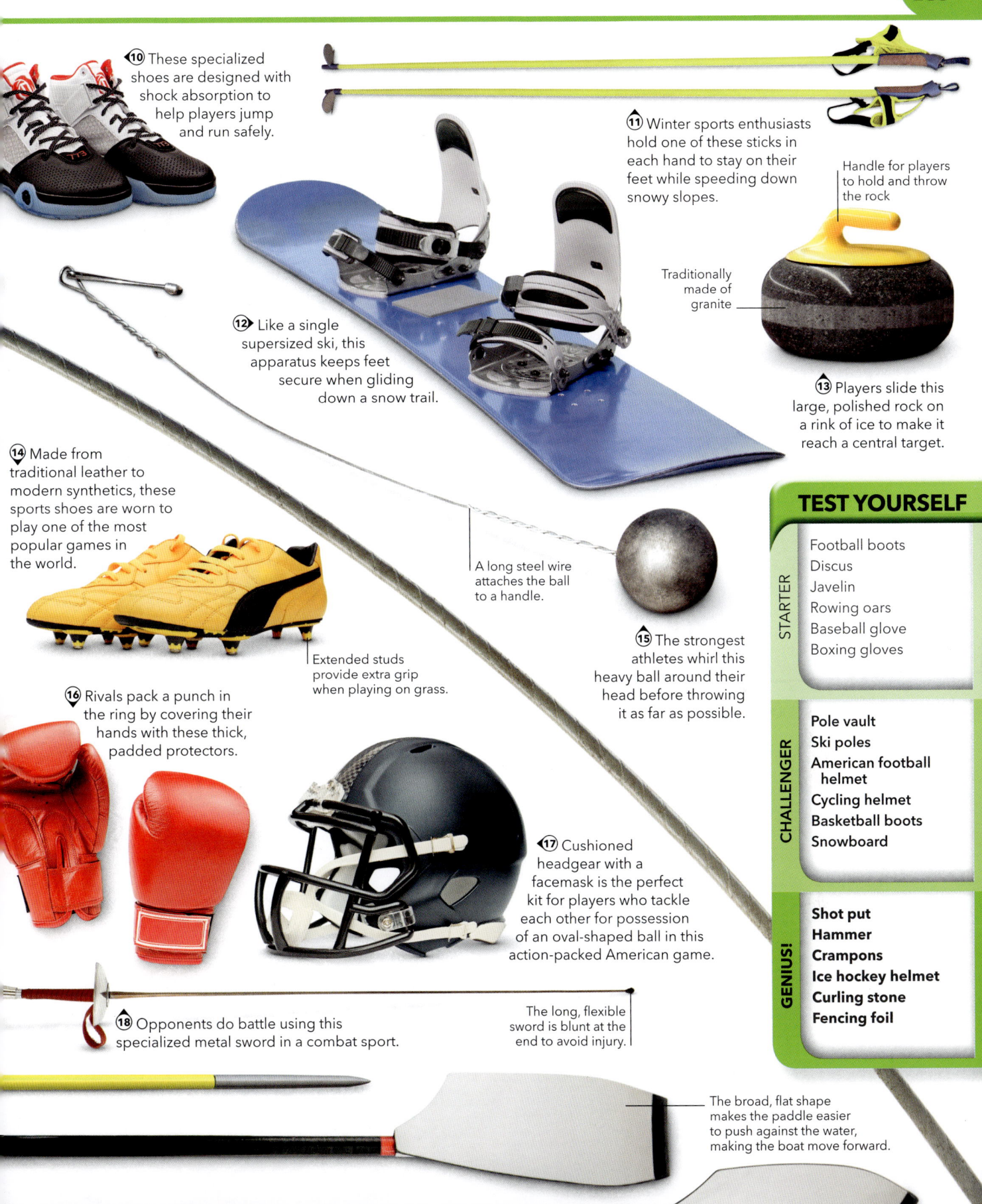

10 These specialized shoes are designed with shock absorption to help players jump and run safely.

11 Winter sports enthusiasts hold one of these sticks in each hand to stay on their feet while speeding down snowy slopes.

Handle for players to hold and throw the rock

Traditionally made of granite

12 Like a single supersized ski, this apparatus keeps feet secure when gliding down a snow trail.

13 Players slide this large, polished rock on a rink of ice to make it reach a central target.

14 Made from traditional leather to modern synthetics, these sports shoes are worn to play one of the most popular games in the world.

A long steel wire attaches the ball to a handle.

Extended studs provide extra grip when playing on grass.

15 The strongest athletes whirl this heavy ball around their head before throwing it as far as possible.

16 Rivals pack a punch in the ring by covering their hands with these thick, padded protectors.

17 Cushioned headgear with a facemask is the perfect kit for players who tackle each other for possession of an oval-shaped ball in this action-packed American game.

18 Opponents do battle using this specialized metal sword in a combat sport.

The long, flexible sword is blunt at the end to avoid injury.

The broad, flat shape makes the paddle easier to push against the water, making the boat move forward.

TEST YOURSELF

STARTER
- Football boots
- Discus
- Javelin
- Rowing oars
- Baseball glove
- Boxing gloves

CHALLENGER
- Pole vault
- Ski poles
- American football helmet
- Cycling helmet
- Basketball boots
- Snowboard

GENIUS!
- Shot put
- Hammer
- Crampons
- Ice hockey helmet
- Curling stone
- Fencing foil

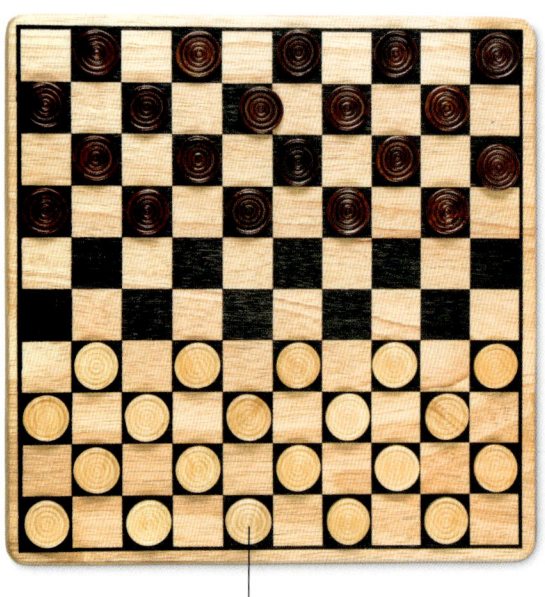

CULTURE VULTURE

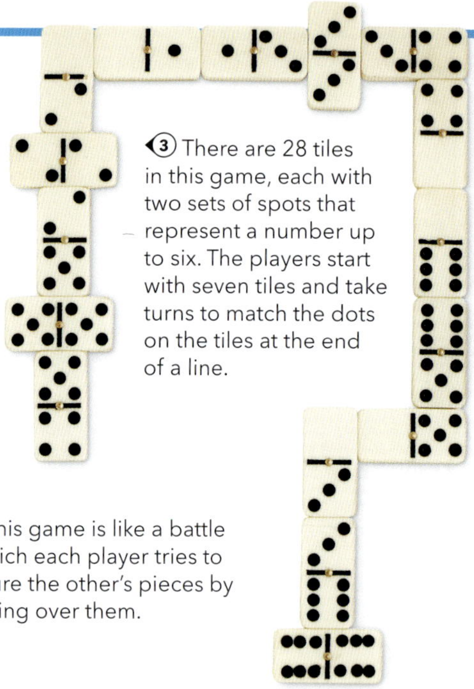

③ There are 28 tiles in this game, each with two sets of spots that represent a number up to six. The players start with seven tiles and take turns to match the dots on the tiles at the end of a line.

② This game is like a battle in which each player tries to capture the other's pieces by jumping over them.

The pieces can only move diagonally.

① Pegs are placed on a board to keep the score in this card game. Players score points by laying down cards in turn.

This card is worth 10 points.

Your turn!

For thousands of years, people all over the world have played games for fun. In many of them, players move pieces around a board, while others are played with cards, dice, tiles, glass balls, or sticks. Perhaps you have played some of them?

④ Players bounce the ball and while it is still in the air, they have to pick up a set number of pieces and catch the ball – in one hand.

Ancient Romans used sheep's knucklebones for the pieces.

⑤ This Chinese game is usually played with a set of 144 tiles, decorated with dots and symbols.

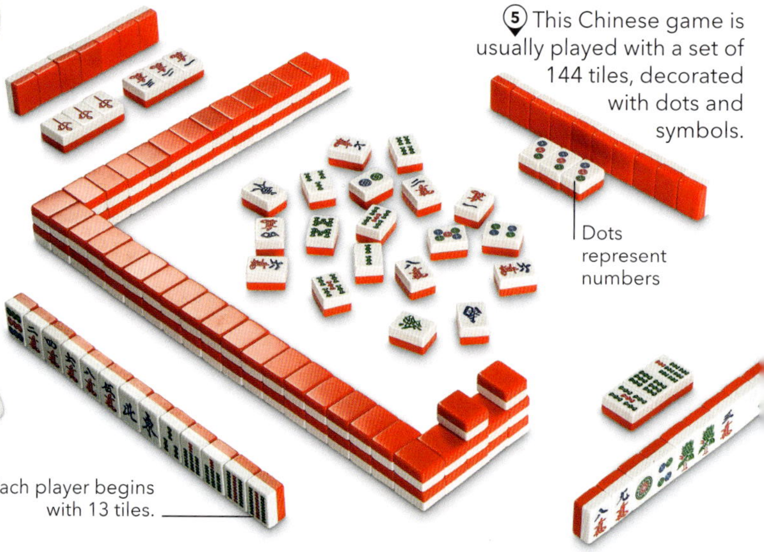

Dots represent numbers

Each player begins with 13 tiles.

ANSWERS: 1. Cribbage 2. Draughts 3. Dominoes 4. Jacks 5. Mahjong 6. Backgammon 7. Spillikins 8. Snakes and Ladders 9. Go 10. Chess 11. Marbles 12. Mancala

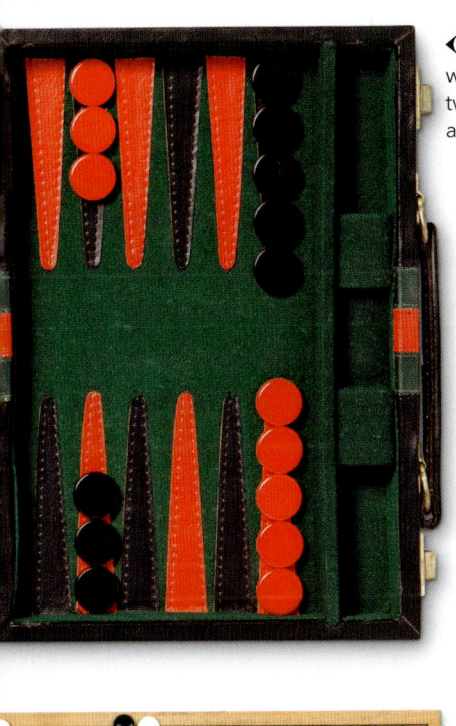

6 One of the oldest board games in the world, this is played by two players. They roll two dice to move the pieces along the board and the first player to clear all their pieces wins.

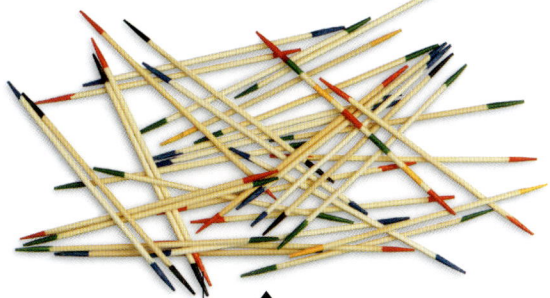

8 Players race their pieces around a board to get to the finish point first. Some squares can help the player to skip rows and climb up the board, while other squares can send them sliding back down.

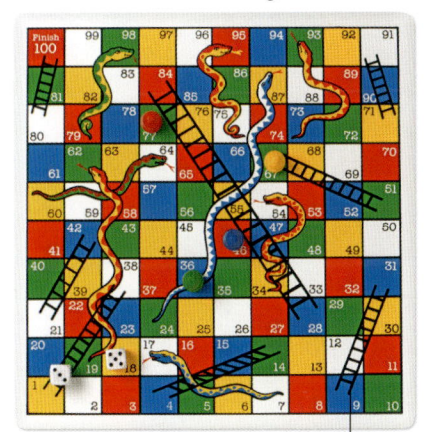

Different coloured sticks are worth different points.

7 Sticks are tossed in a pile and players try to pull them out – one by one – without moving the pile.

The ladder helps the players take shortcuts up the board.

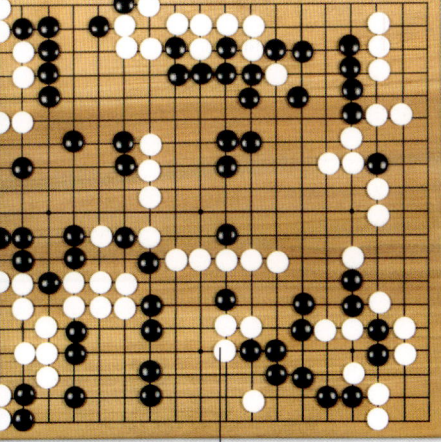

The king is checkmated when no other pieces can save the king from capture.

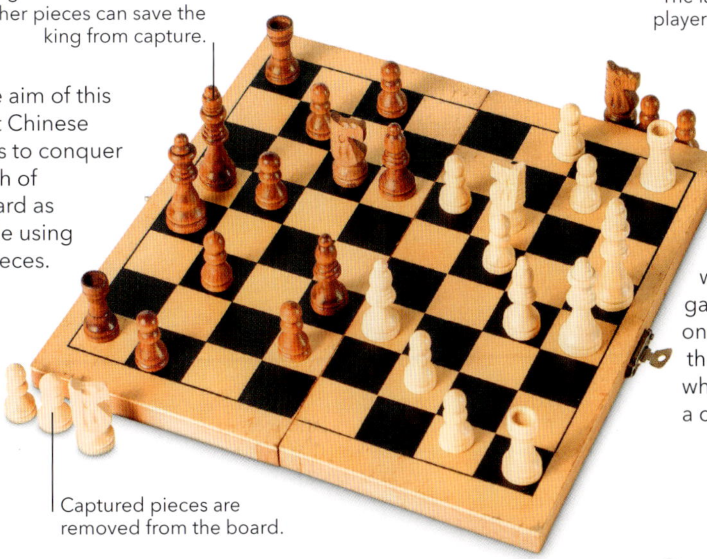

9 The aim of this ancient Chinese game is to conquer as much of the board as possible using your pieces.

10 This battle game has six different pieces each with its own way of moving. The game continues until one player captures the other's king – which is called a checkmate.

Pieces, placed where lines cross, are used to build territories or surround enemy pieces.

Captured pieces are removed from the board.

12 In this ancient African game, players move stones, seeds, nuts, or shells along pits on the board and try to collect the largest pile.

11 Many different games can be played with these colourful glass balls, most involving rolling them across the floor.

The board has twelve hollows or pits.

Little balls have been used in games for thousands of years.

TEST YOURSELF

STARTER	CHALLENGER	GENIUS!
Chess	Draughts	Go
Marbles	Backgammon	Mahjong
Dominoes	Cribbage	Spillikins
Snakes and Ladders	Jacks	Mancala

Index

A

aircraft 30-31, 36-37
  carrier 38-39
  see also transport
amphibians 78-81
  eyes 94-95
  see also reptiles
ancient civilizations 144-45
  games 178-79
  gods see gods
  languages 174
  lost cities 146-47
  mythical creatures 150-51
animals
  behaviour 88-89
  dinosaurs see dinosaurs
  eyes 94-95
  mammals 50-51
  polar bear in the Tower of London 153
  prehistoric creatures 48-49
  reptiles see reptiles
  tracks 90-91
  and weather 133
  see also birds; reptiles
armour
  helmets 158-59
  swords and shields 156-57
  see also warfare
art and artists 166-67
  great masters 164-65, 168-69

B

berries 100-01
  see also plants
birds 66-67
  dino birds 43
  eggs 92-93
  eyes 94-95
  and feathers 67, 68-69
  of prey 70-71
  tracks 90-91
  see also animals
board games 186-87
boats 30-31, 38-39
  see also oceans and seas; transport
bones 20-23
  see also human body
buildings 119, 120-21
  castles and forts 152-55
  see also cities
butterflies and moths 40-41, 60-61

C

capital cities 124-25
  see also cities; countries
card games 186-87
cars 30-33
  see also transport
castles 152-55
  polar bear in the Tower of London 153
  see also buildings; kings and queens
cats, big 52-53
chemical elements 16-19
cities 118-19
  capital 124-25
  lost 146-47
  skylines 122-23
  see also buildings
clouds 134-35
  see also weather
countries 116-17
  capital cities 122-23
  flags 6-7, 128-31
crocodiles 72-75
  eyes 94-95

D

deserts 104-05, 106
  see also Earth

dinosaurs 42-43
    carnivores 44-45
    eggs 92-93
    plant-eating 46-47
    see also prehistoric creatures

E

Earth 106-07
    cities *see* cities
    countries 116-17
    deserts 104-05, 106
    mountains 112-13
    oceans 108-09
    rivers 110-11
    satellite views 126-27
    weather *see* weather
    wonders of the world 114-15
    see also planets
eggs 92-93
elements 16-19
    see also rocks and minerals
exercise *see* sports
eyes 94-95

F

fish 82-83
    behaviour 89
    eggs 92-93
    eyes 83, 94-95
    freshwater 84-85
    invertebrates 58-59, 62-63
    saltwater 86-87
    shellfish 58-59, 62-63
    see also mammals, aquatic; oceans and seas; rivers
fitness *see* sports
flags 6-7, 128-31
flowers 98-99
    see also plants
forts 152-55
    see also buildings
fossils 42-43
    see also rocks and minerals
fruit 100-01
    see also plants

G

galaxies 10-11
    see also space
games
    board games 186-87
    sports *see* sports
gemstones 140-41
    see also rocks and minerals
gods
    mythical creatures 150-51
    Roman 148-49
    see also ancient civilizations
government 160-61
    political leaders 162-63
    revolutionaries 161, 162-63

H

hello, saying 176-77
    see also languages
helmets 158-59
    see also armour
human body 20-21
    bones 20-23
    eyes 94-95
    magnified 24-25

I

insects 40-41, 58-61
    behaviour 88-89
    eggs 92-93
    eyes 94-95
invertebrates 58-63

K

kings and queens 160-61
    see also castles

L

languages 174-75
    saying hello 176-77
lizards 72-75
    see also reptiles
lost cities 146-47

musical instruments 172-73
orchestral 170-71
mythical creatures 150-51
see also ancient civilizations

N

nuts 100-01
see also plants

O

oceans and seas 108-09
see also Earth
orchestral instruments 170-71
see also musical instruments

P

paintings see art and artists
palaces see castles
planes see aircraft
planets 12-13
Earth see Earth
see also space
plants 96-97
flowers 98-99
fruit 100-01
trees 97
vegetables 102-03
politics see government
precious gemstones 140-41
see also rocks and minerals

prehistoric creatures 48-49
see also dinosaurs
primates 54-55

R

rail transport 30, 34-35
see also transport
reptiles 72-75
eggs 92-93
eyes 94-95
snakes see snakes
see also amphibians; animals
rivers 110-11
satellite views 126-27
wonders of the world 114-15
see also Earth
road transport 30-33
see also transport
rocks and minerals 136-39
fossils 42-43
precious gemstones 140-41
see also elements
Roman gods 148-49
see also ancient civilizations

S

satellites 126-27
see also space
sea creatures 62-63
aquatic mammals 50-51, 56-57
fish see fish
seas and oceans 108-09
see also Earth
shapes 28-29
see also maths
ships 30-31, 38-39
see also oceans and seas; transport

M

mammals 50-51
aquatic 50-51, 56-57
see also animals; fish
maths 26-27
see also shapes
meteorites 138-39
see also rocks and minerals; space
monkeys 54-55
motor vehicles 30-33
see also transport
mountains 112-13
satellite views 126-27
wonders of the world 114-15
see also Earth

skeleton 20-23
   see also human body
snakes 76-77
   behaviour 89
   eggs 92-93
   eyes 94-95
   tracks 90-91
solar system 10-13
   see also space
space 10-11
   galaxies 10-11
   golf on the Moon 178
   meteorites 138-39
   moons 12-13
   planets *see* planets
   satellites 126-27
   solar system 10-13
   spacecraft 14-15
spiders 64-65, 89
sports 178-79
   balls 180-81
   equipment 182-85
   golf on the Moon 178
storms *see* weather
swords 156-57
   see also armour; warfare

T

tortoise 72-75
   eggs 92-93
trains 30, 34-35
transport 30-31
   boats 30-31, 38-39
   cars 30-33
   rail 30, 34-35
trees 97
   see also plants

V

vegetables 102-03
   see also plants

W

warfare
   armour *see* armour
   and castles 152-53
   weapons 156-57
   world leaders 160-63
weapons 156-57
   see also warfare
weather 132-33
   clouds 134-35
   see also Earth
whales 56-57
wonders of the world 114-15
   see also Earth
world leaders 160-63

Answers

Now that you've had a go at the chapter picture quizzes, look below to see if you got the answers right.

CHAPTER 1:
SCIENCE GEEK
You can find the constellation of Orion the hunter by looking for the three stars that make up his belt.

CHAPTER 2:
NATURE KNOW-IT-ALL
Did you spot the imperial moth? Its leaf-like colour and markings help it keep camouflaged within the leaves.

CHAPTER 3:
GEOGRAPHY GENIUS
If you look at this picture closely, you can see five camels trotting through the Sahara desert.

CHAPTER 4:
HISTORY BUFF
There are two routes to the centre of the maze – one in blue and one in yellow.

CHAPTER 5:
CULTURE VULTURE
The artist has hidden a skull in this painting. If you look closely from the right-hand side of the picture, the skull becomes clear.

ACKNOWLEDGMENTS

Acknowledgments

The publisher would like to thank the following people for their help with making the book:
Hazel Beynon for proofreading; Margaret McCormack for indexing; Charvi Arora, Sarah Edwards, Chris Hawkes, Sarah MacLeod, Anita Kakar, Aadithyan Mohan, and Fleur Star for editorial assistance; David Ball, Kit Lane, Shahid Mahmood, Stefan Podhorodecki, Joe Scott, Revati Anand, and Kanupriya Lal for design assistance; Simon Mumford for cartographic assistance; Martin Sanders for illustrations; Mrinmoy Mazumdar for hi-res assistance; and Chris Barker, Alice Bowden, and Kristina Routh for fact-checking.

Picture Credits
The publisher would like to thank the following for their kind permission to reproduce their photographs:

(Key: a-above; b-below/bottom; c-centre; f-far; l-left; r-right; t-top)

123RF.com: Valentyna Chukhlyebova 22-23, costasz 173clb, Jozsef Demeter 95br, dique 128bc, Davor Dopar 182cr, Oleg Elagin 111cra, fxegs / F. Javier Espuny 174l, gresei 170tr, jejim 111tc, kajornyot 69tl, Malgorzata Kistryn 149cb, Turgay Koca 181tr, long10000 / Liu Feng 120cr, Krisztian Miklosy 5tc, 120tr, Luciano Mortula 125tr, picsfive 168cr (Frame), 168br (Frame), 169tc (Frame), 169cl (Frame), Song Qiuju 58fbr, 189bl, Ricky Soni Creations 103cb, Natalia Romanova 10-11, jakkapan sapmuangphan 181cb, solarseven 107cl, poramet thathong 58clb, Mark Turner 42fbl, 46bl, vvoennyy 168tr (Frame), 168cl (Frame), 168bl (Frame), 169cla (Frame), 169cb (Frame), 169bl (Frame), 169bc (Frame), 169br (Frame), Maria Wachala 121cr, Sara Winter 114clb, Feng Yu 114-115 (Thumb tacks), Тимур Конев 26clb, 刘嘉跃 84ca (Silver arowana); **akg-images:** Pictures From History 163tc; **Alamy Stock Photo:** Aerial Archives 119fbl, Allstar Picture Library 178clb (Serena Williams), Aaron Amat 167cr, 167fcra, 167fcr (Turquoise brush stroke), 167fcrb, 167fbr, Amazon-Images 55tl, Antiquarian Images 169cl, ARCTIC IMAGES 133br, Art Reserve 149ca, Aurora Photos 112bl, Auscape International Pty Ltd 67crb, Avpics 36cla, B.O'Kane 149bl, Quentin Bargate 155clb, Guy Bell © Succession Picasso / DACS, London 2018. / © DACS 2018 168cr, BIOSPHOTO 80br, 81ca, blickwinkel 65cb, 77cra, 78clb, 78clb (Gaboon Caecilian), 84cl, 85ba, BlueOrangeStudio 51r, Richard Brown 35cra, Peter Carroll 129bl, CBW 8-9, 191fbl, Classic Image 161br, classicpaintings 166cra, 167rc, color to go 156ca, Richard Cooke 30-31t (Red Arrows aerobatic team), CTK 179l, Cultura Creative (RF) 142-143, 191br, Ian Dagnall 169cla, 169br, Ian G Dagnall 158cr, dbimages 113crb, Phil Degginger 16crb, Susan E. Degginger 138cra, Danita Delimont 167cra, Dinodia Photos 167cl, 173c, discpicture 76bl, Dorling Kindersley ltd 5ca, 157tc, dpict 35tr, Redmond Durrell 81tc, adam eastland 162cla, Edalin 95tr, Stephen Emerson 115tr, EmmePi Travel 156-157bc, Entertainment Pictures 175bc (Avatar), Kip Evans 127cla, Excitations 111br, Shaun Finch - Coyote-Photography.co.uk 32cra, fine art 34crb, FineArt 168br, Framed Art 166ca, Granger Historical Picture Archive 162-163cb, 168bc, 169bl, Randy Green 109cra, Kevin Griffin 36br, Hemis 194cl, The History Collection 156cb, Peter Horree 164-165, D. Hurst 137tc, IanDagnall Computing 162c, imageBROKER 36cl, 51cb, 65bc, 110clb, INTERFOTO 144ftl, 157ftl, Izel Photography 167tc, Juniors Bildarchiv GmbH 177cra, H Lansdown 51clb, Lebrecht Music & Arts 38clb, Melvyn Longhurst 27clb, Mint Images Limited 119fbr, Nature Picture Library 50, 77b, 88-89b, Andrey Nekrasov 154-155bc, Ivan Nesterov 155ca, Newscom 178bl, Niday Picture Library 166cla, North Wind Picture Archives 26crb, Novarc Images 132tl, PAINTING 166b, Alberto Paredes 43br, Peter Adams Photography Ltd 119bc, Photo 12 175br, Pictorial Press Ltd 160-161bc, 175bc, 191fbr, Picture Partners 167br, PjrStudio 138cla, Andriy Popov 137tr, tawatchai prakobkit 118b, roberthardng 39cla, 109tl, 188bl, Prasit Rodphan 153bc, Stephane ROUSSEL 124clb, Arthur Ruffino 121c, Isak Simamora 187cr, Sklifas Steven 145bc, Superstock 183l, Thailand Wildlife 60br, Hugh Threlfall 182bc, tilt&shift / Stockimo 27cla, TP 129tc, Don Troiani 156cra, V&A Images 37cb, Westend61 GmbH 137ftl, Jan Wlodarczyk 109clb, World History Archive 126br, 127clb, 161tc (Russian Revolution), 168tr, www.BibleLandPictures.com 167tl, Xinhua 14cb, xMarshall 185tl, Solvin Zankl 82crb; **Ardea:** Pat Morris 85br, Joseph T. Collins / Science Sour 79crb; **Bridgeman Images:** Wahaika rakau, hand club (wood), New Zealand School (18th Century) / Mark and Carolyn Blackburn Collection of Polynesian Art 157clb; © **DACS 2018:** © Succession Picasso / DACS, London 2018. 168cr; **Depositphotos Inc:** Steve_Allen 129tl, Camilla Casablanca 122tr, 122c, 122clb, 122bl, 123crb, 123bl, 123cla, nelka7812 54cla, tehnik751 121br, Violin 182cl; **Dorling Kindersley:** 4hoplites / Gary Ombler 156ftr, Thomas Marent 78crb, Thomas Marent 78bc, The Bate Collection / Gary Ombler 172-173tc, Andrew Beckett (Illustration Ltd) 4tr, 54tl, 54tc, 54tr, 54bc, 54br, 55tc, 55c, 55clb, 55cb, 55bl, 68cr, Board of Trustees of the Royal Armouries / Gary Ombler © The Board of Trustees of the Armouries 156tc, © The Board of Trustees of the Armouries 158ca, © The Board of Trustees of the Armouries 159tl, Booth Museum of Natural History, Brighton / Dave King 92cb (Tachyglossus aculeatus), Bristol City Museum and Art Gallery / Gary Kevin 42bc, Cairo Museum / Alistair Duncan 144tc, Courtesy of Dorset Dinosaur Museum / Andy Crawford 43bl, Dan Crisp 42ca, Ermine Street Guard / Gary Ombler 156cb (Gladius), Shane Farrell 65clb, Harzer Schmalspurbahnen / Gary Ombler 30cl, Hellenic Maritime Museum / Graham Rea 38cla, Holts Gems / Ruth Jenkinson 140tr, 140cl, 140cb, 140bl, 141tl, 141c, 141clb (Gem Opal), Peter Minister and Andrew Kerr 49tl, Barnabas Kindersley 67cla, 184clb, James Kuether 42bl, 44cr, 44-45bc, 45tc, 45clb, 45crb, 47cb, Liberty's Owl, Raptor and Reptile Centre, Hampshire, UK 94tl, 94cb, Jamie Marshall 106bl, The Museum of Army Flying / Gary Ombler 37br, NASA / Arran Lewis 106-107c, National Music Museum / Gary Ombler 170tl, 173tr, National Railway Museum, New Dehli 35cla, The National Railway Museum, York / Science Museum Group 35bl, Natural History Museum, London / Colin Keates 42br, 42fbr, 83cr, 83crb (Porcupine Fish Scales), 93tc, 137tl, 138ca, 141cla, Natural History Museum, London / Frank Greenaway 57br, Natural History Museum, London / Harry Taylor 139cr, Natural History Museum, London / Peter Chadwick 67cla (Owl feather), 92cra, Natural History Museum, London / Tim Parmenter 2cl, 92clb, 93crb, 138c, 140-141bc, 141cla, Oxford University Museum of Natural History 138tr, David Peart 95cla, Pictac 182tc, Jean-Pierre Verney / Gary Ombler Collection of Jean-Pierre Verney 158cl, Linda Pitkin 58br, 63tr, Pitt Rivers Museum, University of Oxford / Dave King 157cra, Powell-Cotton Museum, Kent / Geoff Dann 156tl, Railroad Museum of Pennsylvania 34-35tc, RGB Research Limited / Ruth Jenkinson 16clb, 16cb, 16fclb, 16fcrb, 17fclb, 18tr, 18cra, 18cl, 18bl, 18bc, 18br, 19tl, 19tc, 19tr, 19ca, 19cr, 19clb, 19cb, 19b, 138br, Royal Botanic Gardens, Kew / Gary Ombler 76tc (Leafs), 76tr (Leafs), Safdarjung Railway Station / Deepak Aggarwal 34cra, Senckenberg Gesellschaft Fuer Naturforschung Museum / Gary Ombler 42-43c, Senckenberg Nature Museum, Frankfurt / Andy Crawford 43tr, Universitets Oldsaksamling, Oslo / Peter Anderson 159rc, University of Pennsylvania Museum of Archaeology and Anthropology / Gary Ombler 145tl, Vikings of Middle England / Gary Ombler 157c, Matthew Ward 32-33cb, Peter Barber Lomax / Matthew Ward 32bc, Weymouth Sea Life Centre / Frank Greenaway 87bl, Chris Williams / James Mann 33tl, Jerry Young 2bl (Nile crocodile), 82clb, 84cra; **Dreamstime:** 111cla, Aberration / Petr Malyshev 94cra, Adogslifephoto 65cl, 78cra, Aetmeister 61tl, Aiisha 115bl, Albund 184-185cla, Aldodi / Aldo Di Bari Murga 181cb (Baseball), Alessandro0770 153cb, Alhovik 129cb, Amphaiwan 100tr, Andersastphoto 153br, Leonid Andronov 154tr, Andylid 4tc, 36cr, Arapix 155tl, Artmim 94br, Aruna1224 102crb, Asterixvs / Valentin Armianu 104-105, 191bc, Atman 21, 100tl, Pavlo Baishev 171crb, Folco Banfi 185cra, Bbgreg 162-163 (Frames), Beijing Hetuchuangyi Images Co., Ltd. 34cla, Dean Bertonceij 185cb, Olga Besnard 32cl, Andrii Bielikov 96tr, Lukas Blazek 86tc, Stanislav Bokach 107br, Bolotov 114-115, Martin Brayley 156c, Darryl Brooks 172-173bl, Lynn Bystrom 70tr, Anat Chantrakool 84ca, Chinaview 173ca, Mohammed Anwarul Kabir Choudhury 180cla, Cleanylee 72cla, Cowardlion 125crb, Atit Cumpeerawat 121bl, Cynoclub 61cra, Davidwatherwithernsea 34b, Daviesjb 70tl, Ivo De 33tr, Dejan750 / Dejan Sarman 107bc, Destina156 16cra, Dezzor 131tl, Digitalfestival 172-173ca, Cristina Dini 98cb, Diomedes66 / Paul Moore 138bc, Dmuratsahin 100cra, 101ca, Dreamer4787 109cla, Drflash 131cb, Drknuth / Kevin Knuth 59crb, Dtfoxfoto 133bl, Mikhail Dudarev 68tc, Oleg Dudko 184cl (Ice Hockey), Diana Dunlap 146clb, Dvmsimages 32cra (Model t), E1ena 5bl, 98bc, Elena Elisseeva 96ca, Elnur 185cl, Emicristea 115cla, EPhotocorp 145br, Erlrive 5tl, 68tr, Sergey Eshmetov 172cl, Maria Luisa Lopez Estivill 114bl, Exiledphoto 58bl, F11photo 147cb, Farinoza 81cla, Fckncg 130crb, Iakov Filimonov 70br, Jiri Foltyn / Povalec 95clb, Frenta 154crb, Ruslan Gilmanshin 148cb, Joseph Gough 130cra, Aleksandr Grozdanovski 171bl, Henrikhl 65bl, Birgit Reitz Hofmann 101clb, Björn Hovdal 129bc, Hupeng 33ccrb, Orcun Koral Iäyeri 130-131c, Igorkali / Igor Kaliuzhny 140bc, Igor Ilnitski 131crb, Imparoimparo 94crb, Ipadimages 129r, Iprintezis 39tl, Iquacu 100br, Isselee 2ca, 64cr, 69bc, 71cla, 74cr, 74tr, 93cr, 176bl, Vlad Ivantcov 130ca, Miroslav Jacimovic 131ca, Shawn Jackson 51ca, Janpietruszka 94bc, Javarman 115tc, John Jewell 35crb, Jgorzynik 3tl, 37cl, Jgroup / James Steidl 27tl, Johncarnemella 69cb, Johnsrood7 186crb, Jooools 19tl, Julialine 69cb, Yuliya Ermakova 107bl, Juliengrondin 99cr, Acharayon Kamornboonyarush 60bl, John Kasawa 184cla, Raymond Kasprzak / Rksprzak 120tc, Pavel Kavalenkau 154cla, Kazoka 78ca, Cathy Keifer / Cathykeifer 94bl, Surachet Khamsuk 85ca, Liliia Khuzhakhmetova 185tr, Kichigin / Sergey Kichigin 27cb, Mikhail Kokhanchikov 22clb, 181tl, Kostiuchenko 98br, Katerina Kovaleva 101br, Ralf Kraft 49c, Matthijs Kuijpers 95tc, Alexey Kuznetsov 74tr, Kwerry 95cb, Volodymyr Kyrylyuk 38b, Richard Lammerts 156tr, Richard Lindie 72tl, Liumangtiger 103crb, Renato Machado 121tc, Anton Matveev 85cla, Aliaksandr Mazurkevich 109bl, Boris Medvedev 170tc, Mgkuijpers 5cla, 80c, Borna Mirahmadian 147bl, Mirkorosenau 84tl, Ml12nan 38tr, Mlhead 186bl, Mohdoqba 103bc, Pranodh Mongkolthavorn 155br, Paul Moore 157tl, Konstantinos Moraitis 32br, Mrallen / Steve Allen 131c, Stanko Mravljak / Stana 94clb, Mrdoomits 157cla, Shane Myers 72cla (Green Sea Turtle), Viktor Nikitin 184crb, William Michael Norton 112cra, Nostone 97bl, Anna Om 146tc, Ovydyborets 160bc (Vintage Paper Background), 160bc (Vintage Paper Background), 161br (Vintage Paper Background), Pahham 99cr, David Park 33cr, Jim Parkin 185cr, Svetlana Pasechnaya 5cra, 148bc, Anastasiya Patis 149cc, Martin Pelanek 78cl, Denis Pepin 180-181bc, William Perry 120ca, Petrlouzensky 156bl, Chanawat Phadwichit 39c, Suttiwat Phokaiautjima 173cla, Dmitry Pichugin 113bl, Pictac 5tr, 181tc, Pilens / Stephan Pietzko 106bc, Pincarel / Alexander Pladdet 180bc, Presse750 111crb, Pressfoto / Lvan Sinayko 120bl, Mariusz Prusaczyk 111clb, Pudique 131c (France flag), 131bl, Björn Wylezich 19cb (Sulfur), Prasit Rodphan 180bl, Rostislav Ageev / Rostislavv 31br, Somphop Ruksutakarn 100bl, Sandra79 / Sandra Stajkovic 160cb, Sborisov 121clb, 145pbr, Scaliger 147cra, Scanrail 125tl, Sally Scott 102ca, Shsphotography 131cb, Serhiy Shullye 101cl, Piti Sirisriro 34clb, Solarseven 17r, Sombra12 68br, Sportfoto / Yury Tarasov 107bc (River Volga), Srlee2 113cra, Sssstocker 128-129bc (Hands), Staphy 106br, Stevenrussellsmithphotos 61br, Stillfx / Les Cunliffe 181bc, Stu Porter 95bl, Surandhi 25 59cra, Kamnuan Suthongsa 81cb, Oleksii Terpugov 180tr, Tessarthetegu 95ca, Thawats 74-75cb, Thediver123 / Greg Amptman 82bl, George Tsartsianidis 130cb, 131tc, Lillian Tveit 76br, 189tr, V0v / Vladimir Korostyshevskiy 167bc, Vacclav 146br, Valentyn75 101tc, 141cb, Verdateo 172cla, Dan Vik 30-31t, Viktarm 10cla, Vivellis 4b, 33cra, Vladvitek 86-87cb, Volkop 183clb, Weather888 147cdb, Wlad74 128tl, Wojciech Wrzesień 38-39cb, Yinghua 99cr (Lotus leaf), Yinglina 34tl, Yocamon 5tc (Shuttlecock), 180cl, Yurakp 3ca, 101bl, Zaclurs 185clb, Zelenka68 141crb, Yifang Zhao 170c, 171cl, Alexander Zharnikov 113tl; **ESO:** https://creativecommons.org/licenses/by/4.0 11cla (Barnard's Galaxy), https://creativecommons.org/licenses/by/4.0 / M. Kornmesser 15ca; **FLPA:** Biosphoto / Regis Cavignaux 85bc, Imagebroker / J.W.Alker 62cla, Chris Mattison 79tr, Minden Pictures / Birgitte Wilms 63cra, Minden Pictures / Pete Oxford 81bc, Minden Pictures / Piotr Naskrecki 64tr, Minden Pictures / Ron Offermans, Buiten-beeld 84bl, Minden Pictures / Wil Meinderts 62bc; **Fotolia:** robynmac 181cla, Juri Samsonov / Juri 93cra, uwimages 87cla; **Getty Images:** Lambert-Sigisbert Adam 148cl, Agence France Presse / AFP 163bc, Ayhan Altun 155cla, Per-Anders Pettersson / Hulton Archive 163tr, Marie-Ange Ostré 68bl, Apic / RETIRED / Hulton Archive 163cra, The Asahi Shimbun 97cb, Erwin Aslander / 500px 97br, James Balog / The Image Bank 89ca, Barcroft / Barcroft Media 31cr, Barcroft Media 76ca, Bettmann 27fclb, 160clb, Walter Bibikow 154bl, Manuel Blondeau - Corbis 183br, Bloomberg 87cb, Charles Bowman 155tr, Marco Brivio / Photographer's Choice 109br, C Squared Studios 173tc, 183tl, Carsten Peter / Speleoresearch & Films / National Geographic 137br, China Photos / Stringer / Getty Images News 15cr, Giordano Cipriani 95bc, Dean Conger / Corbis Historical 119tr, Sylvain Cordier / Photolibrary 72ca, De Agostini / A. Dagli Orti / De Agostini Picture Library 162clb, DEA / A. DAGLI ORTI / De Agostini 144bl, DEA / A. VERGANI 121tl, DEA / ARCHIVIO J. LANGE / De Agostini 174ca, DEA / G. DAGLI ORTI 148r, 149crb, DEA / G. DAGLI ORTI / De Agostini 144crb, DEA / G. NIMATALLAH / De Agostini 179bl, DEA / PUBBLI AER FOTO 110bl, DEA PICTURE LIBRARY / De Agostini 162bc, Digitaler Lumpensammler / Moment 109cr, DigitalGlobe 126cra, Elena Duvernay / Stocktrek Images 42crb, ESA / Handout / Getty Images Publicity 126cla, Fine Art Images / SuperStock 162crb, Flickr / Jason's Travel Photography 145fbl, Fuse / Corbis 21br, Mauricio Handler 87cb, Matthias Hangst / Getty Images Sport 178cl, Martin Harvey 114crb, PREAU Louis-Marie / hemis.fr 70-71ca, Heritage Images / Hulton Fine Art Collection 169bc, Schafer & Hill 114cla, IMAGEMORE Co., Ltd. 65tr, Imágenes del Perú / Moment Open 144tr, David C Tomlinson / Lonely Planet Images 108crb, John W Banagan / Lonely Planet Images 124br, Joel Sartore, National Geographic Photo Ark 74bl, Layne Kennedy 110c, Izzet Keribar 115tl, kuritafsheen / RooM 73cla, Kyodo News 39b, Danny Lehman 155crb, Holger Leue 112cl, David Madison 184-185bc, Reynold Mainse / Design Pics 95bc, 189bc, Joe McDonald 54bl, 76tr, MelindaChan 115crb, László Mihály / Moment 125bl, mikroman6 / Moment Open 94-95c, Nikolai Galkin / TASS 17cb, John Parrot / Stocktrek Images 161tl, Peter Zelei Images / Moment 119cb, PHAS 149tc, Photo by K S Kong 68tl, Mike Powles / Oxford Scientific 66clb, Print Collector 149bc, Fritz Rauschenbach / Corbis 78-79cb, Roger Viollet Collection 26crb, Yulia Shevchenko / Moment 167cla (Flamingo), Frédéric Soltan / Corbis News 124tl, Paul Starosta 63cb, Paul Starosta / Corbis Documentary 84tc, Stringer / Jack Thomas / Getty Images Sport 179tr, Stringer / Yasser Al-zayyat 95cl, suebg1 photography 77crb, Chung Sung-Jun / Getty Images Sport 178cb, David Tipling 70bl, UHB Trust / The Image Bank 21cla (Ultrasound), Universal History Archive / Universal Images Group 152-153bc, 168cl, Dr. David M. Phillips / Visuals Unlimited 21cl, Grey Villet / The LIFE Picture Collection 161tr, Visions Of Our Land 120tl, VolcanoDiscovery / Tom Pfeiffer 115cra, Weatherpix / Gene Rhoden / Photolibrary 132-133c, Ben Welsh / Corbis 178-179bc, Westend61 115cga, 136cra, ZEPHYR / Science Photo Library 21cla, Jie Zhao 70cl, Jenner Zimmermann / Photolibrary 102cra; **iStockphoto.com:** 1001slide 112cb, 2630ben 133fbl, 3D_generator 130bl, 3dmitry 130tl, AK2 124tr, Dmytro Aksonov 184-185 (Pole Vaulting), Alan_Lagadu 146crb, Orbon Alija 119bl, allanswart 184tr, amustafazade 171cl (Oboe), AndreaWillmore 112crb, artisteer 182br, bendenhartog 68bc, biometar 167cr (Medicine bottle), Derek Brumby 130c, cinoby 147cla, clicksbyabrar 120bc, Coica 97bc, CreativePhotoCorner 130tc, dem10 146tl, DigitalBlind 132bl, dreamnikon 88cla, duncan1890 161tc, EarthScapeImageGraphy 35cr, Elenarts 99cla, Frankonline 34cl, Freder 21fb, Gannet77 158-159bc, Gregory_DUBUS 133fbr, holgs 145tv, ivkuzmin 68cla, JoeGough 131bc, JUN2 172crb, Katerina_Andronchik 122crb, 122br, 123tl, 123cl, 123clb, kikapieridies / E+ 167cla, kjorgen 55cr, kkant1937 3bl, 158bl, Mark Kostich 2bl, 77tr, 80bc, kurkul 111cr, liseykina 147crb, LPETTET 130bc, MaboHH 124cr, macca236 68cra, mantaphoto 110br, marrio31 86cl, mazzzur 153bc (Mehrangarh fort), mbolina 67sr, mdesigner125 135tc, menonsstocks 131ca (Indian Flag), MikeLane45 69cl, mysticenergy 135crb, Nikada / E+ 125br, olgagorovenko 51crb, omersukrugoksu 167fcr, pawel.gaul 110tr, Perszing1982 133bc, reptiles4all 64cl, Richmatts 88cl, selimaksan 161bc, SL_Photography 130br, stuartbur 180cra, subjug 146-147 (Black corners), tbradford 146bl, TerryJLawrence 147tl, Thurtell 183tc, vistoff 130clb, vwalakte 125bc, walik 185ca, wsfurlan 97bc (Victoria Amazonica), Xantana 109tc; **James Kuether:** 44bc, 45br, 46clb, 49ca; **Longform:** Cartier 140tl; **Mary Evans Picture Library:** 153tr; **NASA:** 14tl, 14tc, 14ca, 15cra, 15crb, 15bl, 15br, 119tr, 126cb, 128-129c, Ames / SETI Institute / JPL-Caltech 11br, Jacques Descloitres, MODIS Rapid Response Team, NASA / GSFC 108ca, ESA / Hubble & NASA 111tl, Hubble & NASA, Acknowledgement: Flickr user Det58 10bl, Bill Ingalls 10-11bc, JPL 15tl, JPL / DLR 13bl, JPL / University of Arizona 13bl, JPL-Caltech / MSSS 14cr, NASA / GSFC / LaRC / JPL, MISR Team 127br, NASA / JPL 126ca, NASA / U. S. Geological Survey / Norman Kuring / Kathryn Hansen 59r, NASA Earth Observatory image by Jesse Allen and Robert Simmon, using EO-1 ALI data from the NASA EO-1 team. Caption by Mike Carlowicz 127tr, NASA image by Jeff Schmaltz, LANCE / EOSDIS Rapid Response. Caption by Kathryn Hansen 126bl, NASA image created by Jesse Allen, Earth Observatory, using data obtained from the University of Maryland's Global Land Cover Facility. 127cb, Jeff Schmaltz 127tl, SDO / GSFC 10tr; **National Geographic Creative:** Michael Nichols 97tr; naturepl.com: Eric Baccega 114cb, John Cancalosi 73cra, Jordi Chias 82-83c, Stephen Dalton 3tr, 69ca, Alex Hyde 60ca, 64cb, Gavin Maxwell 59rc, Pete Oxford 40-41, 191bl; **NRAO:** AUI / NSF 10cb (Fornax X); **Rex by Shutterstock:** 31cra, imageBROKER / SeaTops 72-73bl, Kobal / Paramount Television 175bl, Magic Car Pics 33cl, Quadrofoil / Bournemouth News 31cra (Quadrofoil speedboat), Unimedia 31br (Rinspeed sQuba); **Rijksmuseum, Amsterdam:** 157tr; **Robert Harding Picture Library:** M. Delpho 66-67c, Michael Nolan 75crb, 86br; **Photo Scala, Florence:** courtesy of the Ministero Beni e Att. Culturali et del Turismo 149cla; **Science Photo Library:** Thierry Berrod, Mona Lisa Production 25bl, Dr Jeremy Burgess 25bc, Dennis Kunkel Microscopy 24c, 25ca, Eye of Science 83crb, Dante Fenolio 86cra, Steve Gschmeissner 24tr, 24clb, 24crb, 24br, 25crb, Michael Long 49br, Martin Oeggerli 25cl, Power and Syred 25tr, Science Source 24la, Millard H. Sharp 43fbl, 138-139tc, VEISAND 22bl; **SD Model Makers:** 3br, 38cra, 38crb, 39ca (Viking Ship); **SuperStock:** 4X5 Collection 169cb, age fotostock / Juan Carlos Zamarreño 146tr, hemis.fr / Hemis / Delfino Dominique 89tc, imageBROKER / Helmut Meyer zur Capellen 148bl, Juniors 84cla, Marka 163cr, Minden Pictures / Colin Monteath 108cb, Minden Pictures / Fred Bavendam 86bl, Minden Pictures / Kevin Schafer 114tr, Minden Pictures / Konrad Wothe 55cra, Minden Pictures / Stephen Dalton 94tr, NHPA 80t, roberthardng 146cra, roberthardng / Lizzie Shepherd 38c, Science Photo Library 65cr, Universal Images 51br, Stuart Westmorland 83tr; **The Metropolitan Museum of Art:** Bashford Dean Memorial Collection, Bequest of Bashford Dean, 1928 159tr, Bequest of Benjamin Altman, 1913 145ftl, Bequest of George C. Stone, 1935 158bc, The Michael C. Rockefeller Memorial Collection, Bequest of Nelson A. Rockefeller, 1979 145tc, Rogers Fund, 1904 158tr, Rogers Fund, 1917 144ftr, Rogers Fund, 1921 158br; **Wellcome Collection**: http://creativecommons.org/licenses/by/4.0/: 21ca

All other images © Dorling Kindersley
For further information see: www.dkimages.com